Goldsmiths
and Silversmiths
of England

Paul De Lamerie: the 'Great Seal' salver, 1728–29. Victoria and Albert Museum. (Crown Copyright).

Goldsmiths
and Silversmiths
of England

CHRISTOPHER LEVER

HUTCHINSON OF LONDON

Hutchinson & Co. (Publishers) Ltd
3 Fitzroy Square, London W.1

London Melbourne Sydney Auckland
Wellington Johannesburg Cape Town
and agencies throughout the world

First published 1975
© Christopher Lever 1975

Set in Monotype Bembo
Printed in Great Britain
by Ebenezer Baylis and Son Ltd
The Trinity Press, Worcester, and London

ISBN 0 09 121220 0

To the goldsmiths of England
past, present and to come,
this book is respectfully dedicated.

Contents

List of Illustrations   9
Foreword by Arthur Grimwade, F.S.A.   11
Acknowledgements   13
Introduction   15

Paul De Lamerie   21
Hester Bateman and her Family   57
Matthew Boulton   74
Paul Storr   97
Augustine Courtauld and his Family   126
Garrard & Co.   140
The Hennell Family   163
Anthony Nelme   181
David Willaume   185
Paul Crespin   190
Thomas Heming   196
The Provincial Goldsmiths   201

Bibliography   243
Index   249

List of Illustrations

Frontispiece Paul De Lamerie: the 'Great Seal' salver, 1728–29

1 Paul De Lamerie: the Treby dressing-table service, 1723–24

2, 3 Paul De Lamerie: helmet-ewer and basin, 1741–42

4 Paul De Lamerie: the Sutherland wine-cistern, 1719

5 Paul De Lamerie: the Newdigate centrepiece, 1743–44

6 Paul De Lamerie: silver-gilt two-handled cup and cover, 1739

7 Paul De Lamerie: silver-gilt tea-caddy, 1747

8 Hester Bateman: tea-caddy, 1785

9 Hester Bateman: teapot, 1783–84

10 Hester Bateman: cruet and stand, 1788–89

11 Hester Bateman: salver, 1783

12 Peter and Anne Bateman: the Nelson Cup, 1790

13 Peter and Anne Bateman: goblet, 1799

14 Peter and Anne Bateman: the Wantage Cup, 1795

15 Portrait of Matthew Boulton; artist unknown

16 Matthew Boulton and John Fothergill: pair of candlesticks, 1768

17 Matthew Boulton and John Fothergill: mazarine, 1769–70

18 Matthew Boulton and John Fothergill: flagon, chalice and paten, 1774

19 Matthew Boulton and John Fothergill: one of a pair of sauce-tureens, 1776

20 Matthew Boulton: cassolette, 1779

21 Portrait of Paul Storr: artist unknown

22 Paul Storr: the Nile Cup, 1799

23 Paul Storr: a fruit bowl from the Wellington service, 1810–11

24 Paul Storr: the Theocritus Cup, 1812–13

25 Paul Storr: standing cup and cover, 1833

26 Portrait of Augustine Courtauld: artist unknown

27 Portrait of Louisa Courtauld, by Zoffany

28 Portrait of Samuel Courtauld the Younger: artist unknown

29 Samuel Courtauld: tea-urn, 1760

30 Augustine Courtauld: the State Salt of the Corporation of the City of London, 1730

31 Self-portrait of George Garrard, A.R.A.

32 George Wickes; silver-gilt epergne, 1745

33 Garrard & Co.: gilt table-centre, designed by Prince Albert, 1842

34 Robert Garrard: one of a set of four gilt shell salts, 1867

35 Garrard & Co.: soup-tureen, 1824

36 Portrait of David Hennell; artist unknown

37 Portrait of Robert Hennell III; artist unknown

37a Portrait of Robert Hennell IV; artist unknown

37b Portrait of James Barclay Hennell; artist unknown

38 Robert and David Hennell: coffee-pot made for Lord Nelson, 1799

39 Robert Hennell: wheatear basket, 1850

40 Hennell Ltd: pair of gilt and silver rosewater bowls, designed by Anthony Elson, 1970

41 Anthony Nelme: one of a pair of silver-gilt altar-candlesticks, 1694

42 Anthony Nelme: 'Pilgrim' wine-bottle, 1715

43 'The Ancestor', a presumed portrait of Paul Crespin, 1720–40

44 Paul Crespin: tureen-centrepiece, 1741

45 David Willaume: helmet-ewer, 1700

46 David Willaume: teapot, 1706–7

47 Extract from an account giving details of work carried out by David Willaume for Lady Irwyn in 1726

48 Thomas Heming: tea-kettle and stand, 1761–62

49 Thomas Heming: silver-gilt toilet-service, 1766

50 William Cobbold: the Reade Salt, 1568

51 Robert Rowe: the Eddystone Salt: 1698–1700

52 Nathaniel Bullen: tobacco-box, late seventeenth century

53 Marmaduke Best: gold goblet, 1671

54 William Ramsey: tankard, circa 1670

55 Portrait of George Lowe, founder of the family firm of Lowe and Sons, Chester

56 Peter Edwardes: monteith, 1686–90

57 Ralph Walley: punch-jug, 1690–92

Foreword

by Arthur Grimwade, F.S.A.

IT is now 110 years since William Chaffers, in his *Gilda Aurifabrorum*, first provided collectors of English silver with any clues as to the identity of the goldsmiths whose marks must have hitherto seemed so tantalizing to early students of the subject. But it was still a long time before the names behind the marks were more than mere labels – just enough to make comparisons of different goldsmiths' work possible for the discerning. Even after the researches of that most industrious writer on English silver, Alfred Jones, in the first four decades of the century, there was still in 1953 (when my own thoughts first turned to the conception of a dictionary of London goldsmiths) only Jones' study of the Courtauld family, Philip Phillips' brilliant biography of Lamerie and H. W. Dickinson's absorbing *Matthew Boulton*. These were, however, followed soon after by Norman Penzer's *Paul Storr* in 1954 and David Shure's *Hester Bateman* in 1959 and one began to feel that at last English goldsmiths were gaining their due to be studied as individual artists, reflecting or even establishing the taste of their day and revealing powers of business organization and expansion worthy of their more commercial and scientific contemporaries in the great days of the Industrial Revolution.

Mr. Lever, who is the first to acknowledge his indebtedness to the above-mentioned authors and others, has conceived the plan of what I find to be a most readable volume of the careers and achievements of the protagonists in London and the chief provincial centres of the craft from the days of the Huguenot invasion after 1685 onwards. His book will, I am sure, prove a fascinating introduction to the subject for the ever growing band of enthusiasts for English silver and spread even wider the pleasure and satisfaction of learning something of the man or woman behind the 'maker's mark'.

A.G.G.

Acknowledgements

MY sincere thanks are due first and foremost to Mr. Arthur Grimwade, F.S.A., for most generously making time from his busy life at Christie's and his own literary activities, firstly to read my manuscript and point out the various pitfalls into which I had fallen and a number of factual inaccuracies, and secondly for kindly agreeing to provide a Foreword. To him I am deeply grateful.

I am indebted to Mr. J. G. Shearlock, Mr. W. H. Summers, Mr. Alex Styles and Mr. Frederick Eyles of Garrard & Co., for the help given me in writing the chapter on Garrards. I am also most grateful to Mrs. Jean Meade-Fetherstonhaugh for kindly allowing me to examine her collection of family papers, which enabled me to draw up the Garrard pedigree.

My thanks are due to Mr. Percy Hennell, who made available to me his private collection of family papers, and Mr. Keith Grant-Peterkin of Hennell Ltd. for their assistance in writing the chapter on the Hennell family.

To the Wardens of the Worshipful Company of Goldsmiths I extend my grateful thanks for kindly allowing me to consult the Company's records at Goldsmiths' Hall; I am also indebted to the Librarian, Miss Susan Hare, for her generous help and advice.

My thanks are due to Mrs. Shirley Bury of the Department of Metalwork at the Victoria and Albert Museum for permitting me to examine the Garrard ledgers and the Elkington records.

For their help in various ways I am grateful to the following: Mr. J. W. Brunger of the Worshipful Company of Grocers; Mr. J. W. Dermit, Clerk to the Chamberlain's Court at Guildhall; Miss M. A. V. Gill, Keeper of Applied Arts at the Laing Art Gallery and Museum, Newcastle upon Tyne; Mr. Arthur Morrison, Dean's Verger at St. Paul's Cathedral; Mr. D. F. Petch, Curator of the Grosvenor Museum,

Chester; Sir Robert Wilmot, Bt.; Heming and Co. Ltd. of London; Lowe & Sons of Chester; Mr. D. G. Allen, Town Clerk, Borough of Monmouth; Mr. Geoffrey N. Barrett; the Marquess of Bath; the Revd. N. M. Bedford, vicar of St. Michael the Archangel, Warfield; Mrs. Elizabeth Berry, Chester City Archivist; Mr. Anthony J. Camp, Director of Research at the Society of Genealogists; Mr. Ralph Collier, President of the Campbell Museum, Camden, New Jersey; Mr. David H. H. Felix of Philadelphia; the Duke of Devonshire; Mr. Denis Farr, Director of the Birmingham Museum and Art Gallery; Lieutenant-Colonel Gordon Ilderton; Mr. G. J. Levine; the Duke of Marlborough; Mr. Charles Oman; Canon Maurice H. Ridgway, F.S.A.; Mr. W. A. Taylor, Librarian of the Birmingham Central Reference Library; Miss Robin M. Thomas, Keeper of Art at the City Museum and Art Gallery, Plymouth; the Duke of Wellington, and Mr. A. H. Westwood, Assay Master at the Birmingham Assay Office.

My thanks are due to the following for kindly permitting me to quote extracts from the works referred to:

B. T. Batsford Ltd; *Paul De Lamerie* and *Paul Storr*.

Lord Clark and John Murray Ltd; *Civilization*.

Mr. Arthur Grimwade and *The Connoisseur; Silver at Althorp*.

Mr. Arthur Grimwade, and Mr. Richard Vander of the Society of Silver Collectors: *The Garrard Ledgers*.

Mrs. Margaret Holland and David & Charles Ltd; *Old Country Silver*.

The Wardens of the Worshipful Company of Goldsmiths; *The Plate of the Worshipful Company of Goldsmiths* by J. B. Carrington and G. R. Hughes.

For kindly allowing me to include material which first appeared in 1974 in *Country Life, The Connoisseur* and *Apollo* I am grateful to the editors, Mr. Michael Wright, Mr. Bevis Hillier and Mr. Denys Sutton.

A book such as this must inevitably be based to a considerable extent on the original research of others, and I acknowledge my debt to the various authors mentioned in the bibliography.

I should also like to express my thanks to Miss Emma Hogan and Mr. Ronald Davidson-Houston of Hutchinson & Co. Ltd. for so ably acting as midwives to this book; and to Miss Marian Berman for her diligent work in researching the illustrations.

Finally my thanks are due to Mrs. Ann Trevor for her patience in typing my at times almost indecipherable manuscript.

Introduction

WHAT exactly is a 'goldsmith'? Dr. Johnson's definition in his *Dictionary of the English Language* (1755) is: '1. One who manufactures gold. ... 2. A banker'; the *Oxford English Dictionary* gives: 'A worker in gold; one who fashions gold into jewels, ornaments, articles of plate, etc. ... down to the 18th c. these tradesmen acted as bankers.' Yet, with respect to these two great works, neither gives a wholly satisfactory answer to the question.

Until the early eighteenth century when banks were becoming firmly established goldsmiths were, indeed, usually both bankers and craftsmen. In *The Fortunes of Nigel* Sir Walter Scott puts the following words into the mouth of Master George Heriot (d. 1624; Royal goldsmith to James I) when speaking to Nigel: 'I am a goldsmith and live by lending money as well as by selling plate. I am ambitious to put an hundred pounds to be at interest in your hands, till your affairs be settled.' In 1674 Lord Clarendon (1609–74), in his ... *Life* ... *and* ... *Continuations* ... published in 1759, wrote: 'They [Bankers] were for the most Part Goldsmiths.' In 1690 Sir Josiah Child (1630–99) in his *Discourse on Trade* (1694) wrote that 'His Majesty ... has been enforced to give above the usual rates to goldsmiths.' In the second edition (1713) of his *Guardian* Sir Richard Steele (1672–1729) recorded that 'he gave me a Bill upon his Goldsmith in London'. Six years later the Wolverhampton ironmaster William Wood (1671–1730) observed that 'all our large Payments are made generally in Exchequer Bills, Bank or Goldsmiths' notes'. Sir Francis Child (1642–1713), referred to by Thomas Pennant as 'the father of the profession', is said to have been the first banker to abandon the goldsmith's business. Manufacturing goldsmiths, however, continued for some years to deal in 'running-cashes', i.e. act as bankers, within the trade.

In practice the term 'goldsmith' has seldom been confined solely to craftsmen who made only objects of gold: for financial and other reasons, most goldsmiths have at some time or another worked in silver or even in base metal. The members of the Worshipful Company of Goldsmiths, for example, work principally in silver, but are always referred to as goldsmiths. A goldsmith may on occasion work in bronze and paint in enamel, and cut and set precious and even semi-precious stones, but he remains distinct from the sculptor, artist, or jeweller, even though their work may at times overlap.

Goldsmiths have traditionally been surrounded from early times with a unique aura of mystery. No other workers in the decorative arts figure so prominently in ancient literature and legend. Bezaleel and Aholiab, makers of the Ark of the Covenant, table, mercy-seat, candelabrum and liturgical vessels for the Israelites, are referred to in the Book of Exodus, chapters 25–31. According to the Acts of the Apostles 19:24, 'a certain man named Demetrius, a silversmith, which made silver shrines for Diana [of the Ephesians] brought no small gain unto the craftsmen'.

The earliest known reference to an English goldsmith is thought to be that of Aelfric 'the Grammarian' (c. 955–c. 1020) when in about the year 1000 he mentions one 'Tubalcain . . . ye goldsmith and ironsmith'. The French saint Eloi (588–659), patron of the craft, served his apprenticeship with the Master of the Royal Mint at Limoges, subsequently becoming 'coiner' to Clotaire II, King of the Franks, and treasurer in the household of his successor, Dagobert. Both monarchs entrusted him with important commissions, among which were the construction of the bas-reliefs which decorate the tomb of St. Germain, Bishop of Paris, and the manufacture (for Clotaire) of two gem-studded golden chairs, which are generally regarded as having been his greatest *oeuvres*: he is also said to have been responsible for a number of reliquaries, though none remains today.

The English saint Dunstan (a Glastonbury-born monk who spent most of his life in Winchester and is the patron saint of English goldsmiths) is referred to in the translation, published in 1387, by John de Trevisa (1326–1412) of the *Polychronicon* by Ranulf Higden (c. 1299–c. 1364): 'He telleth that Donstan [*sic*] . . . made in tyme a chalys by goldsmethes craft.' St. Dunstan is also said to have made the crown used at the coronation of King Edgar at Bath in 973. The hermit St. Bilfrith is reputed to have fashioned a jewel-encrusted cover for a Book of the Gospels, which survived until the seventeenth century.

Referring to 'the first Christians who came to the West' Kenneth Clark asks:

what kept that wandering culture alive?... the answer comes out in the poems: *gold*. Whenever an Anglo-Saxon poet wants to put into words his ideal of a good society he speaks of gold.

> 'There once many a man
> Mood-glad, gold bright, of gleams garnished
> Flushed with wine-pride, flashing war-gear,
> Gazed on wrought gemstones, on gold, on silver,
> On wealth held and hoarded, on light-filled amber.'

The wanderers had never been without craftsmen; and all their pent-up need to give some permanent shape to the flux of experience, to make something perfect in their singularly imperfect existence, was concentrated in these marvellous objects. They achieved, even in the casting of a torque, an extraordinary intensity. . . .

This love of gold and wrought gemstones, this feeling that they reflected an ideal world and had some kind of enduring magic, went on right up to the time when the dark struggles for survival were over. It is arguable that western civilization was saved by its craftsmen. The wanderers could take their craftsmen with them. Since the smiths made princely weapons as well as ornaments, they were as necessary to a chieftain's status as were the bards whose calypsos celebrated his courage.[1]

In the Middle Ages the goldsmith was, indeed, the most highly respected of all creative artists, principally because he worked in the most intrinsically valuable mediums (gold, silver and precious stones), whose possession had from ancient times represented, to their owners and others, prestige, power and wealth: 'More to be desired are they than gold, yea, than much fine gold' (Psalms 19:10). Gold, it will be remembered, was the first-named of the gifts presented by the 'wise men from the east' after the birth of Christ (Matthew 2:11). The attraction of precious metals and stones lies not only in their rarity, but also in their weight, appearance and sense of permanence; it is virtually impossible to damage seriously or to destroy the materials from which jewellery and gold and silver-plate are made. Gold and silver were the obvious metals from which to make important objects for ceremonial occasions, and ornaments of great variety and elaborate workmanship still exist today.

Dr. Jacob Bronowski writes:

1. *Civilization* (London, 1969), pp. 8–9.

Gold is the universal prize in all countries, in all cultures, in all ages ... gold for greed, gold for splendour, gold for adornment, gold for reverence, gold for power, sacrificial gold, life-giving gold, gold for tenderness, barbaric gold, voluptuous gold. . . . The Chinese put their finger on what makes it irresistible. Ko-Hung said, 'Yellow gold, if melted a hundred times, will not be spoiled.' In that phrase we become aware that gold has a physical quality that makes it singular. ... It is easy to see that the man who made a gold artefact was not just a technician, but an artist.[2]

With the coming of the Renaissance, attitudes towards goldsmiths changed; attention was paid more to the artistic skill with which an object was made than to its intrinsic worth. Eventually, great artists disdained to create their masterpieces in a medium which, in time of need, could be broken up or melted down to provide ready cash; and patrons of the arts came to regard gold and silver as inferior mediums for artists to work in when compared with intrinsically less valuable materials.

It is frequently alleged that English craftsmen in general, and goldsmiths in particular, seldom if ever invent their own style of workmanship. They borrow designs from whomever has enough inventive genius to establish a new fashion, and it is certainly true that English craftsmen have always been ready to assimilate the ideas of foreigners. Since the Renaissance English goldsmiths have relied to a considerable extent on foreign originality for both shape and ornamentation. Most of the existing design-books are of foreign origin, and most English wrought plate exhibits a distinct element of Continental and, in the case of *chinoiserie*, of Far Eastern taste. In addition, English goldsmiths have for hundreds of years been subject to the invasion of alien craftsmen who, for various reasons, came to work in this country. There were, for instance, Germans working in London as early as the sixteenth century; the Dutchman, Christian van Vianen, was in about 1660 appointed 'Silversmith in Ordinary to His Matie for chastework within His Maties Closett and Bedchamber and also the Closett and Bedchamber of the Queen.' The reigns of Charles II and William of Orange saw the great influx of Huguenot refugees, many of whom were already, or later became, highly skilled goldsmiths and engravers – their arrival coincided with what is perhaps the acme of English goldsmithery. The Huguenots were followed by further French influence in the form of the rococo style, which was in turn succeeded by the great classical revival (inspired by ancient Greece and Rome) and later still by the influence of ancient Egypt.

2. *The Ascent of Man* (London, 1973), p. 134.

Yet, in spite of the undoubted influence of foreigners on English gold-smiths, whether indigenes or immigrants, it is difficult to mistake an English piece of plate for the work of an alien hand. English silver has an indefinable and subtle quality of form, decoration and craftsmanship, which is easily recognizable to the experienced eye.

In the majority of European and American cities goldsmiths were (and in the United Kingdom, still are) required by law to stamp their products with a distinguishing 'maker's mark' (introduced here in 1363), usually consisting of the first two letters of the surname, or initials of forename and surname. It must not be thought, however, that makers' marks are in any way comparable to the signature of an artist on a painting: indeed, the only thing which a maker's mark and an artist's signature have in common is that neither necessarily guarantees the authorship of a work of art.

Few people imagine that the signature of an artist on a picture is proof that that particular picture was painted by the hand of the artist whose name it bears; everyone has heard of forgeries, and most connoisseurs know of the practice of great artists signing works painted by assistants in their studios, in order to enhance their value. Yet many people imagine that every piece of plate bearing the maker's mark of, say, Paul De Lamerie or Paul Storr, was actually fashioned by the master's own hand; a moment's thought will show, however, that this could not possibly have been the case. Enormous quantities of plate were made bearing the mark of an individual craftsman who, with all his other business and administrative duties, could not conceivably have made each item himself. The maker's mark (supported by standard and assay marks) was, and still is, a guarantee only that the item so marked is of the correct legal alloy, and that it is of a sufficiently high degree of craftsmanship to have been sponsored at the Assay Office by the goldsmith whose mark it bears. Needless to say, no craftsman worthy of the name would wish to have his mark punched on a piece of plate made from sub-standard metal or of inferior workmanship.

Not only is the maker's mark no firm guarantee that a particular piece was made by the man whose mark it bears, it does not even signify that it was made in his workshop; it may simply be the mark of the man who sent it to be assayed or 'touched'; in the late seventeenth century a number of native-born English goldsmiths submitted to assay the work of some of their refugee Huguenot *confrères*. To complicate matters further, since 1842 every gold or silver object of foreign manufacture has had to be assayed and re-marked on importation into England, a practice not unnaturally objected to by leading Continental craftsmen, e.g. Carl Fabergé (1846–1920).

In England, goldsmiths eventually sank from the level of craftsmen to tradesmen (as they are described in the *Oxford English Dictionary*), and over the course of hundreds of years came to be regarded as of no more artistic merit than cabinet- and clock-makers, potters or glass-blowers. Indeed, the *Dictionary of National Biography*, begun in the late nineteenth century, lists numerous insignificant painters and sculptors, but cannot find room even for Paul De Lamerie or Paul Storr.

Today a higher status is still accorded to artistic genius than to skilled craftsmanship: that this is true is shown by the vast sums of money given for paintings by great, and even not so great, painters, when compared with the comparatively modest amounts required to purchase a piece of silver by, for instance, De Lamerie or Storr. In this highly materialistic age, the appreciation of art has come to be an excuse for escaping from the crude values of everyday life to a higher plane where values are indefinable and intangible. The plane on which the craftsman operates is regarded as being somehow inferior to that achieved by the artist: that a goldsmith may well show as much genius in the creation of a piece of gold- or silver-plate as does an artist in his painting, is generally ignored.

All questions of taste, however, are subject to that vague and fickle thing called 'fashion': in early times, as we have seen, craftsmen and artists were regarded as equals, and this was true again in eighteenth-century France. In 1868 John Ruskin wrote: 'True goldsmiths' work, when it exists, is generally the means of education of the greatest painters and sculptors of the day'; perhaps, who knows, in due course the wheel will turn full circle, and those who love and appreciate works of art in silver and gold will see the artist-craftsman restored to the honoured position he formerly held as a creator in the decorative arts.

C.L.

1478–1821

From 1822

Paul De Lamerie

(1688-1751)

IT is thanks to the 'Sun King' Louis XIV and the revocation, on 18 October 1685 of the Edict of Nantes that the English, rather than the French, are able to claim as their own Paul De Lamerie, the finest worker in silver and gold that England has ever known.

The Edict, promulgated on 13 April 1598 by Henri IV (Henry of Navarre), had at last given total religious liberty, which they had long been seeking, to his Protestant subjects, the Huguenots: the strong religious and political position which they thereby secured was strongly objected to by ardent Catholics and even by the more moderate, and the salaries paid by the state to their ministers came to be regarded with growing concern. By about 1660 a powerful movement had arisen for a return to the *status quo*. Proclamations and declarations were announced which gradually deprived the Huguenots of their hard-won rights; their position was further rendered intolerable by a series of restrictions and persecutions culminating in 1683 in the notorious *dragonnades*, an iniquitous system whereby regiments of dragoons, notoriously the most ill-disciplined of French troops, were quartered on Protestant families in towns with large Huguenot populations. Louis, who had long been opposed to the liberal tendencies and Calvinist doctrines of the Huguenots, ultimately revoked the Edict, thus finally withdrawing from the Protestants in France all the civil and religious liberties which they had hitherto enjoyed. This added fresh impetus to the emigration of Huguenots, mainly to America, Holland and England, which had been going on for a number of years, and resulted in the loss to France of some fifty thousand of her most industrious families, amounting to almost a quarter of a million people.

Thus it was that the family of Paul De Lamerie, after a brief sojourn in Holland, arrived in England as refugees from France. Evidence that they came in this way is to be found in the Register of Baptisms of the Walloon Church of Bois-le-Duc, or 's Hertogenbosch (said to have been the birthplace of Hieronymus Bosch (*c.* 1450–1516)), to give it its Dutch name, the capital of Northern Brabant situated at the confluence of the rivers Dommel and Aa. Under the year 1688 in the register appears:

Le 14e d'avril a esté baptisé Paul Jaques (né le 9e dito) fils de Paul Souchay de la Merie, et de Constance Roux, présenté par Mr· Jean Souchay de la Chancellerie et Madame Copes, en la place de Jaques Bourse demeurant à la Haye, son parrain, et de Marguerite Vignon, demeurant à Amsterdam, sa maraine.

This entry in the register of baptisms is the first known record of Paul De Lamerie (as he came to be known), and gives in addition to his godparents and their proxies, the names of his parents. His mother was descended from a very old French family, one of her ancestors, Jean Le Roux, having been raised to the nobility by Louis XI in 1475. His father's full name was Paul Souchay de la Merie, one of the proxies being his uncle Jean Souchay de la Chancellerie. Documents held in Dutch government archives show that the two brothers had been officers in the army which had supported William III of Orange, Stadholder of the Netherlands: that they were also *gens de condition*, of the *petite noblesse*, is shown by their differing territorial names. When a French landowner who was also the scion of a house of the minor nobility had several sons, he would normally divide his estate into an equal number of different *fiefs*, giving one to each son, who subsequently added the name of his particular *fief* to his family name. Some, like Paul De Lamerie, eventually dropped the family name altogether, retaining only the name of their *fief*.

The date when De Lamerie's parents first arrived in Bois-le-Duc is unknown, but they are recorded as having joined the Walloon church there on 2 June 1686, and had thus lived in the city for at least two years before the boy's birth. It seems likely that they were able to live there comfortably, as the father had in February 1686 received the considerable sum of 650 florins as a reward for his military services.

The de Lameries were clearly influenced in their decision to leave Holland by the departure for England in 1688 of William III, and by favourable reports which must have come filtering back across the Channel from those of their fellow Huguenots who had accompanied him. Thus on 23 March 1689, when the future goldsmith was not yet one year old, the family, armed with a copy of the boy's baptismal certificate and written evidence of their membership of the Walloon church (both valuable documents for prospective immigrants), left Bois-le-Duc for a new life in England.

The first mention of the de Lameries in England occurs in 1691 when the father's name (written as Paule Lemurre) appears in the poor-rate book of the parish of St. James, Westminster, as paying the rate on a house in Berwick Street, Soho, which runs between Shaftesbury Avenue and Oxford Street. As indicated above, the family seems to have abandoned the name Souchay on arrival in England, being known simply as de Lamerie, which the father wrote delamerie.[1] Even among the Huguenots themselves there were widely differing ways of spelling the same name, and in a generally illiterate age it was not easy for the average Englishman to spell correctly from French pronunciation. Thus, between 1692 and 1696 for example, the name is written in the rate-book as Paule Lemurrey.

It seems likely that during their early days in England the de Lameries were able, in common with the majority of their fellow Huguenots, to live in comparative comfort. They were mostly of good families and may be presumed to have brought with them some, if not all, of their worldly possessions; in addition a number, like De Lamerie's father, had been well rewarded financially for their military services. Thus, while funds lasted, it is not unreasonable to suppose that they were able to live without the necessity of finding work, from which their social position had hitherto precluded them.

After 1696 the name de Lamerie disappears from the rate-book altogether (although the family was in fact living in the adjoining parish of St. Anne), possibly because, through growing impecunity, they were forced into lodgings. It seems clear that at about this time the family fell on hard times, from the fact that in the Irish Letter Books of the Signet Office the family of La Merie were, in common with numerous other Huguenot refugees, granted an annual pension (amounting to £45. 12s. 6d.) from August 1701 to 1704 from the Civil List of the Crown out of funds provided by Irish revenues. After the latter date pensions ceased for those who did not live in, or were unwilling to travel to, Ireland. In addition, Huguenot refugees who could provide proof of their membership in England of the French Protestant Church, were eligible for financial aid

1. A lower-case 'd' has been used here when referring to members of the family other than the goldsmith himself, who always used an upper-case 'D'. When quoting from an original source, the usage therein has been followed.

from the Royal Bounty, which was supplemented out of the Privy Purse. In order to claim this assistance De Lamerie's father had first to join the church of his faith in London, which he could only do by producing the attestation papers which he had brought with him from Bois-le-Duc. In the Relief List of the Royal Bounty of 1703 the name Paul de Lamerie appears as having received the sum of £6.

Paul Souchay de la Merie, having been a soldier and of the *sang pur* in France, was socially debarred from entering his son into the majority of trades: that of goldsmith, however, was one of the few in which it was permissible for the family of a gentleman to engage, which is one reason why there were at that time in England so many distinguished goldsmiths of Huguenot origin. Exactly what circumstances led Paul De Lamerie into becoming a goldsmith is uncertain: most probably his father was advised by Huguenot friends already in the trade that it would be a suitable business for his son to enter; and he would doubtless have been influenced by the success which they had achieved since coming to England. Accordingly, on 24 June 1703 the names of the father and his fifteen-year-old son appear on the Roll of Denizations. This was an essential first step for the boy to take before he could be accepted as an apprentice by the Guild of Goldsmiths, founded in 1180 during the reign of Henry II, and incorporated as 'The Wardens and Commonalty of the Mystery of Goldsmiths of the City of London' by Letters Patent granted by Edward III in 1327. Although there was no legal requirement for his father to take out denizenship, he doubtless felt that, as his son's guardian in the new country of his choice, he might be better able to help the boy in his chosen career were he to do so.

Among the records of the Worshipful Company of Goldsmiths of the City of London appears the following entry:

6 Aug. 1703. Memorand that I, Paul de Lamerie, son of Paul de Lamerie, of ye parish of St. Anne's, Westminster, Gent, do put myself apprentice to Peter Plattell, Citizen and Goldsmith of London, for the term of seven years from this day.

A certificate produced of his denization, dated 7 July 1703, signed by Thomas Lawrence, Notary Public, and also testified to be a certificate for the son and not for the father, by Mr. Plattell.

Under the terms of his apprenticeship it was stipulated that an apprentice 'shall do no damage to his said master nor see it to be done of others but to his power shall let or forthwith give warning to his said master of

1   Paul De Lamerie: the Treby dressing-table service, 1723–24. Ashmolean Museum, Oxford.

2 & 3 Paul De Lamerie: helmet-ewer and basin, 1741–42. The Worshipful Company of Goldsmiths.

4 Paul De Lamerie: the Sutherland wine-cistern, 1719. The Minneapolis Institute of Art: The James S. Bell Memorial Fund, 1961.

5 Paul De Lamerie: the Newdigate centrepiece, 1743–44. Victoria and Albert Museum.

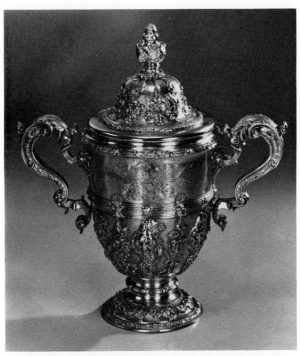

6 Paul De Lamerie: silver-gilt, two-handled cup and cover, 1739. The Worshipful Company of Goldsmiths.

7 Paul De Lamerie: silver-gilt tea-caddy, 1747. The Worshipful Company of Goldsmiths.

8 Hester Bateman: tea-caddy, 1785. Courtesy, Museum of Fine Arts, Boston.

9 Hester Bateman: teapot, 1783–84. City Art Gallery, Manchester.

10 Hester Bateman: cruet and stand, 1788–89. Victoria and Albert Museum.

11 Hester Bateman: salver, 1783. Lancaster Corporation. (*Photo: Peter W. Joslin.*)

12 Peter and Anne Bateman: the Nelson Cup, 1790. Borough of Monmouth. (*Photo: D. H. Jones.*)

13 Peter and Anne Bateman: goblet, 1799. Borough of Monmouth. (*Photo: D. H. Jones.*)

14   Peter and Anne Bateman: the Wantage Cup, 1795. Philadelphia Museum of Art; given by
Mrs Henry B. Du Pont.

same. . . . He shall not haunt taverns or play houses nor absent himself from his master's services day or night unlawfully.' Thus it can be seen that an apprentice was not only his master's pupil, but was also expected to perform the duties of guardian of his master's person and property.

No account of the life of De Lamerie would be complete without some mention of the distinguished master who was to have so great an influence on his future career. Peter Platel (as his name is now usually spelt) received no fee for taking the boy as his apprentice, and it therefore seems reasonable to infer that he was a fairly close friend of the family. From Platel the young De Lamerie learnt the art of working in silver and gold, and to him he owed in great measure his future fame. Surviving specimens of his work show that Peter Platel was a fine craftsman with a sure hand and possessed of a most fertile imagination.

Pierre Platel was the scion of the noble French family of Platel du Plateau, Sieurs d'Ecrose St. Dizier, formerly of L'Isle (Lille) in Flanders. In about 1465 one of his ancestors had been in the service of René I ('the Good') (1409–80), King of Jerusalem, Sicily and Naples, Duke of Anjou, Lorraine and Bar, Count of Provence and Piedmont, a noted patron of the arts. Sieur Batiste Bertrand Platel du Plateau of Ecrose St. Dizier was a Huguenot refugee who in 1685 fled from France to Flanders, whence his two sons (one of whom was Pierre) arrived at Brixham, Devon, in 1688, shortly after the landing at Torbay on 5 November of William III of Orange. They became English citizens on 8 May 1697. When and where Peter learnt the trade of goldsmith is unknown, but it was probably before his arrival in England. On 14 June 1699 he became a Freeman of the Goldsmiths' Company 'by Redemption', i.e. by payment rather than by serving an apprenticeship, and entered his maker's mark at Goldsmiths' Hall later in the same year. He was elected to the Livery of the Company on 26 October 1708, but never became a member of the Court. His workshop, where De Lamerie was apprenticed, was in the fashionable neighbourhood of Pall Mall. The exact date of his death is unknown, but he was buried at St. James's Church, Westminster, on 21 May 1719.

Nothing appears to have been recorded of De Lamerie during the term of his apprenticeship, but if his later life is anything to judge by he must have been an industrious worker and a promising and attentive pupil.

The first mention of him after the expiration of his articles is to be found in the records of the Goldsmiths' Company under 4 February 1712, when it is recorded that 'Paul de Lamerie, apprenticed to Peter Plattell, is made Free by Service.' On the following day 'Paul de Lamerie entered his maker's mark at Goldsmiths' Hall, being described as in Windmill Street near the Hay Markett.' In the book kept for that purpose in Goldsmiths' Hall may be seen the entry in De Lamerie's own handwriting, including the earliest example of his somewhat flamboyant signature, with its curious curling finish to the dot over the 'i', and squirl below. He always used an upper-case 'D' for De, and never joined the preposition to his territorial name as his father had done.

On 25 March 1697 the New Sterling Act had come into force: it had been introduced in order to prevent the practice, current among manufacturing goldsmiths of the day, of melting down coin of the realm to produce silver (of which there was at the time a shortage) for making into plate. The new Act had instituted a higher standard of silver (958 parts of pure silver to 42 parts of alloy), known as the 'Britannia' standard, than that which had been used previously. In addition it was decreed that 'the maker's mark to be expressed by the two first letters of his surname, the marks of the mystery or craft of the Goldsmiths, which, instead of the Leopard's head and the Lion, shall for this plate be the figure of a woman, commonly called Britannia, and the figure of a lion's head erased'.

Accordingly, De Lamerie's first maker's mark consists of the letters LA surmounted by a crown with a *fleur-de-lis* below, in the style current at the time among Parisian goldsmiths; he presumably chose this design in order to emphasize his French origin, of which he was at the time doubtless proud. The figure of Britannia and the lion's head erased were also incorporated in the punch-mark.

Later in the same month the minutes of the Chamberlain's Court at the Guildhall of the City of London record that 'Paul de Lamerie is admitted a Freeman of the City by Servitude through the Goldsmiths' Company'.

De Lamerie's first home in (Great) Windmill Street, Soho, a favourite district for Huguenot goldsmiths in the eighteenth century (native English craftsmen were still at this period working mainly within the

City or in Clerkenwell to the north-west), is unknown, unless it was the same as that which he occupied in 1716, as the poor-rate books for the parish of St. James, Westminster, are missing from 1708 to 1715. In 1716 he appears in the rate-book as Lamerrie and in the following year as Mr. Lamerrie, when he is rated for two houses, the third and fourth on the left going north.

It is unlikely at this early stage in his career that shortage of workspace alone would have caused him to require a second house. That this assumption is at least in part correct is borne out by the fact that in early February he had applied, through the Vicar-General's Office, to the Archbishop of Canterbury for what today would be called a Special Marriage Licence.

Seaventh Febry 1716 which day appeared psonally Paul [Delamare][2] de Lamerie of S[t]. James Westm[r] aged twenty eight year and a Bat[r] and alledged that he intendeth to marry with M[rs][3] Louisa Juliott of S[t]. Gyles in the feilds in the S[d][4] County aged above twenty one years and a Spinster. . . . Not knowing or believing any Impediment by reason of any prcontract Consanguinity affinity or any other Lawfull means whatsoever to hinder ye said intended marryage of ye truth of ye premisses he made oath and prayed Licence for them to be marryed in ye [parish Church of] any of the French Churches or Chapels within the City of London or Suburbs thereof.

This document disproves the oft-repeated myth that De Lamerie's wife was the daughter of Peter Platel. She was in fact the child of André Juliott de la Châtagueraie of Poitou, and of Margueritte Majou, and was born on 27 March 1694. Her parents were both descendants of two very old French families of the lesser nobility, and she traced her descent from the De La Douespe family who left Caen in Normandy some time during the sixteenth century to settle in Bas Poitou. There they established and entrenched themselves, frequently inter-marrying and forming numerous branches. After the Revocation of the Edict of Nantes some fled to England where they either entered the Church or one of the trades open to those of their social position. Louisa was one of six children, her father being a mercer of Earle Street in the parish of St. Giles.

An entry in a register of marriages, formerly held by the French Chapel of the Savoy in the Strand, but now at Somerset House, records that:

2. Words in parentheses deleted in original document.

3. Usual abbreviation of the time for Mistress, i.e. Miss.

4. Sd (said) an error, as no County previously mentioned.

Paul de Lamerie, et Louifa Juliott, ont reçu la benediction nuptialle, dans l'églife de Glafshoufe Street le 11 Fevrier 1716/7 par Mr. Jean Majou, Ministre, en vertue d'une licence de Mylord Archevêque de Cantorbery en date du 7 fevrier 1716/7.

The officiating minister was Louisa's maternal uncle.

So now, at the age of twenty-eight, De Lamerie was established with his young wife in their own home in Windmill Street with, it may be assumed, his place of business next door. To them were born during the succeeding thirteen years six children: Margaret on 9 December 1718; Mary on 1 November 1720; Paul on 24 March 1724; Daniel on 12 November 1727; Susannah on 12 April 1729, and Louisa Elizabeth on 20 November 1730. Of these, both of the boys and the eldest girl died before reaching the age of five years, an all too common occurrence of the time. The births are all recorded in the register of baptisms of St. James's Church, Westminster (the surname appearing as De La Merie, Lemarie, De Lamarie, Lemerie, and De Lemerie, not once, be it noted, as spelt by the father). The burials are recorded in the appropriate register of St. Anne's Church, Westminster, where Daniel's surname is given as Lamiere. In passing we may perhaps be excused for feeling a pang of sympathy and sadness that, with the death of his two sons, the great goldsmith had no male heir to whom to bequeath the prosperous business which he eventually built up.

Only five months after his marriage the following entry appears in the records of the Goldsmiths' Company: 'July 18, 1717. At a Court of Wardens, appeared, according to summons, Mr. Paul Lammerie, and being discoursed with by ye Wardens about his admission into the Livery, he accepted thereof.' This was a most important first step towards reaching the heights of the governing body of his guild, and shows clearly in what high esteem, at the comparatively early age of twenty-nine, he was already held by the senior members of his chosen profession.

The first important piece of silver made by De Lamerie after being elected to the Livery of his guild (and indeed probably the first important commission of his career), which he received from John Leveson-Gower, 1st Earl Gower, whose grandson George Granville (1758–1833) was created 1st Duke of Sutherland in 1833, was a splendidly proportioned and superbly executed oval wine-cistern hallmarked for 1719, measuring 38 in. long, 25 in. wide and 18 in. high, and weighing no less than 700 oz.

The massive recurving and scrolled handles of the bowl terminate in fiercely snarling lions' masks. On either side of the bowl, beneath the rim, are luxuriantly bearded masks clothed with heavily chased scrolls. On the middle of the outside of the bowl richly chased shells and more masks, surrounded by further scrolls, lie on a matted ground. The whole bowl, which rests on high oval feet, is enriched with fine and delicate chasing which encircles its upper parts.

This magnificent example of the goldsmith's craft was for many years in the collection of the Duke of Sutherland: in 1961 it was sold at Christie's for the then record sum of £27,000 (equalled in 1971 by the price paid for a superb sideboard dish by De Lamerie in the first sale of the Plohn collection at Sotheby's), and is now in the collection of the Minneapolis Institute of Art.

A few years later De Lamerie received the first of a number of highly important commissions for silver-plate from the Czars of Russia. The initial order from Peter I (the Great, reigned 1689–1725) was for a wine-fountain, which bears the hallmark for 1720–21.

Phillips describes 'this outstanding piece' as being:

based on others of a similar class of the two previous reigns which are renowned in the history of English silverware, but it is more ornate in design. The simple vertical straps with their interconnected outlined mouldings on the upper and lower bulbous parts and the band of enlarged gadrooning on the base are pleasing reminders of such work on plate of an earlier period, but the deep band of vertical leaves on the central portion of the body and the narrower band of leafage on the top are not in keeping and distract the eye. The concave neck is encircled by a narrow moulded band, and the two hinged and moulded handles are supported on applied ornament on the shoulder of the upper part. The domed cover, with its knurled edge and band of leaf ornament and pine-apple finial, seems to be out of mode, as it is quite unusual to find this form of decoration so early in the 18th century. The additional applied ornament of shells etc. on the deep moulding above the middle portion of the body, and the dolphin top to the grotesque spout, set on a roundel of shells and leaves, are foretastes of what De Lamerie produced in his later rococo work.

Some parts of the decoration recall the designs of the end of the 17th century and the first years of the 18th century. Others are forerunners of what was to come within the next 20 years. In this wise De Lamerie showed singular individuality, albeit apparent inconsistency.[5]

Peter the Great's successors placed further orders with De Lamerie, and he subsequently despatched to the Russian Court a wine-cistern

5. p. 77.

(1726-7) for Peter's wife, Catherine I (reigned 1725-7), and two chandeliers (1734-5) for his niece Anne (reigned 1730-40). These important items were in the same highly elaborate style, and were clearly designed to blend harmoniously with the extravagant architecture and rich setting of the Kremlin.

It was in about 1720, at the time when the young De Lamerie was employed in making Peter the Great's wine-fountain, that he met for the first time the even younger William Hogarth (1697-1764), then working as a silver engraver.

Hogarth had been apprenticed in 1712 to Ellis Gamble (whose trade-card, now in the British Museum, he was later to engrave) of Cranbourne Street or Alley, Leicester Fields (now Leicester Square), who worked at the sign of the 'Golden Angel' as a silver-plate engraver to the trade. 'In Mr. Gamble's shop the fine solid plate of the early eighteenth century was enriched with the intricate armorial devices of its wealthy purchasers, the heraldic beasts that supported the coat of arms, the shield itself subdivided in a complex chequerwork, the crest that surmounted it, and the family motto beneath.'[6] Hogarth's apprenticeship expired in 1718 and he set up on his own in the following year, registering his trade-card on 23 April 1720. In *Anecdotes of William Hogarth, written by himself* he shows that, although he produced a quantity of masterpieces of the engraver's art, his heart was never in the business which he regarded solely as a means to an end:

It was therefore conformable to my own wishes that I was taken from school, and served long apprenticeship to a silver-plate engraver. I soon found this business in every respect too limited and I determined that silver-plate engraving should be followed no longer than necessity obliged me to it.

The fashion of engraving on silver-plate (usually coats-of-arms and normally within a baroque cartouche) was, like the design of the plate itself, largely due to French influence. In his early days Hogarth based much of his engraving, as indeed did De Lamerie himself, on French designers such as Jean Bèrain (1638-1711) and on the pictorial influence of Jacques Callot (1592-1635), and soon won for himself the reputation of being the finest engraver of his day.

Exactly how much of the engraving on De Lamerie's silver, the bulk of which at this time consisted of simple pieces with large flat un-

6. Peter Quennell, *Hogarth's Progress* (London, 1955), p. 23.

decorated surfaces in the so-called 'Queen Anne' taste, was actually done by Hogarth's own hand is not known, as engravers seldom signed their work. Engraving was regarded as a subsidiary of the goldsmith's craft, and many goldsmiths either acted as, or themselves employed, their own engravers, who frequently copied Hogarth's style. It is also certain that a craftsman of the calibre of De Lamerie would himself do much of his own engraving. Thus, although it is known that Hogarth engraved many pieces of plate with his own hand, it is difficult to pinpoint with accuracy any of his work: in many instances one can only estimate the origin of a piece of work from the style, design and quality of craftsmanship.

Silver by De Lamerie on which the engraving is of the very highest quality and is in the so-called 'Hogarthian' style, and is moreover within the period when Hogarth was still engraving on silver-plate, and which may therefore possibly be by his own hand, includes cups and covers of 1718–19 and 1720–21; salvers of 1720–21 and 1721–2; a sideboard dish of 1722–3; and the Treby dressing table set of 1723–4 and punch-bowl of the same year, described below.

Among the engravings listed by John Nichols in his *Biographical Anecdotes of William Hogarth* published in 1781 is 'The Great Seal of England with a distant view of London; an impression from a large silver table.'[7] This refers to one of the few engravings which it is reasonably certain is by Hogarth himself, the masterpiece of the silver-plate engraver's art on De Lamerie's 'Great Seal' salver of 1728–9. This superb salver was made for Sir Robert Walpole (1676–1745) out of the Exchequer Seal of George I, which had been given to him on its replacement in 1728 by that of George II, who had re-appointed Walpole to those offices which he had held since 1721, *viz* Prime Minister and First Lord of the Treasury and Chancellor of the Exchequer.

The following is a description, taken from Phillips, of this impressive square salver (now in the Victoria and Albert Museum) 19⅜ in. in diameter which, with its superb engraving and well-documented provenance, is perhaps the most historic and romantic piece of English silver extant:

The curved raised rim is indented at the corners and has an edging of quatrefoils set between upright husks above a moulded step, divided in the centre of each side by an applied ornament formed of a rosette between two cusps with a scroll on either side and capped by a fan-shaped shell; the curve of the rim is flat chased with diapered panels separated by quatrefoil panels engraved with a classical head and with a leaf between foliated scrolls at the bisection of each

7. p. 148.

corner. The flat surface has a bold flat chased border of sixteen panels of diaper work with husk drops set horizontally, within a shaped and moulded frame, connecting with an intertwined frame of four concaved sides out-lining acanthus foliage, husk drops above and below, dividing each two on each side. In the centre of each side of this border is a foliated and scrolled shield with a shell at the base enclosing, each within two rows of husks, a mask representing one of the four Seasons, Spring, Summer and Autumn being each that of a female, Winter that of a male. In each of the corners of the border is a similar but larger shield, with a husk at the base and a shell at the top, with an inner row of husks on the shield reserved for engraving. It rests on four moulded and scrolled feet.

The centre of the salver is engraved with a large circular shield with a border of scrolled foliage enclosing rosettes, containing side by side two circular replicas of the obverse and reverse of the Exchequer Seal of King George I, parted in the centre by a four-stalked leaf set crosswise, the spaces above and below filled with allegorical subjects. In the former are two draped female figures reclining on clouds, one resting her elbow on a capital and grasping with her right hand a column of entwined snakes, and a flying cherub crowning her with a laurel wreath held in his right hand and holding a ring in his left hand, representing 'Fortitude'; in the latter a central upright figure of Hercules supports in his hands, with arms outstretched, the two circles of the Seal; at the right is seated a chained figure of a man holding a flaming torch ('Calumny') and at the left inclining forward on the ground is the chained figure of a vicious looking woman grasping in her right hand a snake ('Envy') with a view in the background of London and the Bridge with shipping on the River, from Southwark Bank, representing 'Strength'. Two of the four corner shields are engraved with the cypher of Sir Robert Walpole K.G. one with his Arms, one with his Crest, all within the Garter.[8]

The allegorical subjects and view of London in the engraving represent the fortitude and strength with which, in spite of calumny and envy, Walpole had during his previous tenure of office upheld the rights of the State in Parliament.

Another splendid example of Hogarth's engraving which dates from about 1720, shortly after he and De Lamerie met for the first time, is the book plate (in the Royal collection at Windsor Castle) which he designed showing De Lamerie's coat-of-arms. These are blazoned as 'Or 3 tree-stumps indented and erased proper 2 & 1'. These arms were apparently adopted from those borne by a branch of the Souchay family in earlier times and were, as is so often the case, a *jeu de mots* on the name of the bearer.[9] Nichols, in the 1833 edition of his *Anecdotes of William Hogarth*,

8. p. 86.   9. The French for 'tree-stumps' is 'souches'.

refers to the 'Arms of Paul De La Marie. These are beautifully engraved and have two seasons, Autumn and Winter, as terms.'[10] Hogarth, who was so successful as an engraver that in 1735 he was able to persuade the House of Commons to pass the so-called Copyright Act to prevent the piracy of his prints, finally abandoned silver-plate engraving in favour of painting in about 1735.

It seems strange that neither Hogarth, nor so far as is known any other engravers of the calibre of Simon Gribelin (1662–c. 1733; one of his finest engravings is that on the salver made for the Chancellor of the Irish Exchequer, Henry Boyle, in 1702), Benjamin Rhodes (author of *New Book of Cyphers*, 1723), or Joseph Simpson (who signed his superb engraving on a salver of 1717 by William Lukin), ever designed either trade-cards or bill-headings for De Lamerie. If any ever existed, which appears unlikely, they have never come to light; the only invoices which still exist, those for the Treby silver and for George II's christening present to Lord Lincoln's son, referred to below, are written on ordinary pieces of paper.

The next event of note in De Lamerie's career is of considerable interest, and throws at least two shafts of light on the character of the man. Without warning, and through no apparent fault of his own, he suddenly found himself drawn within the tentacles of the law. The civil action in which he appeared as defendant has become case-law on the subject of 'trover'.[11] It will perhaps best be explained by quoting verbatim from Smith's *Leading Cases*; 'Armory v Delamirie:[12] Hilary, 8 G.I. (1722)':

The finder of a jewel may maintain trover for a conversion thereof by a wrong-doer. A master is answerable for the loss of a customer's property intrusted to his servant in the course of his business as a tradesman. Where a person who has wrongfully converted property will not produce it, it shall be presumed, as against him, to be of the best description.

The plaintiff, being a chimney-sweeper's boy, found a jewel, and carried it to the defendant's shop, (who was a goldsmith) to know what it was, and delivered it into the hands of the apprentice, who, under a pretence of weighing it, took out the stones, and calling to the master let him know it came to three half-pence, the master offered the boy the money, who refused to take it, and insisted to have the thing again: whereupon the apprentice delivered him back

10. p. 293.

11. Common-law action to recover value of personal property wrongfully taken or detained.

12. Yet another variation in the spelling of the goldsmith's name.

3

the socket without the stones. And now in trover against the master these points were ruled:

1. That the finder of a jewel, though he does not by such finding acquire an absolute property or ownership, yet he has such a property as will enable him to keep it against all but the rightful owner, and consequently may maintain trover.

2. That the action well lay against the master, who gives credit to his apprentice, and is answerable for his neglect.

3. As to the value of the jewels, several of the trade were examined to prove what a jewel of the finest water that would fit the socket would be worth, and the Chief Justice directed the jury, that unless the defendant did produce the jewel, and show it not to be of the finest water, they should presume the strongest against him, and make the value of the best jewels the measure of their damages, which they accordingly did.

Apart from the purely legal aspect of the case there appear to be two points of interest here concerning the character of De Lamerie. Firstly, he made no attempt, as a lesser man might well have done, to produce a jewel of a low quality claiming it to be the original, in an attempt to mitigate his financial loss: and secondly he appears singularly free from vindictiveness in omitting to make any mention of the name of his dishonest apprentice.

The following is a list, quoted by Phillips from the records of the Worshipful Company of Goldsmiths, of De Lamerie's apprentices from 1715 to 1751:

Name	Date Apprenticed	Premium Paid £	Received Freedom
Peter Johnson	1 Feb. 1715	—	—
David Eymars	3 July 1718	35	—
Daniel Mangannell	28 Feb. 1718	35	—
Bennett Bradshaw	21 Apr. 1721	20	—
Thomas Pettet	20 Apr. 1723	35	—
Michael Oliver	15 Dec. 1724	20	—
Samuel Collins	22 Sept. 1732	10	—
William Hume	4 Sept. 1735	10	1 May 1744
Charles Bardin	5 Aug. 1736	31. 10. 0.	6 Feb. 1744
Peter Archambo[13]	5 Dec. 1738	—	3 Feb. 1747
Abraham Portal	3 July 1740	35	7 Mar. 1749
Henry Ainge	2 Aug. 1743	45	—
Samuel Hodgson[14]	2 Oct. 1749	20	—

13. Made over on the same day to his father.
14. Transferred to William Cripps on De Lamerie's death in 1751.

Bearing in mind the dates of their apprenticeship and of the trial it can be seen that only one of the first four, Peter Johnson, David Eymars, Daniel Mangannell and Bennett Bradshaw could have been the dishonest apprentice referred to in 'Armory v Delamirie'. Of the others, two are of particular interest. The best-known in after years was undoubtedly Peter Archambo the son of a noted Huguenot goldsmith and Freeman of the Butcher's Company. From 1749 he was in partnership with Peter Meure at the sign of the 'Golden Cup' in Coventry Street; he died in 1768. Samuel Collins later worked as a journeyman for De Lamerie, who entrusted him with completing work on unfinished silver after his death.

In addition to shedding light on De Lamerie's character, the evidence of 'Armory v Delamirie' is of further interest in showing that he was not only a manufacturing goldsmith, but that he also kept a trading shop open to the public for buying and selling jewellery and presumably silver-plate. So far as is known, however, he never dealt in 'running-cashes', i.e. acted as a banker, as did a number of other leading goldsmiths: nor indeed is there any record of where he kept his own bank-account, though he must surely have had one.

Although the damages and costs of the case must have been consider-able, they do not seem seriously to have affected his financial position, doubtless due to the success his business enjoyed, and his reputation not at all.

That this is correct is shown by the fact that from 1721 to 1725 De Lamerie was engaged in making a quantity of silver for the Rt. Hon. George Treby, M.P. for Plympton from 1708–34, appointed Secretary at War in 1718 and Teller of the Exchequer in 1725.

Among these commissions the dressing-table service, ordered by Treby as a wedding present for his wife, Charity, elder daughter and co-heiress of Roger Hele of Halwell, Southpool, and Fardel Cornwood, Devon, is one of the finest and most complete of its kind in existence. It bears the hallmark for 1723–4 and consists of no fewer than twenty-seven pieces: a silver-framed looking-glass, two large and one small rectangular caskets, two large and two small circular caskets, two whisks and two brushes, one ewer, four salvers, a pair of candlesticks, a pair of candle-snuffers and tray, two pomade jars, two canisters and two silver-topped glass jars.

This highly important set, which is now in the Farrer collection at the Ashmolean Museum, Oxford, is of particular interest because the invoice (a copy of which appears below) showing the cost of metal, fashioning and engraving, etc., is still in existence:

	£	s.	d.
Delivered a fyne sett of dresing plate, fynely carved all over and chased, weighing together 637 oz. 18 dwt.			
at 6s. 2d. per oz.	196.	13.	10.
Fashion 5s. per oz.	159.	10.	0.
Engraving of all ye armes, &c.	6.	6.	0.
For ye glase and wooden frame	5.	5.	0.
For ye 2 glasses for whater	-.	16.	0.
For lyning of ye two comme boxes, ye 2 draughts, and that of ye juelle tronk	2.	2.	0.
For ye locke to ye juelle tronk	1.	1.	0.
For ye tronk for all ye dresing plate	5.	5.	0.
For 4 bruches to clean ye cloth and commes	-.	15.	0.
	£377.	13.	10.

The high cost of five shillings per ounce for fashioning was no doubt justified by the importance of the set and quality of the work involved. It is curious that although groups of similar objects, the rectangular caskets for example, match each other, other unrelated articles are not so matched. The arms, which are very finely engraved in the so-called 'Hogarthian' style, are those of Treby quartering Grange with an escutcheon for Hele in pretence.

The invoices for most of the other items made for George Treby also still exist, and show that between 1721 and 1725 he paid De Lamerie no less than £2,025. 4s. 1d. for silver-plate.

The only other existing invoice relating to De Lamerie's work is one dated 21 December 1750, the year before his death:

Delivered to the Rt. Honble. the Earl of Lincoln [later the second Duke of Newcastle] as a Gift from His Majesty at the christening of his Child [George, Lord Clinton, d. 1752] One gilt Bafon and Ewer.

This *regium donum* weighed 130 oz. 10 dwt. and cost George II £75. 11s. 7d., or 11/6d. per ounce. It seems strange that although De Lamerie presumably received a number of Royal commissions in the course of his distinguished career, and was made a goldsmith to the King in 1716, he was never appointed to the coveted post of Royal Goldsmith: during the early part of his life this position was held by Samuel Smithin, and in later days by Thomas Minors.

One important piece of silver made for George Treby for which the invoice is missing, is a superbly engraved punch-bowl (complete with ladle) hallmarked for 1723–4, 8½ in. high and with a diameter of 13 in. Phillips describes it as follows:

The bowl is circular and perfectly plain, except for the engraved pictorial subjects on its main bulging surface. The constricted top and the high-stepped spreading base without the usual 'neck' are unusual features; the hinged handles are simply moulded and adorned with leaves on their lower surfaces, and hang from moulded brackets on the upper part of the body. The ladle is quite plain, with a deep bowl and has a tapering socket for its wooden handle.

These pieces were made for the Rt. Hon. George Treby . . . as a gift to Arthur Holdsworth of Dartmouth, Devon. The engraving is in the style of Hogarth. In one picture it represents a scene on a quay, with shipping afloat, with a procession of 11 men in costumes of the period, some wearing swords and one a long gown, preceded by 2 mace-bearers, and followed by a young man with a staff and an elderly one with a stick accompanied by a dog, an old woman bearing on a crutch, and a running boy in the rear; above are the words AMICITIA PERPETUA [Everlasting Friendship]. In the picture on the reverse side the same 11 companions are seated in a panelled room at a long table over the 'wassail-bowl'; some are smoking, all have wine-glasses before them, and the actual Punch Bowl is resting in front of the man in the centre; 2 men-servants are in attendance, one bringing in a further bowl to replenish the (presumably) emptied one; in front is a dog sparring at a cat partly under the table-cloth; above are the words PROSPERITY TO HOOKS AND LINES.

These 2 pictorial subjects are said to represent incidents occurring at Dartmouth, where, doubtless, there was established a Company of 'Adventurers in the Newfoundland Fishery Trade', of which both Treby and Holdsworth were members.

The arms against the first picture are those of Holdsworth impaling Lane. Arthur Holdsworth of Dartmouth, married Elizabeth, daughter of Henry Lane, also of Dartmouth, and widow of Captain John Vavasour. He was mayor of Dartmouth in 1725 and died in 1726.

The arms against the second picture are those of Treby quartering Grange. The Rt. Hon. George Treby[15] married in 1684, as his third wife, Dorothy, daughter of Ralph Grange.[16]

Mr. Arthur Grimwade has drawn to my attention a particularly attractive item by De Lamerie in the collection of Earl Spencer at Althorp,

15. [Rt. Hon. George Treby (1644?–1700), appointed Solicitor-General in 1688–9, was the father of De Lamerie's patron.]

16. pp. 79–80.

Northamptonshire. This is a bowl (8 in. in diameter and dated 1725) and stand (1723) first used as a christening-bowl for the baptism of John, 1st Earl Spencer in 1735, and as a font by the family ever since.

While both pieces are of the highest quality and grace, the dish is particularly interesting as showing, in the design of its rim, what I believe to be Lamerie's first tentative effort at the rococo style of which he was to become so great an exponent. Although the actual composition of the border is in fact strictly symmetrical, there is, in the broken scrolls, a liveliness of movement which had not before been seen in English silver, and which was soon to become, under Lamerie's leadership, a noteworthy characteristic of the new style. Impeccably executed, the whole has a truly feminine grace. . . .[17]

The *Daily Journal* of 7 December 1724 and 31 October 1727 reports De Lamerie as voting respectively for a Member of Parliament and for the office of Chamberlain of the City of London. In the *Daily Post* for 3 June 1728 the following notice appeared:

June 1, 1728. Broke open early this Morning, a House in Albemarle Street, and the following Pieces of Plate stolen . . . if offered to be pawn'd, sold or valued, stop them and the Party, and give notice to Mr. Paul de Lamerie, in Windmill-street, near Piccadilly . . . and you shall have . . . 50 l Reward for the Whole, or proportionable for any Part thereof.

In its Craig's Court Minute Book the Sun Fire Office lists an insurance policy taken out by De Lamerie, dated 17 October 1728: the policy covers household goods and chattels and tools employed in his trade in the sum of £200; stock of 'Wrought Plate' (which must have been a considerable quantity), for £800; and clothes and personal effects, presumably including those of his family (and possibly also those of his apprentices who, as was customary in the eighteenth century, doubtless lodged with him), for £100; the premium required was £2. 8s. 0d. This insurance policy is of some interest as it shows that by this early stage in his career, De Lamerie was already a man of considerable wealth and substance.

On 5 May 1731 De Lamerie advanced a step further in his profession, when 'At a Court of Assistants Mr. Paul de Lamerie was chosen to be an Assistant of the Goldsmiths' Company and excused the office of Rentor,

17. 'Silver at Althorp: III. The Hugeunot Period', in *The Connoisseur*, June 1963, p. 91, by A. G. Grimwade, F.S.A. (In this article this item is referred to as a 'porridge-bowl'; Mr. Grimwade, however, tells me that from more recent information the description given above is correct.)

on condition that he paid a fine of forty pounds cash to the use of the Company.' He thus became, at the age of forty-eight, a member of the governing body of his guild.

A little over a year later, on 17 March 1732, a further entry in the Company's books records that 'Paul de Lamerie entered a new maker's mark, being described as "att ye Golden Ball, Windmill Street, St. James".' In a generally illiterate era, when even in London houses had not

yet begun to be numbered, pictorial trade-signs, such as that adopted by De Lamerie, were a useful and often the only means of successfully advertising an address and business. A Royal charter granted by Charles I had given the citizens of London the right to 'expose and hang in and over the streets signs and posts of signs affixed to their houses and shops, for the better finding out such citizens' dwellings, shops, arts or occupations'. In 1716 John Gay (1685–1732), a contemporary of De Lamerie, published a poem entitled *Trivia, or the Art of Walking the Streets of London*, in which occur the following lines:

> Be sure observe the Signs, for Signs remain
> Like faithful Landmarks to the walking Train.

De Lamerie's new mark consists of the initial letter of his Christian and surname separated by a stop, again surmounted by a crown with a *fleur-de-lis* beneath. This mark is occasionally confused with that used, on silver of the 'Britannia' standard, by Peter Platel, i.e. the first two letters of his surname: however, apart from any other consideration, the date letter and assay mark which accompany it should be enough to identify the maker.

On 1 June 1720, as a result of the increase in the supply of silver from the East Indies and through the capture of increasing quantities of Spanish bullion on the high seas, the Wrought Plate Act came into force, and the Act of 1696–7 decreeing the use of the new 'Britannia' standard of silver was amended. In future goldsmiths were free 'without obligation or restraint' to use either the new or the old sterling standard (925 parts of pure silver) in manufacturing their wares. At the same time a new tax of sixpence an ounce was levied on all new plate: in a contemporary broadsheet, presented as a petition to the House of Commons, the writer, arguing against this additional imposition, claimed 'And if 6d. per oz. be laid on Plate the Manufacturer must for all weighty Plate, pay as much, or more than he receives for the Fashion.'[18] Even allowing for the writer's probable exaggeration, this throws an interesting light on the rate charged at the time by makers of silver-plate.

As a result of this new tax a number of working goldsmiths, including De Lamerie, adopted the practice of removing hallmarks from small light objects, and incorporating them into heavier and more important pieces, thus avoiding both the necessity of submitting them to be assayed or 'touched' and the payment of duty. These items became known as 'Duty-Dodgers'. Some two hundred years after they had been made, the suspicions of the officials of the London Assay Office were aroused concerning the legality of an important basin and ewer by De Lamerie: when the base of the ewer was heated, a circle of silver containing the hallmarks dropped out.

The finished product, after being assayed by the Goldsmiths' Company, bore the appropriate mark, the figure of Britannia for the new standard or that used prior to 1696, the lion passant gardant, for the old standard. The maker's mark in the case of plate made of the higher standard continued to be that registered when the higher standard was the only one permitted, i.e. the first two letters of the surname; if however a goldsmith decided to use the old standard of silver, then his mark had to consist of the initial letters of his Christian and surname. Thus a goldsmith could have two different marks in existence at the same time, one for each standard of silver.

Experience showed that plate made with the old standard of silver was more serviceable and durable than that made with the softer new standard, which was however more suited to the production of especially fine work. That De Lamerie did not officially register his new mark until twelve years after the date at which he could have done so, is probably due to the fact that he preferred to work in the higher standard of softer metal which better suited his fine and delicate craftsmanship. He and his patrons doubtless felt that the higher cost thus incurred was fully justified by the fine quality of the product. The date of his adoption of the old standard marks the time at which he decided to change from his earlier simple and pure style to the heavier and more ornate design with its increasing use of rococo decoration, for which he is best known today. As examples of his work exist dated prior to 1732 and stamped with his new mark, it is fair

18. Cf. the cost of fashioning in the Treby dressing-table set, p. 36.

to assume that he used this mark on occasion before it was officially entered, and possibly as early as 1724.

De Lamerie was by now a man of considerable means, and he began to look around for ways of diversifying his financial interests outside his own business. Even as men with capital do today, he eventually decided to invest in property, and to enter the mortgage market. The first of such transactions appears to be one contained in the Middlesex Land Register dated 7 April 1733, in which one Richard Nicholson, a carpenter, assigned land in that county to De Lamerie in consideration of the sum of £200; further deals of the same kind followed in 1734, '39, '41, and '43.

On 15 August 1734 De Lamerie is first recorded as having been sworn in as a member of the jury at a Trial of the Pyx[19] (at which the coinage is assayed), thus fulfilling one of the routine duties of a member of the Worshipful Company of Goldsmiths. Members were apparently only required to undertake this task at infrequent intervals, as the next recorded date on which De Lamerie was present at a Trial of the Pyx was not until 21 May 1740.

On St. Stephen's Day 1735 De Lamerie's father died; he was buried in St. Anne's Church, Westminster, being officially described as a 'parish-pauper'. Nothing is known of him since he received the Royal Bounty in 1703, and he probably remained poor for the rest of his life, gradually sinking lower and lower until finally entering, and ending his days in, the poor-house. While his son remained an apprentice he had clearly been unable to help his father, but we have no evidence to show that he did so once he became his own master. Father and son had presumably at some stage become estranged, and even the former's wife appears eventually to have deserted him, and gone to live with her son and daughter-in-law and their family in Windmill Street; it seems likely therefore that the old man died friendless and alone.

By 1736 De Lamerie was being described in official documents no longer as Mr. but as Captain, and by 1743 as Major. So far as is known he was never a member of any regular military organization such as the Honourable Artillery Company (raised under Royal Charter granted by Henry VIII in 1537), which was the only official regiment open to him

19. The Greek for 'box', in which are placed the samples to be tested. The Trial dates from at least 1248, and probably from Saxon or even Roman times. It was first entrusted to the Company in the reign of James I.

outside the regular army. The train-bands of the Stuart period and the militia had been disbanded, and the latter were not re-formed until 1759. De Lamerie's commission must therefore have been held in some private quasi-military volunteer body, which elected its own officers who were totally unrecognized by the authorities.

In 1737 De Lamerie received his first recorded commission for a piece – or to be exact two pieces – of ecclesiastical plate. The fine pair of candle-sticks, hallmarked for 1738–9, 23½ in. high and with a base diameter of 8½ in., were intended for use in the chapel of Queen's College, Oxford. Their general design is based on late seventeenth/early eighteenth-century taste, but their supporting columns are grouped differently from the style of that period and their bases are of an entirely new conception. The overall impression is late Gothic, the ornamentation high rococo.

Also marked for 1738–9 is a fine oval soup-tureen weighing 140 oz., measuring 17¼ in. long and 10½ in. high. The principal decoration on the bowl is provided by boldly executed lions' mask knees to the ball-and-claw feet, and on each side by an applied elaborate cartouche surrounding a central boss, which bears the arms of Madden impaling Creighton, from which depend, somewhat incongruously, a sheep's head and feet. The cover is decorated with a flat-chased rococo design which surrounds shell, scroll and foliate decoration which in turn encloses a central boss beneath the handle. Ten years later De Lamerie made a pair of smaller tureens, one bearing the arms of Neville, the other those of Pilkington, with indented corners, the finials of the covers being in the form of elaborately cast foliage and flowers. These three tureens are in the collection of the Campbell Museum, Camden, New Jersey, and in 1973 were exhibited at the Victoria and Albert Museum.

Made in the same year (1738–9) as the candlesticks in Queen's College are a fine pair of rococo table-candlesticks, 8½ in. high and weighing 45 oz., which were sold at Christie's in November 1973 for £6,500. Standing on square bases with incurving corners, the sides are each cast with a conch-shell and above with flowers and laurel in panels on a matted ground; the domed centres are decorated in a similar manner and with a band of large oval flutes; the baluster stems have pendant flower sprays, and the shoulders are ornamented with applied scallop shells.

On 19 January 1738 De Lamerie was appointed to a 'Committee [of the Goldsmiths' Company] for Parliament Business', whose duty it was to prepare a Bill to present to Parliament, designed to prevent the 'great frauds [which] are daily committed in the manufacturing of gold and silver wares for want of sufficient power effectually to prevent the same'. On 22 June 1739 the Committee exhibited a report of its proceedings, signed among others by De Lamerie, to the Court of Assistants. The resulting Plate Offences Act reaffirmed the two permitted standards of silver and one of gold, and ordered all manufacturing goldsmiths to enter a new maker's mark at Goldsmiths' Hall forthwith. Accordingly, we find De Lamerie entering his third and final mark: 'June 27, 1739. Paul de Lamerie entered a further maker's mark, being described as of "Garard Street of ye Goldsmith".' This mark departs in style from that in use by Parisian goldsmiths of the day, on which De Lamerie had based his two previous marks. His new mark consists of the letters PL in script, again surmounted by a crown but this time with a pellet instead of a *fleur-de-lis*

below. At the same time he changed his trade-sign from the 'Golden Ball' to that of 'Goldsmith'.

The move to Garard (or Gerrard) Street, though only just around the corner from Windmill Street, represents an important step in the great goldsmith's career. His success had clearly caused him to outgrow the premises in Windmill Street which he had occupied for at least twenty-three years. It was in his new workshop (in the ninth house on the south side starting from the east end) in the then aristocratic neighbourhood of Gerrard Street, that De Lamerie was to fashion the bulk of the imposing rococo plate for which he is best remembered today.

What must have been one of the earliest important pieces of silver emanating from Gerrard Street is today generally accepted as one of his most notable *oeuvres*. The cup-and-cover, 13½ in. high and hallmarked for 1739–40, exhibit a grace of line and novelty in decoration which could only have been produced by a man with outstanding technical skill and the most fertile imagination. Exactly one hundred years after it was made it was presented to the Worshipful Company of Goldsmiths by John Gawler Bridge, of Rundell & Bridge, Crown Goldsmiths, whose arms it bears. In their catalogue of the Company's plate Carrington and Hughes describe it thus:

The body is bell-shaped, plain above and matted below, and is divided into two portions by a broad reeded and strapped band from which hang six pendants of flowers and ribands. Six straps of vine-work enclosing the masks of satyrs rise from the top edge of the foot, which is divided into two parts by a reeded and strapped band. The foot is slightly domed and decorated with leafage and scroll-work on a matted ground and has an ornamental moulding at the edge. The handles are double-scrolled, a somewhat new form at this period.

The cover, with a reeded and strapped edge, rises in a roll to a high matted dome decorated with straps. Pendants of flowers descend from the base of the knob, which is formed of two-leaved scrolls, two ram's heads, and a flower with inverted petals.[20]

Hallmarked for the same year is another highly ornamental cup-and-cover of exceptional quality and with similarly graceful lines. Known as the 'Ashburnham Cup' it bears the inscription, 'Gift of John, Earl of Ashburnham, to Clare Hall in Cambridge'.

Also made by De Lamerie in 1740 is an interesting item of domestic silver: this is the earliest and finest extant English fish-slice, now in the Ashmolean Museum, Oxford: it has a spoon-type handle extending into the blade, which takes the form of a flat oval disc, pierced and engraved with appropriate piscatory motifs.

In the house in Windmill Street De Lamerie had seen both his sons and two of his daughters die; the only sad event which took place in Gerrard Street was the death in January 1740 of his mother, who was buried on the 25th in the church of St. Anne, Westminster. This must have been a melancholy occasion for De Lamerie, as his mother had been living with him and his family for a number of years, and mother and son had presumably been close.

Although now renowned throughout the world as a master of his craft, and even during his lifetime recognized as a fine workman, De Lamerie, like so many other great artists in various mediums, did not receive full recognition until some time after his death. Consequently, not as much is known about his private life as we should like; although there is no evidence to support such a supposition, it is tempting to imagine his two younger daughters, Louisa Elizabeth and Susannah, then aged nine and ten respectively, running into their father's workshop to play while he worked; while their elder sister Mary, aged nineteen, flirted with (and perhaps even sometimes helped) the apprentices on duty in the shop.

20. p. 91.

On 9 December 1741 De Lamerie is mentioned in the minutes of a meeting of the Court of the Goldsmiths' Company, as having been commissioned to make some plate for the Company in memory of a number of its benefactors whose gifts had been melted down and sold in 1667 and 1711 to pay off a number of the Company's debts.

The gilt 'standish' or ink-stand, $16\frac{1}{4}$ in. long and $12\frac{3}{4}$ in. wide, which he produced in answer to this commission and which was designed to hold a bell presented to the Worshipful Company of Goldsmiths by Sir Robert Vyner, Crown Goldsmith in 1667, is among his finest and most decorative creations. Carrington and Hughes describe it as follows:

The Inkstand (1741) is oblong with wavy outlines with four scrolled feet at the corners. There are two hollows on each side for holding pens, and a round hollow in the centre for wafers, on which the bell now stands. On each side of the centre hollow two boxes for ink and sand fit into compartments which are engraved with the Arms of the Company and surrounded by a wreath of snakes entwined with flowers. Both boxes are pedestal-shaped and bear figures of young Mercury and Hercules, and scrolls, straps and flowers, with the Crest and Arms of the Company in relief.

The border of the inkstand is chased with bold plain scroll-work interlaced with wreaths of flowers and drapery and two leopards' heads facing inwards over the hollow. At each corner, over the feet, bold heads of Jupiter, Minerva, Mercury and Juno (or Venus) are placed. Two feet bear the Arms, and two the Crest, of the Company.[21]

The gilt helmet-ewer and basin dated 1741–2 which were also part of the commission and are still in the possession of the Company, are of imaginative design and superlative craftsmanship. The basin, which measures 21 in. across, is described by Carrington and Hughes as:

Circular in form; the border $6\frac{1}{2}$ in. wide has an edge of broken outline formed of bold scrolls united by flowers, helmets, torches, and masks, and other ornamentation in great variety. Inside this border are four oval medallions each filled by boy figures representing Hercules with club and hydra, Mercury with bag and cock, Vulcan with armour and anvil and Minerva with owl, serpent and helmet. Between these medallions are figures of an eagle, a hooded falcon, a lion and a dolphin, and panels of diaper work. In the centre of the dish the arms of the Company appear in bold relief on a plain burnished background. The whole of the decoration, both of the ewer and its dish, is cast in high relief, laid on and chased. The detail which is very intricate and finely modelled is distinctively English though reminiscent of the florid French taste of the period.

21. p. 95.

(The inscription on the shield borne by Minerva reads 'By prudence and good management I am restored'. This refers to the restoration of the benefactors' plate which had been melted down previously and was restored about 1740.)

The lip and edge of the vase (which measures 14¾ in. high) are formed as scrolls with brackets, tendrils and branches, and leopards' heads (one of the badges of the Company) and from the latter hang wreaths of flowers. A highly raised band encircles the body, the lower portion of which is ornamented by a winged mermaid with double tail twisting round the stem and by young tritons floating on waves and blowing conch-shells. The stem, formed in foam-work, rests on a shaped foot with scroll edges surrounding panels in which are placed flowers, shells, a lizard and a snake. The handle is in the form of a marine god clasping in both hands a scroll which is attached to the body. It terminates in another scroll formed from the tail of the god. The arms of the Company are displayed under the lip.[22]

The whole piece, but especially the splendidly modelled (though somewhat over-large) triton handle and sumptuously scrolled base, is strongly reminiscent of the work of the great French designer Juste-Aurèle Meissonnier (1695–1750).

Bearing hallmarks for 1743–4 and of imposing size (length 21 in., width 20 in., height 9⅞ in.) is a most impressive centrepiece, considered by some to be De Lamerie's masterpiece. It is described by Phillips as follows:

The decoration in this example is cast, chased and repoussé. De Lamerie has departed from his flat-chased rococo ornament on flat surfaces, and has definitely become an exponent of more pronounced embellishments. The raised scroll and shell and voluted borders of the dishes, with festoons of flowers and varying panels; the somewhat riotous adornment of the central circular bowl, with its bust, shells, flowers, and scroll and shell bordered panels enclosing landscape views; the cherubs within the flower and scrolled lambrequins below its strap-adorned spreading base; the elaborate scrolled, voluted and foliated brackets with their lion's mask and paw feet supported by voluted scrolls – all in high relief; the scroll and panel decoration inside the dishes – in low relief – show his skill in combining diverse motifs of ornament. The use of the band of strap work around the base of the bowl is a throwback to the work of earlier days, whilst the ringed and intertwined ribbon on the rim is of more recent use.[23]

This superb example of the goldsmith's art is known as the 'Newdigate Centrepiece'; in addition to being engraved on the outside with the arms

22. pp. 94–5.   23. p. 108.

of that family, it bears on the inside the following inscription: 'The Gift of ye Rt. Honble· Sophia Baroness Lempster to S^r· Roger & Lady Newdigate, A.D. 1743'. It is now in the collection of the Victoria and Albert Museum. To adapt the epitaph in St. Paul's Cathedral to Sir Christopher Wren (1632–1723), *Si monumentum requiris, aspice.*

The middle 1740s saw a revival of the fashion for *chinoiserie* decoration. This unusual form of ornamentation, which had originally been introduced at about the time of De Lamerie's birth, appears to have been used to decorate silver only in England, although it was much used on the Continent on porcelain and furniture. *Chinoiserie* was largely inspired by, and freely adapted from, travel books illustrated, and sometimes even written, by those who had never actually visited the Far East, and who therefore had to rely on second-hand accounts from returning merchants and seamen; hence the somewhat symbolist designs. The fantastical figures of Chinese in long, flowing robes, wearing 'coolie' hats and carrying 'mushroom' sunshades as they walk among stylized flowers, Rackhamesque trees in which perch exotic birds, and pagoda-like houses, have an indefinable naïve attraction.

Between about 1680 and 1690 *chinoiserie* decoration was either engraved or flat-chased. When it was revived in the middle 1740s it appeared in the form of high relief, being normally employed to decorate items connected with tea-making, especially sugar-boxes and tea-caddies. A fine pair of silver-gilt caddies by De Lamerie dated 1747 are in the collection at Goldsmiths' Hall; they are profusely decorated with bats'-wing fluting and *repoussé* chasing of harvesting scenes, rustic thatched huts, palm-trees, cherubs' masks and scrolls; the finials are formed as prostrate tea-plants. A very similar pair, 5⅜ in. high, made by De Lamerie in 1744 were sold by Christie's at the Hôtel Richemond in Geneva in November 1972 for £6,257 (Sw. fr. 56,000).

In 1743 De Lamerie took another step upwards in the hierarchy of his guild: 'May 18, 1743. At a Court of Assistants Captain Paul de Lamerie was elected to the office of Fourth Warden'; he took the oath of office on 30 May. He was absent from the Trial of the Pyx on 23 July 1745, but attended that of 1750, the last before his death. On 22 May 1746 'at a Court of Assistants Major Paul de Lamerie was elected to the office of Third Warden', at the same meeting being elected to the Standing Committee of the Goldsmiths' Company. The following year, on 20 May, he was appointed Second Warden, taking the oath nine days later. He was now but one step away from the highest office which the Worshipful

Company of Goldsmiths has to offer, that of the Prime Wardenship; death sadly cheated him of this final honour.

In 1748 De Lamerie made a superbly conceived pair of candlebra which in June 1973 sold at Christie's (from the collection of the Earl of Liverpool) for £22,000; to quote the catalogue: 'the candlesticks on shaped triangular rococo bases chased with swirling scrolls, flowers and foliage on a matted ground, the stems formed as male and female figures holding above their heads a vase-shaped floral socket, with detachable nozzles, engraved with a coat-of-arms [Jenkinson, perhaps for Charles (1693–1750), father of Charles Jenkinson, 1st Earl of Liverpool]. The two-light branches with scroll foliate and female caryatids supporting flower-shaped wax-pans and nozzles, the central flame finial chased below with shells and scalework – 15 in. high ... the sticks 1748, one of the branches 1736 ... 160 ozs.'[24]

29 March 1750 must have been a happy day in the life of the great goldsmith, for on that day he saw his second surviving daughter Susannah, then aged twenty-one, married at the Church of St. Giles-in-the-Fields to Joseph Debaufré, a merchant of Hatton Garden and a member of an old and respected Huguenot family. The bridegroom's grandfather, father and uncle were all noted clockmakers, and were members of the guild of their trade.

On 20 December 1750 De Lamerie attended for the last time a meeting of the Worshipful Company of Goldsmiths; he must by then have been a sick man as his will, drawn up on 24 May 1751, speaks of his 'long and tedious Illness'. He died in his house in Gerrard Street, no doubt surrounded by his family, on 1 August, and was buried six days later, in St. Anne's Church, Westminster.

Although De Lamerie had doubtless been brought up and educated in England as a good French Protestant (his father having joined the church of his faith in London) and was very probably bilingual, he appears never to have joined that church himself, as his name is nowhere to be found on any list of membership or *témoignage*. It is likely that he joined the English church instead, and that he married in a French church only to please his bride and future parents-in-law. All the baptisms and burials in his family took place in the English churches of St. James and St. Anne respectively. Nor, so far as is known, does he seem to have taken part in any Huguenot activities in London. From the time that he abandoned the

24. For a similar pair see Phillips, plate CLIII.

Parisian style when entering his third maker's mark in 1739, it seems that he wished finally to divorce himself from the land of his fathers and adhere solely to that of his adoption.

Following his death a number of obituary notices appeared in London newspapers, of which that published in the edition of the *London Evening Post* for 3–6 August is perhaps the most interesting: '. . . the same day died Paul D'Lemerie, Esq; an eminent Goldsmith in Gerard-Street, Soho; . . . was particularly famous in making fine ornamental Plate, and has been very instrumental in bringing that Branch of Trade to the Perfection it is now in.'

De Lamerie left behind to mourn him a widow and three daughters: his will, which was proved on 8 August, was a somewhat complicated document, and mainly provided for his surviving family.

As he had, through the death in infancy of his two sons, no male heir to whom to bequeath his now flourishing business, he declared that it was to be wound up. An inventory was to be prepared of the stock of finished plate and of work in hand; the latter was to be completed and then all was to be sold by public auction. He appointed as auctioneer Abraham Langford (1711–74), the celebrated playwright and leading auctioneer of the day, who had premises in the north-east corner of Inigo Jones' colonnaded Piazza at Covent Garden, 'If he will do it at the same price that another will.'

There is no record of any auction catalogues in existence which would provide interesting information on the prices obtained for the goldsmith's possessions, but the *Daily Advertiser* of 16 January and 4 February 1752 carried the two following sale announcements: 'All the Genuine, Rich and elegant stock of plate [consisting of "Tables, Terreens and covers, Bread-Baskets, Sauce-Boats, Tea-Kettles, Tea-Chests, Cannisters, Coffee-Pots, Figure and other Candle-Sticks, Girandoles, Cases of Knives, Forks and Spoons, Cups and covers, Tankards, Mugs, Salts, Tea-spoons &c. all enriched and finish'd in the highest taste;"] watches, and valuable jewels' were to be sold *in situ* in Gerrard Street. 'All the genuine and entire stock of curious patterns and tools, with all the mahogany and other presses, counters, drawers, shelves, desks and other fixtures of the shop' were to be disposed of in Langford's rooms in Covent Garden. A number of De Lamerie's patterns and moulds were bought by Philip (or Phillips) Garden. It is worth noting in passing that the stock consisted of watches and jewellery as well as silver-plate; clearly De Lamerie continued to the last to be a trader as well as a manufacturer: it may well be that some at

4

least of his stock of watches were made by the grandfather, father and uncle of his son-in-law Joseph Debaufré, whose products are today much sought after in the sale-rooms.

The sale announcement (and the insurance policy taken out in 1728) show that De Lamerie kept in stock a considerable amount of wrought silver. This is of interest, as it shows that in addition to fulfilling private commissions De Lamerie and his English contemporaries were working for stock for sale over the counter to casual buyers. They were thus, doubtless unconsciously, preparing the way for a system which would eventually lead to the industrialization of their trade. This practice may also possibly have had some bearing on the design and conservative style of the majority of silver produced in England in the eighteenth century. De Lamerie's more splendid and elaborate creations were almost certainly produced in answer to specific private commissions, while his simple and less ornate pieces were intended for stock.

Apart from some personal legacies the remainder of the will contained provisions for the future of his widow and two unmarried daughters. Out of rents received from two freehold houses which he owned in the Haymarket (the sale of some of De Lamerie's leasehold properties of which, as previously mentioned, he owned a number, took place on 27 November 1751), and from interest on other investments, Mary and Louisa were each to receive, during the lifetime of their mother, an annuity of £30 until marriage. De Lamerie clearly wished to keep the family unit intact, and possibly fearing that argument might break out between mother and daughters after his death, left specific instructions for the maintenance of the home. Mary and Louisa were to be permitted to continue to live with their mother in the house in Gerrard Street, where each was to have her own separate apartment with the use of all necessary furniture, and free board and lodging paid for by their mother out of the income she received from the residue of the estate. After her death the house and contents in Gerrard Street and the two houses in the Haymarket were to be divided equally between all three daughters.

Among his personal bequests De Lamerie left the sum of £500 to his daughter Mary, 'in consideration of her dutiful behaviour to me during the whole Course of her Life and for her tender care and affectionate regard for me during a long and tedious Illness'. To his book-keeper, Isaac Gyles, he left the sum of 40 guineas, and to his nurse Sarah Clarke who had cared for him during his final sickness, 20 guineas; to his journeymen Frederick Knopfell and Samuel Collins £15 and £20 respectively, to the latter on condition that he remained in the service of the executors for a period long enough to complete the work in hand. As mentioned above, Collins had been one of De Lamerie's apprentices, and the latter obviously thought highly of his former pupil and trusted him to complete work on the unfinished plate. As executors he appointed his wife, and two Huguenot friends, Charles Fouace and John Malliet, to each of whom he left 10 guineas 'for a Ring or what else they please'.

After his death his family continued to live together, amicably so far as is known, in the house in Gerrard Street until, on 11 November 1754, Mary at the age of thirty-four married John Malliet at St. Anne's Church, Westminster. There is no record of how well the couple knew each other before her father's death, but it seems clear that their friendship increased while he was acting as one of the goldsmith's executors. De Lamerie's widow lived long enough to see the birth in 1759 of one Malliet grand-daughter, Louisa, and two Debaufré grandsons, Joseph in 1754 and Richard in 1756, as well as the death at Richmond, Surrey, on 22 September 1761, at the age of thirty, of her daughter Louisa, before she herself died in the same house in Gerrard Street on 8 June 1765. In her will she left Isaac Gyles and Sarah Clarke, both of whom were presumably still in her employment, an annuity of £12 each for life, and her jewellery to Louisa who had, however, pre-deceased her. The residue of her estate was to be divided among her daughters and grandchildren: she appointed as executors her nephew Solomon Paul Juliott and her son-in-law John Malliet.

Of Paul and Louisa De Lamerie's two surviving daughters, Susannah died on 28 July 1803, and Mary on 15 September 1810: of the former's two sons, Joseph married in 1780 Mary Hodgkin, who bore him two daughters: Elizabeth the elder, born on 13 February 1784, married on 7 June 1804 John Guyon, Royal Navy, seventeen years her senior, one of the twenty-one children of Henry William Guyon of Frognal Hall, Hampstead, and is the progenitor of all those descendants of her illustrious grandfather who are alive today.

We have now traced the career of De Lamerie from his birth in Bois-le-Duc in 1688 to his death in London sixty-three years later: but what of his skill as a goldsmith for which he is today so famous?

In order to be able to evaluate properly De Lamerie's professional skill both as craftsman and designer, and to be able to see his work in its proper perspective in relation to that of his predecessors, contemporaries and successors, one must first appreciate the existing state of the English goldsmith's art as it stood at the start of the eighteenth century.

The most distinctive form of ornamentation of the so-called English 'William and Mary' style was convex and/or concave fluting, normally expressed in the form of vertical, horizontal, slanting or curving parallel lines, usually finished off with a beaded or corded band on the remaining plain surface: this design was sometimes completed with decoration of simple stamped foliage (known as 'cut-card work') and an embossed shield. The so-called 'Queen Anne' style, with its perfectly plain surfaces totally unornamented apart from simple discreet mouldings, was then, and still is today, regarded as the height of good taste, in its fundamental purity and simplicity. This plain, simple and uncomplicated style is essentially of English origin, having evolved over centuries in unbroken line; it is always distinct from plain Continental pieces in both form and proportion.

Flamboyantly ornamental silver with motifs derived from classical mythology; extravagant strap-work; decorative chasing; elaborate moulding; naturalistic casting and engraving in the style which came to be known as 'rococo', is, on the other hand, entirely of Continental origin. All English plate of the period in this taste owes its style to French designers who themselves derived much of their inspiration from Italian influence: such masters as Gilles-Marie Oppenort (1672–1742), Thomas Germain (1673–1748; appointed *orfèvre du roi* in 1723), and Juste-Aurèle Meissonnier (appointed *dessinateur pour les pompes funèbres et galantes* and *orfèvre du roi* in 1724, and *dessinateur de la chambre et du cabinet du roi* in December of the following year by Louis XV) spent much of their early years studying in Genoa and Rome.

In the late seventeenth and early eighteenth centuries many silversmiths working in England were of foreign extraction; prior to 1685 they were mostly of German or Dutch origin, but after the Revocation of the Edict of Nantes in that year they were joined by an increasing number of Huguenot refugees from France. As can be imagined, their arrival in England in considerable numbers was looked upon with much disfavour by the native-born English manufacturing goldsmiths, who naturally enough viewed them not as a stimulating and invigorating influence but as a serious threat to their livelihood. Various petitions were presented to the Worshipful Company of Goldsmiths arguing that Huguenots should not be accepted into the Company nor be made Free of the City, and that the Company should refuse to assay or 'touch' any of their wares: as a result, it was a number of years before Huguenots were assimilated by, and generally accepted as part of, the English goldsmiths' establishment.

The sons of Huguenot immigrants were often apprenticed to masters who were themselves of Huguenot origin, and as was to be expected they absorbed much of their masters' manufacturing skill and designing knowledge: they were thus able themselves to carry a stage further the ideas and designs brought to this country by their masters from France. Due largely to the competition supplied by native-born English craftsmen, and to the inherent need for immigrants to excel indigenes in order to achieve equal recognition and success, Huguenot goldsmiths in England showed noticeable improvements in designing ability and in their formulation of creative ideas once they became established in this country.

In the early days of De Lamerie's career such goldsmiths of Huguenot extraction as Pierre Harache, David Willaume, Augustine Courtauld, Peter Archambo (the father of De Lamerie's apprentice), Peter Platel, Simon Pantin, Louis Mettayer and Paul Crespin, together with the native-born Englishmen Anthony Nelme and Benjamin Pyne, were all producing superb examples of the goldsmith's art: the same may be said of Charles and Frederick Kandler, Samuel Courtauld and Nicholas Sprimont in the second part of De Lamerie's working life. The characteristic style which they evolved was largely based on the designers of the Louis XV taste already mentioned, and on the work of Jean Lepautre (1618–82), Paul Ducerceau (c. 1630–1713), and Jean Bérain, created *dessinateur de la chambre et du cabinet du roi* by Louis XIV in 1674.

There can be little doubt that De Lamerie is the most outstanding craftsman in silver and gold that this country has produced: although of French parentage he came to this country at a very early age, and was thus under English influence for much longer than his working life. His master, Peter Platel, to whom he was apprenticed and who was to have so great an effect on his future work, was himself one of the finest craftsmen of his period, and passed on much of his knowledge to his pupil.

De Lamerie's career can be neatly and conveniently divided into halves; the first lasted for the duration of his first maker's mark from 1712 to 1732; during this period, when the simple baluster style was much in vogue, he worked mostly in the softer 'Britannia' standard of silver, producing exceptionally beautiful and essentially simple pieces of plate, such as George Treby's punch-bowl, with little if any applied ornament and of a more delicate and less elaborate design than he was to make in later life.

The second half of De Lamerie's career dates from the entering of his second maker's mark in 1732 to his death in 1751. With the passing into law of the Wrought Plate Bill of 1719 goldsmiths were permitted to work in either the old or new standards of silver. De Lamerie remained for some time faithful to the softer new standard, believing both that the quality of his wares demanded it and that his patrons' pockets could well stand the higher price which it entailed. Gradually, however, the heavier and more ornate rococo style began to supersede the simpler and more elegant 'Queen Anne' design; being an astute business man and seeing in which direction his future prosperity lay, De Lamerie became one of its prime exponents. That he did not start to produce plate in the rococo taste earlier than he did, is partly explained by his reluctance to change to the harder but lower standard of silver which the heavier new style required, and partly by the fact that the prevailing demand had up to that time been for plate in the 'Queen Anne' taste.

It was his production of silver-plate in the rococo style which was to bring De Lamerie lasting fame; although he freely adapted to his own purposes the designs of such French masters as Bérain and Meissonnier; the *Stil rustique*[25] of Wenzel Jamnitzer (1508–85); the 'auricular' or 'lobate'[26] style of the van Vianens; and indeed on occasion the work of his immediate predecessors and contemporaries in England, he never allowed himself to become submerged by their ideas, and was always able to express his own thoughts through his mastery of detail and craftsmanship. In spite of the fact that he frequently repeated many of his designs, he was always most careful to make changes in the details, sometimes for example substituting a swing-handle for a fixed one, or slightly altering the curve of a spout or the design of a finial.

25. Described by Johann Neudörfer, the chronicler of Nuremberg, as the art of 'casting little animals, worms, weeds and snails in silver . . . so delicate and thin that they move when one blows on them'.

26. Known in Holland as *Kwabornament* and in Germany as *Knorpelwerk*, this seems to be the only decorative style which was developed principally by goldsmiths. It makes use of plastic scrolling motifs, reminiscent of the shape of the ear, to create Bosch-ian fantasies of people and monsters growing out of each other, which contrast sharply with areas depicting mythological scenes in calm and delicate workmanship. This style was pioneered by Adam van Vianen of Utrecht (*c.* 1565–1617), his brother Paulus (*c.* 1568–1613), and his son Christian (b. 1598) who in 1650 published a book of his and his father's designs entitled *Modelles artificiels de divers vaisseaux d'argent*.

If he did not at all times excel in every respect some of his distinguished contemporaries, a number of whom could on occasion rise to great heights, De Lamerie nevertheless remained *primus inter pares*; few of his rivals could emulate his most distinctive characteristic, scrolling foliate chasing on a matted and diapered background; nor could many of them match him for painstaking attention to detail (in, for instance, the apparently minor matter of the piercing of a caster or pounce-box), or, above all, for consistency; De Lamerie had few, if any, failures. Yet some of his work, though never ugly or banal, could become over-elaborate and even somewhat unbalanced: the handle of the ewer in the possession of the Goldsmiths' Company, for example, appears rather out of proportion when compared with the lip on the opposite side, and indeed in relation to the size of the whole piece. De Lamerie could never be accused of poor craftsmanship, only on occasion (as, for example, in some of the decoration on Peter the Great's wine-fountain) of a lapse in taste. The figure, chased in high relief, of Cupid notching an arrow to his bow as he sits amidst rocks, chased flowers and scrollwork, on the body of a kettle made in 1745, accords ill with the reptilian-tailed sea-horse which forms the knop of the cover. It was as if De Lamerie's fertile imagination and sheer virtuosity at times ran away with him; this is especially true in some of his smaller and less important pieces, to which the elaborate rococo style is less well adapted. In his more spectacular creations, however, De Lamerie displayed the touch of a true master and near genius in the manner in which he played off the high relief of rococo with the softness of flat chasing, seen to advantage in the basin belonging to the Goldsmiths' Company.[27]

During the last two or three years of his life the pioneer of the rococo taste, as if wearying of such flamboyance which in others could sometimes amount almost to vulgarity, began to show a return to his earlier and more simple style: the wheel had turned full circle. If at this period in his life De Lamerie had turned his attention from gold and silver to bronze and marble, like the most celebrated of all goldsmiths, the vainglorious Benvenuto Cellini (1500–71), it is interesting to speculate on what masterpieces in these mediums he might have produced.

27. Cf. the 'Newdigate Centrepiece', pp. 46–7.

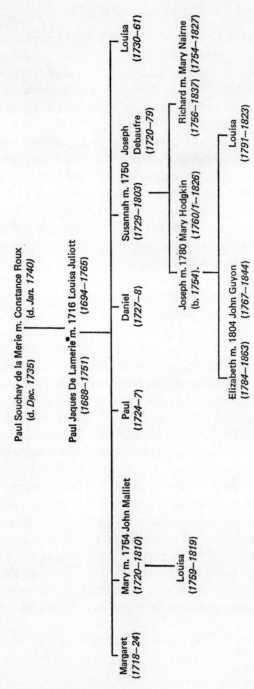

DE LAMERIE PEDIGREE

Paul Souchay de la Merie m. Constance Roux
(d. *Jan. 1740*)

● Paul Jaques De Lamerie m. 1716 Louisa Juliott
(*1688–1751*)   (*1694–1765*)

Margaret
(*1718–24*)

Mary m. 1754 John Malliet
(*1720–1810*)

Louisa
(*1759–1819*)

Paul
(*1724–7*)

Daniel
(*1727–8*)

Susannah m. 1750   Joseph
(*1729–1803*)   Debaufre
(*1720–79*)

Louisa
(*1730–61*)

Joseph m. 1780 Mary Hodgkin
(b. 1754).   (*1760/1–1826*)

Richard m. Mary Nairne
(*1756–1837*) (*1754–1827*)

Elizabeth m. 1804 John Guyon
(*1784–1863*)   (*1767–1844*)

Louisa
(*1791–1823*)

● practised as goldsmith

Hester Bateman

(1709-1794)

and her Family

HESTER BATEMAN, most celebrated of English women goldsmiths, was born in late February or early March 1709, the youngest child of Thomas and Ann Needham; she was baptized in the parish church of St. James, Clerkenwell, on 24 March of that year. It seems probable that Hester's father was well advanced into middle age at the time of her birth, as her mother, Ann Booth, whom he had married at St. Botolph's, Bishopsgate, in May 1703, was his third wife. Hester had an elder brother, William, born in 1704, and a sister Margaret, born in 1708, as well as a half-brother John (for many years landlord of the 'Heathcock' inn in the Strand) and half-sister, Elizabeth. When he died, John left Elizabeth and Hester 'one guinea apiece to buy mourning rings'.

In 1729 Hester married John Bateman, son of the John Bateman, who, in 1697, was registered as an apprentice by the Gold and Silver Wyre Drawers Company, when he was described as 'the son of John Bateman, late of Stafford, Gent.'. The ceremony did not, however, take place in church, but in the no doubt somewhat depressing surroundings of the notorious Fleet prison-house, where numerous legal but 'run-away' marriages were carried out by unscrupulous clerics imprisoned for debt: such marriages remained legal until 1753. In his *Account of London* (1790) the naturalist and antiquary Thomas Pennant (1726–98), friend and correspondent of Gilbert White of Selborne, and contemporary of Hester Bateman, gives the following account of this aspect of life in the Fleet:

Along this most lawless space was hung up the frequent sign of a male and female hand conjoined, with *Marriages Performed Within* written beneath. The parson was seen walking before his shop; a squalid profligate figure, clad in a tattered plaid night-gown, with a fiery face, and ready to couple you for a dram of gin, or roll of tobacco.

John and Hester Bateman's first child, named John after his father, was born in 1730, and baptized at the Church of All Hallows in London Wall on 29 March of that year. On 20 May 1732 his parents were married 'in the sight of God' at the parish church of St. Botolph, Aldersgate. The application for the licence, signed by John himself, was witnessed by Robert Sleeford, Notary Public. In the licence Hester is described as 'aged above twenty-one years and a Spinster', while John is given as 'aged twenty-five years and a Bachelor' of the parish of St. Bartholomew-the-Less: his occupation is given as a 'Gold Chain Maker'. In several documents referring to John Bateman he is variously described as a 'Chain Maker', a 'Watch Chain Maker', a 'Wyre Drawer' and a 'Goldsmith': he did not, however, serve any apprenticeship to these crafts, and was thus never officially qualified to carry on business within the borders of the City of London, where jurisdiction over their members was held by the Livery Companies. It is likely, therefore, that he worked at his home as an 'outworker' for duly qualified masters in the trade.

John and Hester Bateman's next two children were both girls, Letticia and Ann. Ann, the younger, was baptized at St. Botolph's, Aldersgate, in 1736, but we know nothing of Letticia's place of birth nor indeed, until 1740, do we know where John and Hester and their three children were living. On 25 January of that year a second son, Peter, was born in the Batemans' then home in Nixon's Square, in the parish of St. Giles, Cripplegate, a neighbourhood much favoured by 'out-workers' carrying out commissions for craftsmen working within the City. On 8 September 1745 a third son, William, was born in the house in Nixon's Square and was, like his brother Peter, baptized in the church of St. Giles. It is probable, though by no means certain, that he was the 'William Bateman, Goldsmith' who was the father of a daughter, Sarah, whose birth was registered in the parish church of St. Luke, Old Street, in the County of Middlesex, in 1771.

By now it seems clear that the Batemans were prospering in their trade, and in 1747 they moved into larger premises in a more affluent neighbourhood, No. 107 Bunhill Row, near the Dissenters' cemetery in Bunhill Fields, in the parish of St. Luke, a short distance north of the City, another area patronized by 'outworking' craftsmen; here the family was to remain for over a hundred years. Other goldsmiths known to have been working at the time in Bunhill Row are James Howell and Cornelius Bland. A drawing in the possession of Thomas de la Rue & Co. (executed shortly before the house was demolished in 1915) shows No. 107 to have been one of a short row on the west side of the street, slightly smaller than its neighbours, a typical early Georgian house with a formal and dignified classical façade, consisting within of some nine or ten rooms. A house of this size would of course necessitate the employment of a servant, and it is known that the Batemans employed at least one, at a salary of £4. 0s. 0d. per annum. On one side of the Batemans' home, in No. 106, lived Nathaniel Dell, a manufacturer of mathematical instruments; on the other side in No. 108 which was on the corner of Blue Anchor Alley, lived one William Best, whose occupation is unknown.

Shortly after moving to Bunhill Row in 1747, John and Hester Bateman's fifth and last child, Jonathan, was born on 18 November of that year, being baptized at the church of St. Luke in the following month.

During the succeeding thirteen years we hear nothing of John and Hester and their family, but it seems safe to assume that they continued to flourish and their business to expand, John making watch-chains and fashioning silver for master-goldsmiths within the City, helped by his eldest son John, who had entered the trade in 1744. It was doubtless during this period that Hester first got the 'feel' of silver by buffing by hand with a piece of steel the finished items of wrought plate emanating from her husband's workshop, a monotonous and repetitive job invariably assigned to the women of the household.

We next hear of the Batemans in 1760, for on 16 November of that year John died 'of consumption', being buried a few days later in St. Luke's churchyard.

It is at this point in our story that the character of Hester Bateman begins to emerge. To have been widowed at the age of fifty-one was nothing unusual in the eighteenth century; to have carried on her husband's business after his death was commonplace; the *Veuve* Dumas of Paris and the *Veuve* Perrin of Marseilles are examples of successful widows in the field of faience, as is the *Veuve* Clicquot in that of wine; in this country numerous pieces of eighteenth-century silver exist bearing a widow's initials, usually contained within the widow's lozenge-shaped shield. What is exceptional in the case of Hester Bateman is the manner in which she not only continued to run her husband's business but actually managed to enlarge and expand it, and ultimately make an independent name for herself: Hester Bateman was clearly a most determined, shrewd and intelligent woman, and moreover a physically strong one, for she did not retire from the business until she was over eighty years old. What she achieved is made to appear even more remarkable when it is realized that she had received little, if any, formal education, and as a result was totally illiterate. She signed all necessary documents with a simple X, against which a witness would inscribe 'Hester Bateman, her mark'.

It would, of course, be naïve and over-romantic to imagine, as many people do, that silver bearing Hester's – or for that matter any other widow's – mark was actually fashioned with her own hands. Widows were mostly, or even entirely, concerned with the running of the business – with obtaining designs, accepting commissions, marketing their wares, sending out accounts and balancing their books – and would seldom enter their workshops other than to give instructions or approve completed items.

Acting with urgency Hester succeeded in proving her husband's will, in which he specifically bequeathed to his wife the tools of his trade, one of a craftsman's most prized possessions, on the actual day of his death, and at once took upon herself the responsibilities of the business. In this task she was ably assisted by her two eldest sons, John and Peter, and an apprentice named John Linney who, after the death of his master, remained to complete his apprenticeship under his widow.

John Bateman Junr. had been apprenticed in 1744 to James Slater, a Merchant Taylor. On 24 March 1749, however, he was made over by mutual agreement for the remaining years of his apprenticeship to William Shaw, 'Citizen and Goldsmith', becoming Free of the Worshipful Company of Goldsmiths in 1751. He thereupon returned to his parents' home in Bunhill Row, shortly afterwards marrying Alice Case, the daughter of a member of the Carpenters' Company. They had four children: Phoebe, who died at the age of four; Thomas, who later became a 'Goldbeater'; Peter, who became a Freeman of the City of London on 17 April 1797, being described as 'the apprentice of Thomas Claes, Chancellor, Citizen and Cooper, and who his term with the said Thomas Claes he hath faithfully served'; and Hester. John, as the eldest son and a master-goldsmith, would doubtless have inherited the responsibilities of the family business on the retirement of his mother, had he not died in 1778, at the age of fifty-eight, in his home in Mason's Alley, Shoreditch.

Peter Bateman had been apprenticed in 1755 to Richard Clarke 'Jeweller and Goldsmith' (later also the master of Jonathan) who, in July of that year, at the age of about twenty-seven married Peter's sister Letticia. Clarke had been apprenticed to a member of the Company of Needlemakers in 1742, in due course obtaining his Freedom and eventually becoming Warden in 1769 and Master two years later. Before his marriage he had lived near the Heathcock inn in the Strand where, it will be recalled. Hester's half-brother John was landlord. After his marriage to Letticia he carried on business under the sign of the 'Eagle and Pearl' at 9 Holborn Barrs, where presumably both Peter and Jonathan served their apprenticeships. Richard and Letticia had several children; the eldest, a daughter named after her mother, was born in Bunhill Row in 1759 and baptized in the church of St. Luke: their first son, christened after his father, was born in 1764, and entered the Bluecoat School of Christ's Hospital in 1772; two years later another son, John, was born, followed by a third son, Peter, and a daughter, Sarah, who later married the goldsmith Crispin Fuller; the sixth and last child, a daughter named Mary, married one Richard Hoare.

Peter Bateman married in 1763 Elizabeth Beaver, and moved with his wife, who died shortly afterwards, into 86 Bunhill Road: he then returned to his mother's home at No. 107, and on marrying for a second time in 1776 he bought No. 106, where he remained until his death in 1825. Peter also owned the freehold of a house in Newcourt Row and at one time leased from his sister Letticia, after the death of her husband, No. 43 Pall Mall. Peter had no children by either of his wives, and remained close to his mother throughout her life; it was he who engrossed his mother's will and, in addition, kept the books of the family business after the death of his father.

It is hardly surprising that a woman of Hester's determination, with three skilled assistants behind her, would decide to carry on and seek to expand her late husband's business. As a first step towards this end she registered her maker's mark, a cursive H.B., at Goldsmiths' Hall in 1761.

$$\mathcal{HB}$$

This mark was confused by Sir Charles Jackson with that of Henry Bailey; however as Shure points out (p. 14), 'Henry Bailey entered only one mark at Goldsmiths' Hall – H.B. in BLOCK letters, surmounted by a crown. Furthermore, the trade directories of the period list "Henry Bailey, Plateworker, Foster Lane, 1750–1760".' No mark appears in the Registers at Goldsmiths' Hall for Hester's late husband, John, because by the Act of 1738 gold chains were exempt from marking, as also were silver chains until 1790; had Hester wished only to continue John's chain-making business she too need have entered no mark; that she did so in 1761 indicates clearly a decision to manufacture wrought plate for which, since chain-making and wire-drawing was a specialized branch of the trade, she would be unlikely to have received any training from John. Undoubtedly, therefore, she employed journeymen in her workshop, acting herself as an administrator.

Very few pieces of silver bearing Hester's mark are known, however, between 1761 and 1774 when she registered her third mark, again a cursive H.B. The reason for this is simply that in the immediate period

after John's death Hester was more concerned with trying to continue the business as it was, rather than in attempting to branch out as a goldsmith in her own right: as a result the bulk of wrought plate at this period emanating from the workshops at 107 Bunhill Row was made in answer to commissions received from other goldsmiths, who would punch their own mark on Hester's unmarked wares, or overpunch her mark with their own. One of the earliest pieces of silver bearing Hester's unaltered mark is a simple double-ended marrow-scoop bearing the date-letter for 1763.

In the middle 1760s William joined his mother and two elder brothers in the family business in Bunhill Row, to be followed in April 1769 by his younger brother Jonathan, on the completion of his articles to their brother-in-law Richard Clarke. A month later Jonathan, at the age of twenty-one, married Ann, daughter of James and Ann (née Olympe) Dowling, at St. Peter's Church, Cornhill. The Olympes were a Huguenot family who had fled to England from France after the Revocation of the Edict of Nantes, and are thought to have been descended from the Germain family of great French goldsmiths. Ann may well have brought her husband (who left £5,000 when he died) a sizeable dowry, as shortly after their marriage Hester (having re-registered her mark at Goldsmiths' Hall) felt financially independent enough to work increasingly for private clients and less as an 'outworker' for other goldsmiths. Soon after their marriage Jonathan and Ann bought No. 84 Bunhill Row next door to John at No. 85 and but two doors away from Peter at No. 86. All three brothers, and Ann, worked with Hester at No. 107.

In 1778 Hester's eldest son, John, died. Seven years later Jonathan's eldest son, born in 1770 and also named Jonathan, became apprenticed 'to learn his arts of a Goldsmith for seven years' to his father who, having failed to accept the Freedom of the Needlemakers' Company as he was entitled to do, had recently become Free of the Goldsmiths' Company; in 1789 Jonathan's second son William, born in 1774, joined his brother in apprenticeship to their father.

In 1784 and 1785 Hester was commissioned by the Corporation of Chester to provide a pair of unusual ogee-shaped punch-bowls for presentation, together with a 'Corporation Purse', as prizes at the May Westchester Races. The bowl of each is engraved with the city arms and the motto *Antiqui Colant Antiquum Dierum* (Let the Ancients Worship the Ancient of Days) and the name of the mayor in the year of presentation, Henry Hegg in 1785 and John Bennett in 1786. Both these bowls were exhibited during the Chester Festival in 1973 – the former at Lowe & Sons, the latter at the Grosvenor Museum.

By 1786 the Batemans' business had so far expanded as to justify the erection of new and larger workshops at the back of 107 Bunhill Row, thereby causing the rateable value, hitherto about £20, to be increased to some £140. The family, doubtless inspired by the shrewd Hester, appealed to the Vestry Committee against this increase with such success that a reduction to £100 was secured.

In 1790, in her eighty-second year, Hester decided, reluctantly we may be sure, to retire, and went to live with her widowed daughter Letticia Clarke in St. Andrew's, Holborn. One of the last pieces to bear her maker's mark is a fine tea-urn, 24⅜ in. high, stamped with the date-letter for 1790. The body of the urn, which rests on a decorated and indented base standing on four feet, is beautifully chased and engraved with ribbon-ties and flower-swags. A frieze of flower-heads encircles the top: above is a rising cover with an urn finial. This piece is now in the collection of the Museum of Fine Arts in Boston. Hester left the family business, which had become 'Hester Bateman & Co.' in 1789, in the capable hands of her two surviving sons, Peter and Jonathan, who in the same year registered their own joint mark, P.B. over I.B. A bright-cup soup-ladle weighing 5 oz. 18 dwt. bearing this mark and the date-letter for 1790 was sold at Sotheby's in June 1973 for £260. This is the rarest mark to be found on silver emanating from Bunhill Row, as in April 1791, only a few months after it was entered at Goldsmiths' Hall, Jonathan died of cancer, leaving his widow Ann as sole legatee.

In September 1794 Hester died, and was buried in the church of St. Luke on 26 September, surrounded, we may be sure, by her loving children and grandchildren. In her will, twice re-drawn (both times by her son Peter), firstly after John's death in 1778 and secondly in 1792 after the death of Jonathan, she left her estate, amounting to some £1,250, on trust to her three executors, Peter Bateman, Letticia Clarke and her daughter-in-law Ann Bateman, who each received the sum of £200.

After Hester's retirement in 1790 and the death of Jonathan in 1791, Peter was left to manage the family firm without the assistance of a partner. By this time it is clear that Bateman silver was so much in demand that the work and administrative duties were too great for any one individual; accordingly, a few months after Jonathan's death Peter took his widow, Ann, into partnership, the two of them registering a joint mark PB over AB. In the same year (1791) Peter and Ann acquired from William Best

No. 108 Bunhill Row, which was presumably considerably larger than No. 107, as the latter was thereupon leased to one Adam Travers. At No. 108 Peter and Ann, one of the most successful and prolific of the various Bateman partnerships (sometimes referred to in official documents as 'Ann Bateman & Co.') continued to work together until Ann retired at the age of fifty-six in 1805. William, Ann's youngest son, was taken into the firm as a full partner in February 1800, a new mark, PB over AB over WB, being registered in that year.

Jonathan and Ann Bateman had seven children: Jonathan, William, Peter, Letticia, James, Richard and Ann; of these only the two eldest boys and Letticia and Ann survived infancy. On 13 October 1803 Letticia married at St. Luke's Church, Old Street, the Revd. Thomas Palmer Bull, son of William Bull founder of the Dissenters' Academy in Newport Pagnell; the ceremony was conducted by the Revd. Robert Newton, an old and close friend of the bridegroom's father.

On his father's death Jonathan, who it will be remembered had been apprenticed to him in 1784, was made over to his mother to complete his time with her. The indenture of apprenticeship (so called because the paper was torn in two by an indented, not a straight line, one part being retained by the parents of the apprentice, the other by his master) at Goldsmiths' Hall refers to Ann as being 'without commission of court', i.e. she had never become Free of the Company.

In 1797 Jonathan married Ann Willoughby and (Travers presumably having been given notice to quit) moved into No. 107 Bunhill Row, where he died in the following year at the early age of twenty-eight.

In 1799 Jonathan's younger brother, William, obtained his Freedom of the Worshipful Company of Goldsmiths, and was taken into partnership by his uncle Peter and his mother in the following year. In the same year (1800) William married Ann Wilson at the church of St. Matthew in Friday Street. The ceremony was performed by the Revd. John Newton, who had at one time served in the Royal Navy and had been ordained by the Bishop of Lincoln in 1764, and who may well have been related to Robert Newton and was certainly a friend of William Bull. In due course William and Ann had no fewer than eight children, William, Henry, Josiah, Eliza, Mary, Emma, Augusta and Emily.

Five years after William joined the firm his mother, Ann, felt able to retire, and in the same year (1805) Peter and his nephew registered their joint mark at Goldsmiths' Hall, PB over WB.

In 1815 – the same year as Peter's retirement – William's mother Ann died, an end hastened by the onset of dropsy. Her estate was valued at some £2,000, in addition to which she possessed 'certain other assets in the books of the Governor and Company of the Bank of England'. She appointed as her executors her brother-in-law Peter, her son-in-law Thomas Palmer Bull, and her nephew-by-marriage Crispin Fuller, the goldsmith/husband of Sarah, daughter of Letticia and Richard Clarke. Ann bequeathed certain specified items among her household effects to William, on condition that he paid her executors the value thereof, amounting to £51. 5s. od. The bulk of the family plate was to be divided between her unmarried daughter, Ann, and Letticia Bull, who had already received 'six table-spoons, two bottle-stands and two gravy-spoons'. The residue of the estate, including her clothes and personal effects, was left to Ann.

On 19 November 1825 Peter Bateman died at the ripe old age of eighty-five, and was buried later in the same month near the grave of his parents, Hester and John, in St. Luke's churchyard. In his will, drawn up shortly before he died, Peter appointed as his executors the Revd. George Pritchard, the incumbent of the Baptist Church, Stepney; his nephew-by-marriage, the Revd. Thomas Palmer Bull; and Charles Bannister of Godwell Street, who gave as his occupation 'Inspector of Pavements'. He bequeathed the bulk of his estate to his nephew William, on condition that 'he pay back the principal and interest of the money he now owes me'. To his unmarried niece, Ann, he left 'the sum of £50, the property derived from her late mother, being, as I consider, sufficient for her support'. To his nephew Thomas Bateman, 'Goldbeater of Chiswell Street' (the son of his eldest brother John) he bequeathed the sum of £15; and a similar amount to Thomas's sister Hester Marshall, then a widow, of Hoxton, stating that 'they had borrowed from me in my lifetime double or treble the amount they would otherwise have received at my decease'. In addition Peter left a number of charitable bequests, e.g. £50 to the Baptist Church, Stepney, and a like amount to the Evangelical Union, Newport Pagnell.

From the day of his uncle Peter's retirement in 1815, William was for the first time in its history the only Bateman in the family firm in Bunhill Row; in the same year he entered his mark, WB, in two sizes within a

lobed punch, at Goldsmiths' Hall; one of the most distinguished pieces of plate bearing this mark is a finely executed silver-gilt tray, weighing over 281 oz. and measuring almost 3 ft. in length, bearing a contemporary Royal presentation inscription, which was produced in 1837 to the order of the Royal Goldsmiths, Rundell, Bridge & Co. In July 1973 this tray was sold at Sotheby's for £3,400. A silver table centrepiece with scrolling branches for six candles and a central sweetmeat dish, made in 1820 and punched with William's mark, was sold in a provincial sale-room in 1973 for £3,500. In 1828 William was elected to the Court of Assistants of the Worshipful Company of Goldsmiths, becoming a Warden two years later, and Prime Warden in 1836. In 1835 he was one of the Wardens who welcomed the guests (among whom were the Duke of Wellington and Sir Robert Peel) at a banquet given by the Goldsmiths' Company to inaugurate their new Hall. In the middle 1830s William went to live in the then fashionable suburb of Stoke Newington, from where he travelled daily to his workshops in Bunhill Row. In May 1845 he was elected Foreman of the Jury of the Trial of the Pyx and signed the report presented to the Worshipful Company of Goldsmiths.

In 1850 William Bateman died at his home in Stoke Newington. His eldest son, William, had married one Elizabeth Parratt, of whom her father-in-law clearly disapproved: he refused to acknowledge the validity of their marriage, and in his will refers to their son as 'my reputed grandson'. On his father's death William Junr. took into partnership one Daniel Ball, registering with him the joint mark WB over DB; a coffee-pot and stand bearing this rare mark appeared in a London sale-room in 1973. Although the partnership was short-lived (for a few years later William registered his own individual maker's mark at Goldsmiths' Hall) over a century of uninterrupted Bateman ownership and tradition had been broken.

Hester Bateman inherited her husband's business at a time when taste in England was undergoing a change. It was inevitable that any style as elaborate and flamboyant as the rococo would be followed, sooner or later, by a violent reaction in taste; the quest for a purer type of design, which occupied artists and craftsmen from the middle of the eighteenth century, necessitated a return to first essentials, which for them meant Antiquity – the works of ancient Greece and Rome.

In 1732 the Society of Dilettanti was founded in London to promote and encourage the excavation of Greek antiquities. Examination of the ancient sites of Herculaneum, begun in 1711, and of Pompeii, was renewed in 1738, and resulted in the publication of numerous lavishly illustrated works describing their treasures, among them: *Le Antiquità Romane* by Giovanni Battista Piranesi in 1748; *Recueil d'Antiquités égyptiennes, étrusques ...* (Comte de Caylus, 1752–67); *Ruins of Palmyra* (Robert Wood, 1753); *Ruins of Baalbek* [Heliopolis] (Wood, 1757); *Les Ruines des plus beaux monuments de la Grèce* (J. D. le Roy, 1758); *Della Magnificenza ed Architettura de Romani* (Piranesi, 1761); *Antiquities of Athens* (James 'Athenian' Stuart and Nicholas Revett, 1762–1815); and *Monumenti Antichi* by Johann Joachim Wincklemann (1767).

Throughout the second half of the eighteenth century excavations were pursued with relentless enthusiasm by archaeologists from all over Europe.

Sir William Hamilton (1730–1803), ambassador to the Court of Naples, was one of the most energetic English collectors, and the publication in 1766–7 of his *Antiquités étrusques, grecques et romaines* did much to popularize the neo-classical style in England, where the most influential designer was Robert Adam (1728–92); from 1754 to 1762 Adam travelled extensively throughout Italy and Dalmatia (Yugoslavia), and on his return to England was appointed architect to George III. For the next twenty-five years Robert, in partnership with his brother James, was the dominant figure among English neo-classicists, producing designs not only for architects but for cabinet-makers, china-manufacturers, sculptors and goldsmiths. In 1773 the Adam brothers published their *Works in Architecture*, which was based on a series of engravings of their principal designs.

Neo-classical designs contrasted regular sweeping and graduated curves with horizontal and vertical straight lines; regularity and symmetry (the direct opposite of the rococo) was the ideal of each plane and elevation. The delicate lightness and grace of the Greek originals was every designer's ideal, an aim which was achieved partly by using thin gauge metal and partly by the extensive use of decorative piercing. By the 1780s the more advanced goldsmiths possessed their own rolling-mills with which to make sheets of thin pliable silver. The Batemans took full advantage of this rolled silver in fashioning much of their domestic plate.

Another reason for employing light gauge metal at this time was the re-imposition in 1784 of duty at sixpence per ounce on silver plate, and of eight shillings per ounce on gold. The sign that duty had been paid was the punch of the Sovereign's Head, which appears on all but the smallest articles until the duty was abolished in 1890; in 1796 the duty on silver was raised to one shilling per ounce; in 1803 the duty on silver was further increased to one shilling and threepence per ounce, and that on gold to sixteen shillings per ounce; in 1814 the rates were raised yet again to one shilling and sixpence and seventeen shillings per ounce respectively.

Decoration in relief was usually applied or embossed, consisting of shallow spiral or vertical fluting; palmettes; husks; acanthus leaves; paterae; floral scrolls; swags of foliage or fabric draped over oval medallions or tied with ribbon-bows; and later on rams' masks, classic Greek key-patterns and bay-leaf wreaths. Mouldings consisted for the most part of beading, astragals, or reeding. Normal engraving was largely superseded by bright-cut engraving, which produced a brighter and more eye-catching effect. Armorials were placed within true 'shield'-shaped shields; lettering was normally in a classical 'copperplate', using graduated thicknesses of delicacy and precision in marked contrast to the earlier bolder style.

'The life that is well spent is a long life'; so wrote Leonardo da Vinci (1452–1519) in his *Trattato della pittura* (Treatise on painting) first published in Paris in 1551, and he might well have been writing of Hester Bateman.

The neo-classic revival and so-called 'Adam' style almost exactly coincided with the assumption by Hester in 1760 of her late husband's business, and lasted until her retirement in 1790. Over the years the name of Hester Bateman has become, especially in the United States, one of the best known among English goldsmiths: this is not simply because she was a woman (for women goldsmiths, e.g. Elizabeth Tuite, Anne Tanqueray– daughter of David Willaume – Eliza Godfrey and Louisa Courtauld were not uncommon in eighteenth-century England), nor because work bearing her mark is vastly superior to that of her contemporaries; the reason is partly that so many of her pieces have survived to be collected today, and partly because of the high standard of most of the plate emanating from Bunhill Row.

As we have seen, very little Bateman silver is known between 1760 (when Hester's husband John died) and the mid-1770s, as during this period Hester was primarily concerned with keeping the business going rather than with expanding it. She had, in addition, to compete with the discovery in 1743 by Thomas Bolsover, a Sheffield cutler, of what came to be known as 'Sheffield Plate'. Bolsover discovered that by fusing sheets of silver to copper a hard and durable substitute for pure silver resulted. Double plating, with a sheet of copper sandwiched between two layers of silver, was developed between 1763 and 1770. This invention, which put silver-like wares within the reach of the less affluent, resulted in a number of smaller goldsmiths being driven out of business. When Hester did eventually branch out on her own account, she sensibly decided not to attempt to compete with already well-established goldsmiths in the production of important ceremonial plate for aristocratic households, but rather to concentrate on producing well-designed and simple domestic items for the increasingly prosperous middle-class.

Hester's early work consists largely of flat-ware (spoons, forks, ladles and sugar-tongs), numerous examples of which survive today; these show her to have been unsurpassed in this branch of her craft. From flat-ware it was natural that she should progress to the manufacture of other household pieces, such as salts, cream-jugs, sugar-bowls and baskets, tea- and coffee-pots, kettles, urns, trays, salvers, and waiters.

Not all Bateman silver, however, was for ordinary domestic use, and a number of orders for ceremonial and ecclesiastical plate found their way to Bunhill Row. Among the former were pieces for several City of London Livery Companies; the Wheelwrights' commissioned Hester in 1781 to make a snuff-box; the Needlemakers' ordered a two-handled cup and cover, and the Grocers' a large set of spoons; a coffee-urn was presented to the Coopers' by Sir James Esdaile. The Esdailes had fled from France to England after the Revocation of the Edict of Nantes, and had set themselves up in business as 'Military Accouterers'. Sir James, co-founder in about 1780 with his son-in-law Sir Benjamin Hammett, of Esdaile, Hammett & Co., 21 Lombard Street, bankers, was an Alderman of the City of London for Cripplegate Ward, and in 1778 Lord Mayor of London. The family lived at No. 82 Bunhill Row and were thus near neighbours of the Batemans, to whom it is known they gave a number of orders for plate.

In 1783 the city of Kingston upon Hull commissioned Hester to re-fashion a pair of goblets presented to the Corporation in 1723 by William Wilberforce, grandfather of the slavery abolitionist: in addition to the original inscription 'The gift of Mr. William Wilberforce Mayor 1723' these goblets bear Hester's mark and the date-letter for 1783; they are now in the collection of Hull Corporation. Dating from the same year is a fine salver, owned by Lancaster Corporation, which unusually is engraved with a view of the Town Hall.

Hester Bateman's most important piece of ecclesiastical plate is the 'Preacher's Verger's Verge' (incorrectly called a 'wand' by Shure) in St. Paul's Cathedral, which is still today in regular use. It is the oldest verge in the cathedral and used to bear the date-letter for 1781 together with Hester's mark; it was originally 34 in. long but at some time became damaged and is now some two inches shorter, and all trace of marks have disappeared.[1]

Other interesting pieces bearing Hester's mark include a fine inkstand,

1. For information on this verge I am indebted to the Dean's Verger of St. Paul's Cathedral, Mr. Arthur Morrison.

consisting of a tray containing three pots and a candlestick and snuffer, all decorated with delicate beading, dated 1780; it is now in the collection of the Philadelphia Museum of Art. Dating from the same year is a galleried snuffer-tray having an unusual serpentine outline: the gallery, which is finely pierced with a design symbolizing a flight of birds, is surmounted by a beaded rim. Marked with the date-letter for the following year (1781) are an unusual pair of hexagonal-stemmed candlesticks standing on circular bases, with trumpet-shaped sockets, engraved with floral pendants, which in October 1969 sold at Christie's for £2,500. A fine epergne, dated 1786, is an important and unusually large piece of Bateman silver, standing 20¼ in. high and measuring 26 in. long overall. It consists of a central canoe-shaped basket, surrounded at a lower level by eight circular baskets, all of which are petal-fluted with a band of saw-piercing. The festoons between the legs and central base exemplify the direct influence of Robert Adam.

In 1787 Hester Bateman's mark was punched on one of the largest and most elaborate pieces of plate to come from her workshops in Bunhill Row. This is an oval tray, 28½ in. wide and weighing 148 oz. 15 dwt. The centre is unadorned, save for the engraved armorials of the D'Arcy family; the rim is saw-pierced with a repeating pattern of arcading, and is edged with a guilloche border; overlying the pierced arcading are festoons of oak-leaves and acorns, each swag terminating in, alternately, a classical vase and a foliate medallion. Two years later her workshop made a second oval tea-tray with a reeded rim, 23½ in. wide and weighing 110 oz. 3 dwt., engraved in the centre with contemporary armorials (Mabball or Mabbett impaling Julius) within a bound reeded cartouche, standing on four panel supports decorated with anthemion motifs: in June 1973 this tray sold at Sotheby's for £3,600.

Four items bearing the punch of Peter and Ann Bateman are of special interest: a simple elegant two-handled cup made by them in 1790 bears the inscription 'Admiral Lord Nelson from Thomas Hardy 15th. June 1804': it is now in the collection of the Monmouth Borough Council. A particularly attractive boat-shaped sugar-basket dated 1794, with pierced acanthus decoration and reeded swing handle, now mounted on an inscribed plinth of dark-green mottled verdite, was recently chosen by the British Petroleum Company as the trophy for the 'B.P. Shield', a two miles and one furlong handicap hurdle race, the first race on the card on the day of the Grand National at Aintree. Made in the following year (1795) is a fine two-handled cup and cover known as the 'Wantage Cup', originally intended as a horse-racing trophy. The lid is covered with a design of lanceolate leaves which depend from the knop, a motif which is repeated on the base and on the bottom of the cup, which is of classical urn shape in a typically Adam style. A frieze of scrolling foliage encircles the top of the cup, while on the side is engraved a horse-racing scene: this cup is now in the collection of the Philadelphia Museum of Art. Dating from the last year of the eighteenth century is a simple silver goblet with a frieze of paterae around the rim: the coronets of Nelson and Brontë are engraved on the side of the goblet, whose interior is gilded: this goblet is also owned by the Monmouth Borough Council.

All these four pieces made by Peter and Ann Bateman between 1790 and 1799, together with the Kettledrums bearing the joint mark of Peter, Ann and William and the date letter for 1804, which were presented to the Household Cavalry by George III, are of a quality which would not have shamed Hester herself.

BATEMAN PEDIGREE

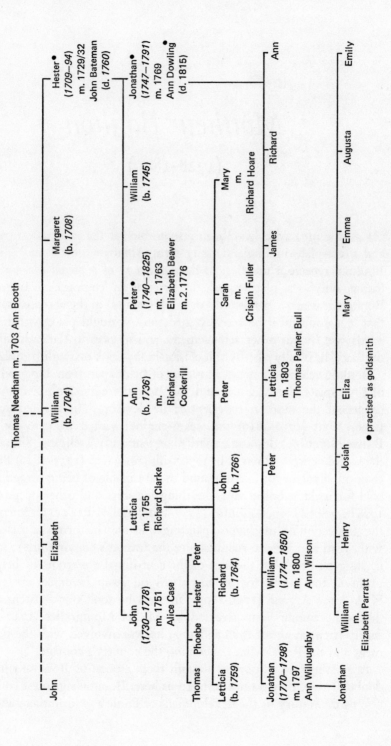

Thomas Needham m. 1703 Ann Booth

John   Elizabeth

William (b. 1704)   Margaret (b. 1708)   Hester• (1709–94) m. 1729/32 John Bateman (d. 1760)

Ann (b. 1736) m. Richard Cockerill   Peter• (1740–1825) m. 1. 1763 Elizabeth Beaver m. 2. 1776   William (b. 1745)   Jonathan• (1747–1791) m. 1769 Ann Dowling (d. 1815)

Letticia m. 1755 Richard Clarke   John (1730–1778) m. 1751 Alice Case

John (b. 1766)   Peter   Sarah m. Crispin Fuller   Mary m. Richard Hoare

Letticia (b. 1759)   Richard (b. 1764)   Hester   Peter   Thomas   Phoebe

Letticia m. 1803 Thomas Palmer Bull   James   Richard   Ann

Jonathan (1770–1798) m. 1797 Ann Willoughby   William• (1774–1850) m. 1800 Ann Wilson   Peter

Jonathan   William m. Elizabeth Parratt   Henry   Josiah   Eliza   Mary   Emma   Augusta   Emily

• practised as goldsmith

Matthew Boulton

(1728–1809)

OF all the men who have been responsible for the production of gold- and silver-plate in England, only two, Abraham Portal and Matthew Boulton, receive a mention in the *Dictionary of National Biography*, the former only as a 'playwright', the latter as an 'engineer'. It is true that Boulton was not a 'goldsmith' or a 'silversmith' in the accepted sense, in that it is doubtful if he actually made any wrought plate with his own hands; yet for his other achievements and services to the craft of gold-smithery, he is fully worthy of inclusion in any book on English goldsmiths.

Boulton achieved fame in a number of fields apart from the production of silver-plate: he was first and foremost the eighteenth-century fore-runner of the modern *entrepreneur*; he developed in partnership with James Watt (1736–1819) the steam-engine; visited in 1776 by James Boswell (1740–95) Boulton remarked sententiously 'I sell here, Sir, what all the world desires – Power'. In 1779 with James Keir (1735–1820) Boulton took out a patent for 'a compound metal capable of being forged hot or cold for making bolts, nails, sheathing for ships and other purposes'; in 1778 he helped Francis Eginton (1737–1805) in the latter's experiments into the production of 'mechanical paintings'; in 1780 he formed a partnership with Watt and Keir to manufacture the former's copying press; in 1788 he suggested to Watt the idea of the centrifugal governor; he helped to promote the patent for an improved oil lamp invented in 1784 by F. P. Aimé Argand (1755–1803); in 1798 he took out a patent for an 'hydraulic engine' ram invented by Michel Montgolfier (1740–1810); finally between about 1786 and 1799 he was involved with the govern-ment and the Royal Mint concerning the country's coinage.

Fascinating and important though these aspects of Boulton's life un-doubtedly are, they do not concern us here. Boulton's greatest contribu-tion to the history of the development of English goldsmithery were his efforts which lead, directly in the case of Birmingham and indirectly in that of Sheffield, to the establishment in those two towns of provincial Assay Offices. But that is to anticipate.

Matthew Boulton's grandfather, John Bolton [sic], who came from Lichfield, may have been a descendant of the Puritan cleric Robert Bolton, rector of Broughton in Northamptonshire from 1609 until his death in 1631. John Bolton married Elizabeth, daughter and co-heiress of Matthew Dyott of Stichbrooke in Staffordshire, and his wife Mary née Babbington of Curborough. Their son Matthew came to Birmingham from Lichfield in about 1710 and set himself up in business there as a 'toy maker' and silver stamper, in an area known as Snow Hill contemporarily described as 'a very rural neighbourhood, only sparcely built upon in close proximity to the open country'. Since most craftsmen in this trade worked in the centre of Birmingham, it can safely be concluded that Matthew senior had only a small workshop.

In the register of marriages of St. Martin's Snow Hill is the following entry: '1723 June 21 Matthew Boulton to Christiana Peers'. There were several children of the marriage but only two need concern us here; Anne, who was to marry Zacchaeus Walker, one of her distinguished brother's managing clerks, and the celebrated Matthew himself.

Matthew Boulton was born on 3 September (O.S.) 1728 in the Boulton family home, No. 7 Snow Hill bordering on Slaney Street; he was baptized fifteen days later in the parish church of St. Philip. He received his early education at a 'Private School' run by the Revd. John Hausted, chaplain of St. John's Chapel, Deritend, from 1715 until his death forty years later. On leaving school he gravitated, as was natural, into his father's business, which was then specializing in the production of shoe-buckles, many of which were exported abroad, particularly to France, whence they were subsequently reimported to this country as à la mode. Boulton junior was taken into partnership in 1749, and was left in sole charge of the business after the death of his father ten years later.

In 1749 Boulton married Mary, daughter and co-heiress (with a half share in a fortune of £28,000) of Luke Robinson, an 'opulent mercer' of Lichfield and his wife Dorothy, daughter and co-heiress of John Babbington of Curborough and of Packington, Staffordshire. As we have seen, Boulton's maternal great-grandmother was née Babbington, so he and his wife were, albeit distant, cousins. In 1759 Boulton suffered a double blow through the death of his young wife (who left no surviving children) and his father. The loss of his wife clearly hit Boulton particularly hard, as is shown by the following note written by him which still survives: 'Upon seeing the corps of my dear Wife Mary many excellent Qualities of Hers arose to my mind which I could not then forebere acknowledging extempory with my pen & depositing in her Coffin.'

From correspondence which still exists it is clear that Boulton maintained a close and warm friendship with his mother-in-law Dorothy Robinson, and it seems likely that he continued to visit her in Lichfield after his wife's death. Hardly surprisingly, in the circumstances, he eventually fell in love with his late wife's younger sister and co-heiress Anne (1733–83), his junior by five years. Here of course, he fell foul of Article 17 of the Marriage Prohibitions in the Prayer Book's Table of Kindred and Affinity. It appears that the Robinson family were divided in their views on the proposed marriage, Anne's brother Luke and their father being anti, Dorothy and Anne being pro: Boulton seems to have been strengthened in his resolve by reading John Fry's *The case of marriage between near kindred particularly considered with respect to the doctrine of scripture, the law of nature and the laws of England* (1756) in which the author gives as his opinion that 'marriage with a deceased wife's sister is fit and convenient being opposed neither to law nor to morals'.[1]

Accordingly we find the following entry in the marriage register of St. Mary's, Rotherhithe: 'Matthew Boulton and Ann [sic] Robinson both of this parish were married in this church by Banns this Twentyfifth day of June, One thousand seven hundred and sixty, by me, Ja. Penfold, Cur.' The witnesses were Boulton's elder sister Mary and the church clerk Stephen Ogle. The couple had presumably been forced to travel for the ceremony as far afield as Rotherhithe, because it was not every cleric who was willing to perform a marriage which, in the eyes of the church, remained illegal and invalid. Boulton and his bride had clearly stayed in the parish for a sufficient time prior to the marriage to establish residence there. There were two children of the marriage: Anne (1768–1829), who had a crippled hip and leg; and Matthew Robinson (1770–1842), a sickly child, who in 1817 married Mary Anne (1795–1820), daughter of William Wilkinson and his wife Elizabeth, *née* Stockdale.

For some time after the death of his father and his first wife Boulton had

1. p. 80.

been turning over in his mind an ambitious scheme for the establishment of a manufacturing complex, where craftsmen in the various branches of the 'toy' trade would work together under one roof, thus enabling him to reap both wholesale and retail profits. Within Boulton's particular trade it was the first step towards 'vertical integration' and modern methods of factory production.

In the spring of 1761 Boulton found, on Handsworth Heath, a little under two miles from Snow Hill on the Wolverhampton Road, the site he was looking for on which to establish his new enterprise: it was conveniently intersected by Hockley Brook (a leader of the Thame) which would supply water power. He subsequently purchased a one-hundred-year lease on the site for the sum of £1,000, from Edward Rushton who in 1756 had himself leased the land from John Wyrley, Lord of the Manor of Handsworth.

The estate on which Boulton was to found his new empire bore the curious name of Soho. Various suggestions have been made concerning the origin of the name 'Soho', which is first mentioned in a deed of 1761 quoting the lease of 1756 between Wyrley and Rushton. The name is reputed to derive from an inn sign depicting a huntsman urging on his hounds with cries of 'So-Ho, So-Ho'. Since a similar origin is attributed to the name Soho in London, the name in Birmingham may have been derived direct from the capital, as e.g. Vauxhall in Birmingham and Piccadilly in Manchester. It is interesting to remember, as we have already seen, that Soho in London was a favourite area for eighteenth-century Huguenot goldsmiths. Since Boulton was himself primarily a manufacturer and businessman he was clearly in need of someone who would act as a travelling salesman to advertise his wares. Accordingly on 24 July 1762 he took into unofficial partnership John Fothergill (the partnership survived until 1781), each of them putting the sum of £5,000 into the business, which moved to Soho in early August of the same year. The new factory was designed to look like a country mansion set in a landscaped park; Boulton and his family later lived in the central block, while the ground-floor wings housed the workrooms, with living accommodation for the employees above.

At first the new partnership concentrated largely on the production of steel 'toys' (made from highly polished facetted steel which was both light-reflective and rust-resistant), and a little later on buttons and buckles made in a variety of substances, including, of course, silver.

B&F

Sheffield plate – entered 1764

Boulton, however, was always highly conscious of the importance of improving the quality of his products; 'How', he wrote to Fothergill, 'can I expect the public to countenance rubbish from Soho while they can procure sound and perfect work from any other quarter?' In order to try to achieve this laudable aim Boulton began late in 1762 to produce articles made in 'Sheffield' plate. In 1743, it will be remembered, Thomas Bolsover (or Boulsover) discovered that if a thin sheet of silver is fused to a thicker sheet of copper and the resulting billet is hammered, a strong sheet of metal with the appearance of silver but costing much less results; he used his discovery mainly in the production of buttons and other 'toys'. In the 1750s his one-time apprentice Joseph Hancock developed the process by producing domestic articles in Sheffield plate. The Soho factory was one of the first to adopt the 'Sterling silver thread' edging introduced by George Cadman and Samuel Roberts in place of the plated edge previously used, which after much buffing and burnishing would reveal the underlying copper. Boulton became a convinced proponent of silver thread edging, stamping his wares 'silver borders' together with his mark of a sun, which he entered in 1784 when the firm was described as 'M. Boulton & Co.'. Sometimes the mark of the sun is stamped twice; alternatively a single sun and his surname in full in upper-case letters may be used.

Boulton soon became the largest manufacturer of Sheffield plate in the country: he started to work in this medium at almost the exact time that Hester Bateman was in the process of assuming responsibility for the running of her late husband's business; like her his wares were predominantly in the prevailing 'Adam' neo-classical designs discussed in the previous chapter. Boulton particularly excelled in pieces with shell and gadroon edges, e.g. snuffer-trays, salvers, waiters, inkstands, coasters, trays, candlesticks and candelabra. A fine collection of Soho Sheffield plate, beautifully designed and made, may be seen in the Ellis Greenberg collection at the City Museum and Art Gallery, Birmingham.

During the 1760s Boulton expanded the business of his manufactory in a number of different directions – in the production of *bijouterie, objets d'art* and *de vertu*, in ormolu, pinchbeck, and tortoise-shell for example, and in the manufacture of clocks. He secured the valuable patronage of George III and Queen Sophia; the Dukes of Richmond and Lennox, and Northumberland; the Earl of Shelburne (later the 1st Marquess of Lansdowne); Lord Dartmouth, Lord Cranbourne and Horace Walpole. In addition he received commissions to provide metal mounts for their wares from some of the leading designers of the day, such as the Adam brothers and Josiah Wedgwood (1730–95).

As a direct result of his success in the production of articles in Sheffield plate, Boulton turned his mind in about 1765 towards the manufacture of pieces in solid silver. He at once encountered a serious obstacle. All silver plate had to be assayed, and the nearest assay office to Birmingham was in Chester, seventy-two miles away to the north-west by rough and dangerous roads, frequented by highwaymen and footpads. There was, in addition, the not inconsiderable cost of transport to be considered, as well as the possible damage to the goods and piracy of their design by the goldsmiths of Chester.

After a visit to Boulton in May 1766 Lord Shelburne on his return to Bowood Park, made the following memorandum: 'Another thing they are in a great way of is an assay master which is allowed at Chester and York; but it is very hard on a manufacturer to be obliged to send every piece of plate to Chester to be marked . . . it would be an infinite public advantage if silver plate came to be manufactured here . . . and that it should be taken out of the imposing monopoly of London.' On 7 January 1771 Boulton wrote to Lord Shelburne to explain the delay in sending his patron two pairs of specially commissioned candlesticks, which it had taken the Chester Assay Office twelve days to 'touch', and which had been packed so badly by them that on their return the 'chasing was entirely destroyed'. Boulton went on to explain that 'we have been obliged to substitute new parts' and that 'it will take near a week's work to make the necessary repairs'. He continues: 'I am so exceedingly vex'd about the disappointment and loss which have attended the two pairs of candle-sticks that altho' I am very desirous of becoming *a great Silversmith*, yet I am determined never to take up that branch in the Large Way I intended *unless powers can be obtained to have a Marking Hall at Birmingham.* This is not the first time by several that I have been served so. I had one parcel of Candlesticks quite broke by their careless packing.'

(In the same letter Boulton goes on: 'it is almost impossible to make some things *very elegant* unless there is a contrast of *Colours*, viz. bright burnish'd parts contrasted with a beautiful white Dead Matt'. This matt effect is characteristic of much of Soho manufactured silver.)

On 1 August 1771 Boulton wrote to the Duke of Grafton to explain the late delivery of a silver cup, known as the 'Thetford Cup', the specifications for which were 'the cup to be made without handles. Three horses running on one side, on the other a medal as you propos'd with the inscription "Thetford Cup / run for in 1771 and won by / Lord Clermont Stewart". To be sent to His Grace the Duke of Grafton Arlington Street before ye one day of July & not to exceed sixty guineas.' The actual cost was £52. 10s. 0d. 'When the Cup was nearly made it was by the carelessness of one of my workmen melted in soddering on of some ornaments (a misfortune that will happen sometimes even to the careful) – Another Cup was made directly but was delayed many days at Chester, where we are obliged to send everything to be essay'd & mar'k'd wch is a grievance that will prevent us (unless removed) from ever establishing an extensive Manufactory of Silverwares upon such a footing as will be most advantageous to this Kingdom.'

On 4 December of the succeeding year (1772) we find Boulton writing to another patron, the Duke of Richmond, in the following terms: 'I am now manufacturing some plate with a degree of Elegance w'ch I flatter myself your Grace would approve, and if Parliament would but grant us at Birmingham the same indulgence as it hath granted to many towns in England . . . I think I could push that article into a cheaper and more elegant style than 'tis now in, and for that purpose I expect the Town of Birmingham will present a petition to Parliament this session praying for the establishment of an Office here for the assaying and marking of wrought plate.'

As soon as the craftsmen of Sheffield got wind of what was afoot, they naturally demanded the same facility for their town also. On 8 December of the same year (1772) Gilbert Dixon, a lawyer by profession, and Clerk to the Cutlers' Company, wrote to Boulton and Fothergill as 'the most principall persons in this Business' saying that 'the establishment of such an Office in Sheffield has been much wish'd for by the Artificers in Silver here, who for some time past have had such a project in contemplation for the convenience of having their Goods assayed and marked without

the trouble expence [*sic*] and delay of sending them to the Goldsmiths'
Hall in London'. Dixon suggested to Boulton that Sheffield should 'go
hand in hand with you to Parliament' to which Boulton, possibly
influenced in Dixon's favour by being referred to as a 'most principall
person', for he is known to have been rather vain, readily agreed, writing
rather pompously in the third person on Christmas Eve that 'he hath no
selfish contracted views but most sincerely wishes to see Sheffield as well
as Birmingham upon a footing with London in that point & likewise
assures them that to the utmost of his power he will assist & promote their
endeavours'.

Sheffield accordingly presented her petition to parliament on 1 February
1773; Birmingham did the same on the following day. A Committee of
the House was set up to examine these petitions, its members receiving
from Boulton a 'Memorial relative to Assaying and marking wrought
plate at Birmingham', which concluded:

Objections may possibly be made by the Corporations of Goldsmiths in
London and in other Marking Towns to such a grant, which, it may be said,
may prove injurious to them, because it may enable others to work in Plate
with as much Convenience as they now do. But as *Birmingham* is not near to
any Market for Plate it can deprive the other Towns of no Part of their Trade
except by working better than they do and cheaper; and against losses of
business by these means the proper Securities are not Privileges, but Excellence
in Design and Workmanship and moderate Prices.

It would be tedious to detail here the objections (mostly alleging the use
of sub-standard silver) raised by interested parties in London, such as the
Goldsmiths' Company and the 'Goldsmiths, Silversmiths and Plateworkers of the City of London', among whom were John Carter, George
Cowles, David Hennell, John Wakelin and Charles Wright, or the
counters from the 'Merchants and Manufacturers of Birmingham' and
their colleagues in Sheffield. On 11 May 1773 Boulton wrote to
Fothergill: 'I was in hopes that I should have been able by this post to have
informed you of a final decision of ye House upon ye Assay Bull [*sic*] but
as it did not b[r]eak up before eleven last night ye Members were so much
fateagu^d that the House hath not sat to-day & our affair is now ajourn^d
till Thursday so that you may expect to hear on Saturday what our fate
will be. The Londoners have engaged two Councelors to plead their
shabby cause at the Bar of the House & are makeing all possable Interest

6

they can. . . . As to the House of Lords I have twice the interest in that House than in ye Lower house. I shall not employ any Council but as I have taken great pains to make proper impressions upon ye Members I shall submitt ye case simply to their decision. Lord Denbeigh took me about with him yesterday in his Chariot to several ministerial Members pressing them to serve us. He says he has talk'd much to the King in my fav^r.' Lord Dartmouth, another of Boulton's clients, and Sir George Savile, M.P., spoke on Boulton's behalf in the Upper and Lower House respectively.

After much debate and a number of amendments the Assay Bill was agreed to by the Upper House on 28 May 1773, on the same day receiving the Royal Assent. Boulton recorded in his diary: 'Set out from London 2 o'clock on Sunday ye 30 May & ariv'd at Soho ye Monday before 8 in ye morning.' He was received by a triumphal peal of bells from Handsworth Church.

It has been suggested that the Birmingham and Sheffield town marks of an anchor and a crown respectively (the Hallmarking Act of 1973 provides for the change from a crown to a rose for the town mark of Sheffield from January 1975), authorized by the Assay Act (13 Geo. III. cap. 52), were decided by the toss of a coin and were derived from the 'Crown and Anchor' inn in the Strand, where the manufacturers of Birmingham and Sheffield are said to have met and conducted their case when in London.

James Jackson was accorded the privilege of becoming Birmingham's first Assay Master, and to him Boulton and Fothergill sent on the first day that his office was open, 31 August, no less than 841 oz. of plate for assaying, of which one piece weighed almost 200 oz. and a second more than 100 oz. Heading the list is a tea-urn (in the collection of the Birmingham City Museum and Art Gallery) of a classically simple shape, with upward curving handles with leaves at either end; the body and cover are partially fluted, and the whole rests on a square plinth which stands on four foliate feet. The partners' joint mark consists of their initials, MB before IF. After Fothergill's death in 1782 Boulton punched his

MB IF

plate with his initials alone. In 1784 the Act was amended to permit manufacturers of plated ware to register their marks at the Assay Office in Sheffield: Boulton accordingly registered the marks of twin suns and his name in full and a single sun, as described above.

We have already seen that some years before Birmingham and Sheffield were granted the right to their own assay offices, Boulton was producing silver mostly decorated in the prevailing rococo taste which he sent to be 'touched' in Chester where his agent was one John Foliott. In 1771 Boulton wrote to Foliott: 'Herewith you'll receive by the Chester coach a silver cup which beg you get marked and return by the same conveyance.' Only three pieces of Chester-marked Boulton silver are extant: a finely pierced mazarine of 1769 12 in. in diameter and weighing 22 oz. 5 dwt., engraved with a contemporary coat-of-arms and motto, and a pair of candlesticks 12 in. high, each weighing some 33 oz., dated 1768 and now in the collection of the Birmingham Assay office; the octagonal bases of these rare pieces are enriched with typically rococo swirls, the columns with acanthus, beading and flower ornamentation.

Boulton was not above luring craftsmen away from their masters to come and work for him at Soho, as we find in a letter addressed to his London agent William Matthews at 'Green Lettice Lane off Cheapside' written on 5 January 1771: 'Mr. Dumee has a cousin in London who is a chaser (tho' a very inordinate one); if he should call on you, pray tell him that Mr. Boulton will employ him if he chooses to come to Soho.' Nicholas Dumee was a fine Huguenot goldsmith who registered his maker's mark at Goldsmiths' Hall in partnership with Francis Butty in 1759. Boulton also attempted to seduce away, from the London goldsmith Thomas Heming, a craftsman of German extraction named Hankle.

The neo-classical revival coincided with Birmingham's and Sheffield's right of 'touch', and as might be expected virtually all of Boulton's Birmingham-marked silver is in this taste: it seems to have appealed to him for a number of reasons; it was fast becoming popular among the aristocracy, and would doubtless soon become so among the prosperous middle class (who usually follow the lead of their social superiors) and for whom Boulton's Great Silver Manufactory was ideally suited; and the new 'Adam' style, which required precise uniformity of texture and shape, and repetitive designs of classical decorative motifs, was better suited to machine work than to hand-raised methods.

Boulton succinctly expressed his opinion of the new style in a letter to the Honble. Mrs. (Elizabeth) Montague (1720–1800; the original Blue-Stocking), *née* Robinson and thus a relation by marriage to Boulton, which accompanied a dinner service which he made for her in 1776: 'I flatter myself its neatness, its simplicity and durability will be more agreeable than French finery or dirty richness.' In the same vein he wrote on 20 January 1776 to the Earl of Findlater, 'I w'd have Elegant simplicity the Leading principal whereas in my opinion such of the Orfèvre of the French as I have generly seen is troy Chargè. But as I have not seen any of the best productions of Monsr. August [Robert-Joseph Auguste, *c.* 1730–1805] I therefore presume I have seen nothing. His fame I am persweded is found in superior Merit because I have heard so many Noblemen of good Tast concur in ye same opinion of him – I therefore am desirous of availing myself of your Lordship's good Offices at Paris in ye Spring. . . .'

An interesting side-light on the prices obtained by Boulton for his wares comes in a letter to a dealer written in 1771: 'plated tankards with lids at 42s. apiece, ditto pints 21s., ditto dobbins [a type of mug] about 9s. 6d. or 10s. 6d. Tea kitchens [tea-urns], in general, containing a gallon at seven guineas, but these may be made of any size.'

In 1774 Boulton received a commission, via a Worcester jeweller/goldsmith named Samuel Bradley, from a group of 'ladies of Worcester' for a large silver tray for presentation to Lady Lewes, wife of Sir Watkin Lewes:[2] according to the records in the Assay Office at Birmingham the weight of this tray was 327 oz. but Boulton, in writing of it in 1775 to one of his patrons, Sir Harbord Harbord, later Baron Suffield, mentions that it weighed 334 oz. In the Thursday, 18 August 1774 edition of *Berrow's Worcester Journal* (England's oldest news-sheet, founded in the 1660s) this tray is described as follows:

Yesterday was presented to Lady Lewes, by the ladies of Worcester, the superb piece of plate mentioned in our last, adorned with many curious and emblematic devices of which the following is an exact description:

The shield
    a) in the middle: Fortitude
    b) beneath: Britannia

2. Practised at Chancery Bar from 1766. Four times unsuccessfully contested Parliamentary seat at Worcester. Knighted 1773. Alderman of City of London, and Lord Mayor and M.P. for City of London, 1780. Inherited estates in Glamorgan and Pembroke through his wife, but died in penury.

c) with Magna Carta in her hand
d) Temperance

The supporters:
a) Eloquence
b) Hope

The crest: Fame
The motto: 'Firm in the glorious enterprize'
Inscription: 'The ladies of Worcester present to Lady Lewes this mark of their esteem in the acknowledgement of the noble and disinterested efforts of Sir Watkin Lewes to destroy the influence of bribery and corruption in the election of members to represent their country in Parliament, and in particular to restore to the citizens of Worcester their rights and priviledges.'

Boulton described it thus to Sir Harbord Harbord: 'This table has a solid border, bending outwards, with festoons of laurels upon it in a section of it. The bottom was an ellipsis whose length was 2 feet $7\frac{1}{2}$ inches, and whose breadth was about 1 foot $11\frac{3}{4}$ inches, or perhaps 2 feet. It measured about $1\frac{1}{2}$ inches wider and longer at the top of the rim, and was 2 inches high about the flat part. In this table, a solid board was pressed on account of its strength, but if a laced border should be required, it will have more work, and become lighter, and in that case, the price will be dearer, say, from 20s. to £2 according to its degree of richness. We made no stand for this table as the "spirit of patriotism" amongst the Worcester ladies did not extend so far. We made designs for a stand of black ebony to be decorated with silver ornaments and suitable to the table but it was never executed.'

Unfortunately all trace has vanished of what must have been a very impressive piece of silver.

Later in 1774 Boulton, presumably feeling that he should seek to widen his horizons, sent the following list of silver plate which he had for sale to retailing goldsmiths and jewellers in London: 'All manner of silver and silver plated articles such as tea kitchens, bread baskets, candle sticks, [and] waiters.'

The most important designers for Boulton plate in the neo-classic taste were Robert Adams and James Wyatt: since the style of these two great men was often remarkably close, one can only say that plate with the 'feel' of Adam and Wyatt, produced by Boulton after the death of Adam in 1792, probably owes its origin to the design of Wyatt.

1776 appears to have been a vintage year for Boulton and Fothergill silver designed by Adam, for in that year were made three of the finest pieces of silver to bear their joint mark, a pair of silver sauce tureens (in the collection of the Birmingham Assay Office) and a silver-gilt helmet-shaped cream jug with lid (in the Museum of Fine Arts, Boston). All three pieces are superbly fluted on their bodies and lids, and all are fine examples of the style of Robert Adam. Each tureen rises from a trumpet-shaped oval base with cast strap and floral motifs; the ribbon-wreathed rims of the bowls, from which rise wide loop handles, are surrounded by a frieze of cast floral and foliate scrolls; on each side of each bowl is an oval medallion containing a coat-of-arms within a shield; the matching covers have each a baluster finial. Each tureen weighs some 28 oz. and stands $5\frac{1}{2}$ in. high. A somewhat similar pair are dated 1773. The jug, which stands $13\frac{1}{2}$ in. high and rests on a circular spreading foot, is encircled by two ornamental straps; the top one consists of paterae, with a row of beading below and a band of ribbon-wreaths above; the bottom band is formed of scrolls within a ribbed border. The high looped handle has a row of beads running along the centre, with ovolo edging.

Another fine jug of 1776 by Boulton (in the collection of the Birmingham City Museum and Art Gallery) stands $13\frac{3}{4}$ in. high on a quadrangular concave-sided base decorated with guilloche moulding; on the four corners of the base are chased flower-heads. The body of the jug, which has a handle similar to that described above, is encircled by a row of beading near the bottom and a band of ribbon-wreathing near the top, with four oval medallions and a coat-of-arms between. Both these jugs are based on the traditional ewer shape of the classical era, and their design was almost certainly inspired by the drawings of Sir William Hamilton's vases by Chevalier P. V. d'Hancarville.

An interesting and rare item made by Boulton, now at Temple Newsam, Leeds, is a cassolette or scent burner dated 1779; the ovoid body, the base of which is embellished with acanthus foliage and which has a scrolling frieze, is supported between the shoulders of three winged demi-caryatids, which rise from three spreading legs terminating in claw-and-ball feet pinned to ebony balusters; the legs are connected by stretchers; between the wings of the caryatids depend swags of drapery with an oval fluted medallion above; the cover, which is topped by a finial of acanthus foliage, is finely pierced to allow the smell of the burnt scent to escape.

Perhaps this was similar to the burners to which Boulton refers when, in writing to his wife in 1770, he mentions that: 'The King hath bought a pair of cassolets, a Titus,[3] a Venus[4] clock and some other things. . . .'

Other references to cassolettes are found in a letter written by Boulton to Fothergill in May 1773: 'Pray order Bentley to forward a pair of cassoletts for the French Ambassadure, well finished and another pair for Lady Hilsborough.' When writing in April 1772 to his London agent William Matthews concerning a sale at Christie and Ansell's in St. James's, where in Boulton's day it was customary for manufacturers of *objets d'art* to send their wares to be sold by public auction by Mr. James Christie, Boulton mentions the following results: 'To Prince of Wales: Winged figure casolets . . . Mr. Dunbar: delivered from the sale: A pair of winged figure casolets with pedestals: £29. 8s. od.'

In 1772 Mrs. Montague describes to Boulton how 'the aromatick gales . . . from these Cassolettes drive away the Vapour of soup & all the fulsome savour of dinner. . . . there is a prettiness of fancy in the Cassolettes which improved into grace & good taste w'd render the sort of thing a beautiful addition to a table. . . .'

At this date cassolettes, which were of French origin, were customarily brought into the dining-room at the conclusion of a meal.

A cup and cover by Boulton and Fothergill dated 1777, standing 12 in. high and weighing 67 oz., is of typical Robert Adam design: the urn-shaped body is decorated with husk-swags and flower-heads, with a frieze of scrolling motifs. A coat-of-arms is engraved on the body, surrounded by ribbon-ties and foliage sprays. The base of the cup, which rests on an octagonal indented base with a guilloche and flower border, has decoration of acanthus leaves rising from a short fluted stem. The handles are formed of intertwining snakes.

A circular bowl on a trumpet stem marked by Boulton and Fothergill but undated, though probably about 1780, also shows unmistakable Adam characteristics: a heavy frieze of guilloche and flower decoration has a boldly beaded border above and a ribbed one beneath. On the body are swags of husks, with classical busts on oval medallions between.

3. 'Titus' clock: ormolu gilded figure of Emperor Titus in toga, leaning his left elbow on vertical rectangular marble clock-case ornamented with classical masks, Imperial eagles and floral swags.

4. 'Venus' clock; described in Christie and Ansell's catalogue for April 1771 as: 'An horizontal time-piece representing Venus at the tomb of Adonis, in marble and or moulu, and on the pedestal is a medalian of his death. . . .'

A superb pair of candlesticks each 10¾ in. high and weighing about 20 oz., made by Boulton in 1789, are wholly Adam in concept: the circular bases are encircled by a fluted frieze and a design of cast foliage. From the base a trumpet foot leads into the foot of the column which rises via a fluted baluster to a similarly shaped and decorated support to the gadroon-bordered sockets.

Another fine Boulton piece probably designed by Robert Adam is an epergne dated 1790, standing 12 in. high and weighing over 55 oz. The oval rest for the cut-glass bowl is heavily cast with vertical fluting, and has a broad gadroon border. Three lions' masks with ring-in-mouth handles rise from the top of each of the three legs, which have shell and anthemion decoration and paw and acanthus terminals. A massively gadrooned central floral finial rises from the middle of the incurved triangular base.

Two magnificently designed ewers, one for wine by Boulton and Fothergill, 1776, 12 in. high weighing 21½ oz., the other for cream by Boulton alone, 1785, 6 in. tall weighing over 5½ oz., also bear the hand-mark of Robert Adam. The former, of classical simplicity, stands on a circular foot; the looped handle, decorated with beading with ogee borders, is joined to the body by cast acanthus leaves. The latter, also on a circular base, has a broadly reeded rib and rim and a plain flat band handle.

The design of a circular salver of 1774 by Boulton and Fothergill, with a diameter of 12 in. and a weight of over 28 oz., is also probably the work of Adam: the pierced and cast border is embellished with festoons of husks, and alternately with inverted palmettes and flower-heads. Another Adam designed piece is a 4½ in. high spool-shaped dish-ring, made by Boulton and Fothergill in 1773: a guilloche band dividing fine piercing bordered by ribbon-wreath edging is typical of Robert Adam. A four-light spirit warmer is set in an oval gimbal supported by four straps, so that the ring can be used from both sides, which are of different diameter to take plates of differing sizes. The turned yew-wood handle is joined to the frame by a silver socket. The pattern for this piece may be seen in the Birmingham Reference Library.

To conclude our examples of Adam designed and Soho manufactured silver let us take a magnificent pair of ecclesiastical ewers made in 1791. The bodies, which are of classical urn form, are encircled by two bands of scrolling motifs, with below the lower one tapering fluting; they bear on each side oval foliage wreaths surrounding oval medallions containing a

Portrait of Matthew Boulton; t unknown. National Portrait ery, London.

Matthew Boulton and John ergill: pair of candlesticks, . Birmingham Assay Office. *to: City Museum and Art ery, Birmingham.*)

17 Matthew Boulton and John Fothergill: mazarine, 1769–70. Birmingham Assay Office. (*Photo: City Museum and Art Gallery, Birmingham.*)

18 Matthew Boulton and John Fothergill: flagon, chalice and paten, 1774. St. Mary's Chapel, Birmingham. (*Photo: City Museum and Art Gallery, Birmingham.*)

19 Matthew Boulton and John Fothergill: one of a pair of sauce-tureens, 1776. Birmingham Assay Office. (*Photo: City Museum and Art Gallery, Birmingham.*)

20 Matthew Boulton: cassolette, 1779. Art Gallery and Temple Newsam House, Leeds.

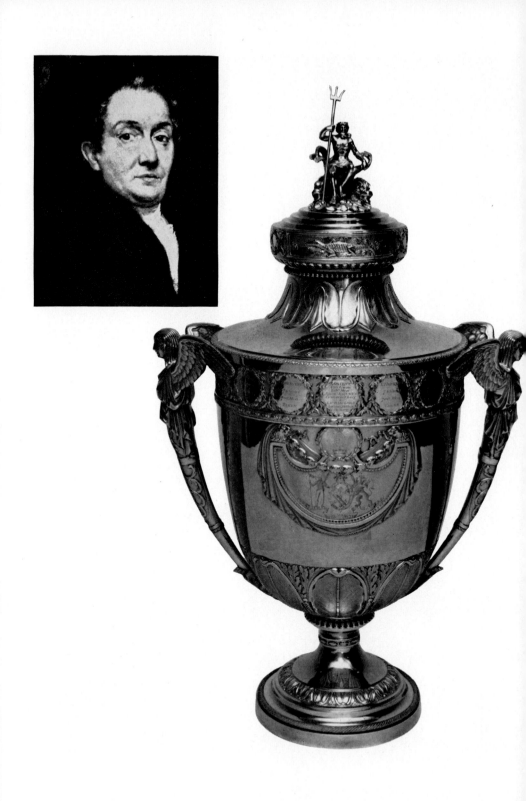

21　Portrait of Paul Storr:
Stapleton-Champneys Collection.

22　Paul Storr: the Nile Cup, 1799.
National Maritime Museum,
Greenwich.

23　Paul Storr: a fruit bowl from the
Wellington service, 1810–11.
Wellington Museum, Apsley House.
(*Crown copyright*.)

24　Paul Storr: the Theocritus Cup,
1812–13. The Royal Collection.
(*Reproduced by gracious permission of
Her Majesty the Queen*.)

25 Paul Storr: standing cup and cover, 1833. The Worshipful Company of Goldsmiths.

26 Portrait of Augustine Courtauld: artist unknown.

27 Portrait of Louisa Courtauld, by Zoffany.

28 Portrait of Samuel Courtauld the Younger: artist unknown.

29 Samuel Courtauld: tea-urn,
1760. (*Photo: courtesy of Christie's.*)

30 Augustine Courtauld: State
Salt of The Corporation of the
City of London, 1730.
(*Photo: Eileen Tweedy.*)

cast figure of Christ; on the front of the body are the letters I.H.S. and a cross within a bright-cut star. The circular bases are decorated with acanthus motifs on ribbon-wreathed borders, and are joined to the body by trumpet-shaped necks with a gadrooned rim. The loop handles are decorated with ribbon-wreathed edging. On the base of each is a contemporary inscription reading: 'For the use of St. Mary's Chapel Birmingham. Boulton and Fothergill fecit 1774.'

Robert Adam died in 1792, and although Boulton continued to produce plate from his designs for a number of years, it is not unreasonable to conjecture that plate not strictly in the Adam taste and perhaps lacking his sophistication and delicacy was designed by Wyatt.

James Wyatt was trained in the same tradition as Robert Adam. After four years spent studying architecture in Rome and Venice, he returned to England in 1766, where he soon became highly successful and a rival to the Adam brothers, being employed extensively by the aristocracy to design and enrich their mansions. He was elected an Associate of the Royal Academy in 1770 and a Royal Academician in 1785. After Robert Adam's death in 1792 it was only natural that Boulton should look to Wyatt for designs for his silver.

Wyatt's designs are, in the main, a little heavier and less delicate than those of Adam, and the design for a number of pieces of Boulton's silver may be attributed to his hand. These include an egg-stand containing a set of six egg-cups and spoons, surmounted by a boat-shaped salt-cellar resting on a wire dome. The octagonal reeded wire stand rests on six ball feet. A pierced 'Gothic' frieze surrounds each egg-cup, which rests on a reeded circular foot. The date of this piece, which weighs 32 oz., is 1792. Also probably to a design by Wyatt is an egg-stand for six of 1808 with a swing handle, contained within a serpentine frame which rests on pillar supports terminating in ball feet; this set, which unusually incorporates a pair of oval covered salt-cellars and a larger matching butter-dish, was sold at Sotheby's in 1973 for £900.

A well designed pair of plain lyre-shaped candlesticks 10 in. high and weighing about 10 oz. each, made by Boulton in 1807, are almost certainly of Wyatt origin, as are at least two other pairs of candlesticks dated 1792 and 1797, both of which are of rather more conventional form. A nice and very small taper-stick only 1¼ in. high, rising from a circular reeded pan, made by Boulton in 1804, was probably also designed by

Wyatt, who almost certainly was responsible for a splendidly conceived chamber candlestick of 1805, 4 in. in height. The slightly everted tray has a heavily gadrooned border, which is repeated on the rim of the sliding socket which rises from a plain column. The conical extinguisher, heavily reeded at the base, and topped by an acorn finial, has a right-angled bracket which fits into the circular thumbpiece of the broad band handle.

Two inkstands made by Boulton in 1803 and 1801 are also probably from a design by Wyatt. The former, of canoe shape, has a reeded border and rests on four plain feet; it contains an ink-pot, a pounce-pot and a central plinth, on which stands a taper-stick, complete with chained extinguisher, with plain ring handle. The latter consists of a deep oval tray on four feet with a pair of containers for ink- and pounce-pots. A bell-shaped taper-stick, with slightly everted socket, rises from a baluster-knop on the reeded handle.

A matching cream-jug and sugar-basin made by Boulton in 1795, and probably part of a complete tea service, also owe their origin to Wyatt. Both are of *bombé* outline and rest on a cast circular foot. The top half is enriched with broad fluting above acanthus leaf decoration, which encircles each piece. The handles are enriched with shell terminals and lions' masks. The lip of the cream-jug has a reeded everted rim, with scrolling acanthus leaf ornamentation at either side.

Among pieces of Boulton's silver possibly designed by Wyatt (who died in 1813) before the death of Adam in 1792, mention must be made of two plain drum-shaped teapots of 1775 and 1776, and a curious *bombé* sugar-vase dated 1774, decorated all over with a swirling *repoussé* rococo confection of flowers and foliage, with an open flower finial. It was intended to be *en suite* with a pair of tea-caddies made by Samuel Taylor in 1749.

In spite of the undoubted excellence of his silver, this side of the business was not a financially profitable one for Boulton; this was due partly to the imposition of a tax of sixpence an ounce on silver which was re-introduced in 1784, and partly because the production of Sheffield plate reached its acme between about 1785 and 1800. The financial lack of success was certainly in no way due to the manner in which the Soho manufactory was managed. Paying apprentices were not accepted; instead, as Boulton explained in a letter to James Adam written on 1 October 1770, 'I have train'd up many and am training up more plain Country Lads, all of which that betray any genius are taught to draw, from which

I derive many advantages. . . .' In this way Boulton obtained not only Soho-trained craftsmen, but also designers. He clearly placed as much importance on design as on craftsmanship, and in addition to obtaining designs from Adam and Wyatt he also employed John Flaxman and Sir William Chambers, as well as draughtsmen within his firm, of whom the finest was a man named Hooker. A large collection of drawings contained in the Soho Manufactory Pattern Books may be seen in the Birmingham Reference Library.

Boulton also made sure, largely through the installation at Soho in 1776 of a steam-driven engine, that his craftsmen were supplied with the most advanced technological inventions. Boulton himself perfected a means of wire-drawing, which enabled a length of wire of uniform diameter to be produced; two cake-baskets made entirely of silver-wire dated 1780 and 1788 and a sweetmeat-basket of 1774 with a grape and vineleaf border, prove the efficacy of Boulton's system.

Among the departmental managers (who received a wage of £9 per week) at Soho concerned with the production of silver-plate were: James Cook in 1781, apprenticed in 1779; one Caldecott, a master-piercer, who was probably responsible for the Temple Newsam cassolette; S. Athos and John Bownas (1782); John Watson, Thomas Dixon and William Hancock (Sheffield plate); James Watt, John Bingley, William Chamberlain (died 1798), John White (Sheffield plate), and John Haywood (a master-piercer; 1783). Apprentices included John Hodges in about 1768, originally a managing clerk and later manager of the silver department, who died in 1808; Isaac Abbot (who was apprenticed to Benjamin Smith, currently working for Matthew Boulton); John Fellows, a candlestick-maker; John Fenton, a silver-wire drawer, apprenticed in 1767 and articled in 1770; Henry Gillings, a chaser, articled in 1775; Hannah Owen, a burnisher and polisher, whose agreement is dated 1769; Edward Pardoe, a chaser (agreement 1768); Thomas Bunbury of Dublin, articled as a 'silversmith' in 1771; Elizabeth Allen, a burnisher and polisher (agreement 1768), and Joseph Burton, a chaser articled in 1768. The period of apprenticeship at Soho was from three to five years. Mention of the two women 'burnishers and polishers', Hannah Owen and Elizabeth Allen is of interest (cf. Hester Bateman, p. 59).

Towards the end of his life Boulton concentrated his energies increasingly on his iron-founding, steam-engine and coinage interests, although his

Soho manufactory continued to produce silver and Sheffield plate of a uniformly high quality of workmanship and design.

On 11 July 1783 Boulton's second wife, Anne, to whom he was clearly devoted, was tragically drowned in the ornamental lake below Soho House; the loss must have affected Boulton deeply, and in order to regain mental and physical stability, his doctors prevailed upon him to take a fifteen-week recuperative holiday in Ireland and Scotland.

On his return to Soho, Boulton once again immersed himself in his various business interests, in which he took an active part until shortly before his death. Having previously enjoyed excellent health, from about 1802 he suffered increasing pain from kidney-stone, which the waters of Cheltenham Spa could alleviate but not cure. Late in 1807 Boulton had a serious attack, from which he only slowly recovered. In March 1809 he suffered another setback which was eventually to prove fatal; he died peacefully on Thursday, 17 August 1809, only sixteen days before his eighty-first birthday. On the day after his death the *Birmingham Herald* contained the following obituary notice: 'His life has been an uninterrupted application to the advancement of the useful arts. . . .'

Boulton's funeral, 'furnished in the handsomest manner avoiding ostentation', took place exactly a week later, and cost the immense sum of £544. 17s. 2d. The hearse was followed by nine mourning-coaches and six hundred of Boulton's employees, to the most senior of whom was accorded the honour of bearing their late master into the parish church of St. Mary, Handsworth. To each person present was given a memorial copper medal, with on the obverse the inscription 'Matthew Boulton, died August 17th 1809 Aged 81 [*sic*] years' and on the reverse, surrounded by a palm-wreath 'In memory of his obsequies August 24th 1809'. His son, Matthew Robinson, erected a bust (by John Flaxman) in memory of his father in St. Mary's Church, together with a mural plaque engraved with a one-hundred-and-eleven-word panegyric.

Boulton's will, engrossed on 23 June 1806 and witnessed by James Watt, was proved by his son who was his sole executor, in the sum of £150,000 on 15 September 1809. He left his unmarried daughter Anne £5,000 on trust; to his nephew Zacchaeus Walker Junr. he bequeathed the sum of £500, and to his sister Ann £50; his niece Mary Mynd and his nephew George Nunn received £200 and £500 respectively, and John Thomas and Charles, the sons of his late partner John Fothergill, each were left £100. His workforce and domestic staff were also remembered, among them his works managers and managing clerks, and his housekeeper, valet and coachman. After a number of other small bequests, the residue of the estate, including a diamond ring presented to him by Emperor Alexander of Russia and a second ring which he had received following the death of Nelson, was left to his son, Matthew Robinson, who went to live at Tew Park, Great Tew, Oxfordshire.

Matthew Robinson continued to use his late father's maker's mark on Soho silver until 1842, when he was succeeded by his son Matthew Piers Watt (1820–94), who managed the silver workshop there until it finally closed in 1848, when a number of the dies were purchased by Thomas Bradbury & Sons of Sheffield.

One of the finest pieces of silver produced by the 'Boulton Plate Company' (as the silver department at Soho came to be known after the death of Matthew Boulton) is a four-light candelabrum, standing 29½ in. high and dated 1811. The perfectly plain cylindrical column, which has a capital of the Composite Order, rises from a rectangular plinth from which it is divided by a spool-shaped collar which rests on a stepped base. The four curving ribbed branches have sockets ornamented with beading and neo-classical foliage, below which are gadroon-edged drip-pans. The centre of the top of the column is decorated with beautifully cast and chased acanthus and feather embellishment, above which a flame-finial rises from a gadroon-bordered fluted base. The overall spread of the branches of this formal but pleasing piece is 17 in. The designer was most probably James Wyatt.

Matthew Boulton in his working life was a man of diverse talents and eclectic taste, matched only by the variety of his friends and the distinctions which he achieved.

Among the former he numbered Dr. Erasmus Darwin (1731–1802), the great radical scientist, and Dr. William Small (1734–75), described by Benjamin Franklin (1706–90), the distinguished American diplomat, statesman and scientist, as 'an ingenious philosopher and a most worthy honest man'. Franklin himself came to know Boulton during his second visit to England from 1757 to 1762, and they continued afterwards to correspond on scientific matters. John Roebuck (1718–94), chemist, iron-founder and mine-owner, and his partner Samuel Garbett (1715–1803); Josiah Wedgwood (1730–95) for whose pottery Boulton provided metal mounts; James Adam (1728–94) the great neo-classical designer; James

Watt (1736–1819), who in partnership with Boulton developed the steam-engine; James Keir (1735–1820), soldier, chemist and glass-manufacturer; John Wilkinson (1728–1808), England's greatest eighteenth-century iron-master; Dr. Joseph Priestly (1733–1804), discoverer of oxygen in 1774 and a distinguished experimental chemist; and Richard Lovell Edgeworth (1744–1817), the writer – all were friends or business associates of Matthew Boulton.

If the number of Boulton's friends was legion, no less so were the various distinctions with which he was honoured: in 1766, at the age of thirty-eight, he became co-founder with Darwin and Small of the Lunar Society (so called because meetings were held at the time of the full moon, in order that members should have light on their way home afterwards) for scientific and social intercourse: members included John Baskerville (1706–75), the printer; Samuel Galton (1719–99), the Quaker merchant; Thomas Day (1748–89), the author; Dr. William Withering (1741–99), the botanist; and John Whitehurst (1713–88), the horologist, as well as many of Boulton's friends and associates mentioned above.

In 1783 Boulton was elected a Fellow of the Royal Society of Edinburgh, and in the following year a Fellow of the Royal Society. In 1792 he became an Honorary Member of the Society of Civil Engineers (founded in 1771 by John Smeaton). In 1794 Boulton's name was 'pricked' by the King (incidentally with a gold bodkin) as High Sheriff for the County of Staffordshire in the following year. In 1800 Boulton was elected as one of the original Proprietors of the Royal Institution of Great Britain, founded by Count Rumford. According to Professor P. P. Zabarinsky, Boulton was a member of the Voluntary Economical Society of St. Petersburg (1765–1917), Russia's most senior scientific society.

A number of portraits and busts of Boulton are known; among the former are a painting in oils by Charles Frederick von Breda, R.A. 1792 (in the collection of the Institution of Civil Engineers), which depicts him holding one of his Soho medals in his left hand, a magnifying-glass in his right hand, and with a view of the Soho Manufactory in the background; a painting by Lemuel Abbot, owned by the Corporation of the City of Birmingham, and a third, dated 1801, by Sir William Beechey, R.A. Among the latter are the Flaxman memorial in St. Mary's Church, Handsworth, mentioned above; those on a Mint Medal (1798) and a

Memorial Medal (1819), and a gilded ormolu plaque produced at Soho in about 1780. Two wax portraits of Boulton by Pieter de Rouw (1771–1852), signed and dated 1803 and 1814 respectively, are in the Victoria and Albert Museum.[5] Together, these give us a fair idea of Boulton's personal appearance: he was well built and of about medium height, with a somewhat receding forehead, high-bridged nose, firm chin, and blue-grey eyes which gave him a determined yet pleasant expression.

Concerning his character and abilities, let James Watt, his friend and partner for thirty-five years, have the final word: in a Memorandum dated 17 September 1809, written at the request of Boulton's son, Watt speaks of him as follows:

Mr. Boulton was not only an ingenious mechanick . . . but possessed in a high degree the faculty of rendering any new invention . . . useful to the publick.

His conception of the nature of any invention was quick. . . .

When he took any scheme in hand he was rapid in executing it. . . . He was a liberal encourager of merit in others. . . .

To his family he was a most affectionate parent. He was steady in his friendships, hospitable & benevolent to his acquaintances & indeed I may say to all who came within his reach . . . & to sum up humane and charitable to the distressed.

In respect to myself, I can with great sincerity say that he was a most affectionate & steady friend & patron with whom during a close connection of 35 years I have never had any serious difference.

5. From the Mary Bate Collection and the gift of Charles Vine respectively.

BOULTON PEDIGREE

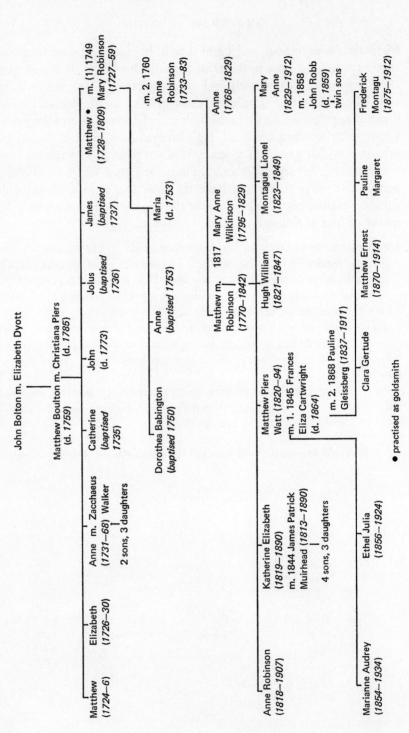

John Bolton m. Elizabeth Dyott

Matthew Boulton m. Christiana Piers
(d. 1759)   (d. 1785)

Matthew   Elizabeth   Anne   m.   Zacchaeus   Catherine   John   Jolus   James   Matthew ●   m. (1) 1749   Mary Robinson
(1724–6)   (1726–30)   (1731–68) Walker   (baptised   (d. 1773) (baptised   (baptised   (1728–1809)   (1727–59)
                                                            1735)   1736)   1737)

                                 2 sons, 3 daughters
                                                                                                                                m. 2. 1760 Anne
                                                                                                                                            Robinson
                                                                                                                                            (1733–83)

                             Dorothea Babington   Anne   Maria
                             (baptised 1750)   (baptised 1753) (d. 1753)   Anne
                                                                                                                                            (1768–1829)

                                                                      Matthew m.   1817   Mary Anne
                                                                      Robinson   Wilkinson
                                                                      (1770–1842)   (1795–1829)

                                           Matthew Piers   Hugh William   Montague Lionel   Mary
                                           Watt (1820–94)   (1821–1847)   (1823–1849)   Anne
                                                                                                                                        (1829–1912)
                                           m. 1. 1845 Frances
                                           Eliza Cartwright   m. 1858
                                           (d. 1864)   John Robb
                                                                                                                                        (d. 1859)
                                           m. 2. 1868 Pauline   twin sons
                                           Gleissberg (1837–1911)

Anne Robinson   Katherine Elizabeth   Clara Gertude   Matthew Ernest   Pauline   Frederick
(1818–1907)   (1819–1890)   (1870–1914)   Margaret   Montagu
                                                                                                                      (1875–1912)
                   m. 1844 James Patrick
                   Muirhead (1813–1890)

                   4 sons, 3 daughters

Marianne Audrey   Ethel Julia
(1854–1934)   (1856–1924)

● practised as goldsmith

Paul Storr

(1771–1844)

IN the same way that Paul De Lamerie was the dominant figure among eighteenth-century goldsmiths, so another Paul, Paul Storr, reigned supreme as artist and craftsman during the Regency period one hundred years later.

It has not proved possible to trace the ancestry of Paul Storr with any certitude further back than his grandfather Edward, a publican and victualler of Tothill Street, Westminster. There is in existence a certificate of baptism for one John Storr, a hat-maker, whose brother Thomas was the father of Paul; this certificate reads:

> This is to certify that John Storr son of Edward by Elizabeth was born the 9th and baptized the Thirteenth of January one thousand seven hundred and forty one as appears by the Register of Baptisms belonging to the parish of St. Margaret's Westminster this 4th July 1787.
> Signed: Jos. F. Fox.
> Parish Clerk and Register Keeper.[1]

John died in 1792 and the business, situated at 12 Union Street, which runs between King Street and Margaret Street off (New) Palace Yard in the City of Westminster, was subsequently carried on by his widow Ann and their two sons, William and John II, Paul's first cousins.

On the morning of Wednesday, 3 October 1804 a disastrous fire ravaged Union Street, and No. 12 and most of its contents were a total loss: Ann Storr and her two sons consequently moved first to No. 6 Bridge Street (one street north of Union Street) in the following year (where from 1807 they described themselves as 'Hat Makers & Furriers'), and subsequently in 1816 south again to Little Peter Street.

1. Penzer, pp. 34–5.

William Storr appears to have died unmarried. John II (1781–1854) married in 1819 and had a son, John III, born in 1821, who in turn had three sons and a daughter.

In 1757 John's younger brother, Thomas, became apprenticed for the comparatively modest premium of £5 to John Christopher Romer, a silver-chaser of St. James's, Westminster. In 1753 one Edward Norton Storr had been apprenticed to Romer; he was presumably a third son of Edward and Elizabeth, and his middle name may well have been his mother's maiden name.

We do not hear of Thomas again for over thirty years, when he is described in the lease of a house in Horseferry Road, dated 18 April 1788, as 'Thomas Storr of Union Street in the parish of St. Margaret's Westminster Victualler . . .'.[2] From this it is clear firstly that at some unknown date prior to 1788 he had abandoned the career of silver-chaser and had assumed that of his father, and secondly that he had by that date joined his brother John in the latter's home in Union Street.

Now from 1783 to 1786 Thomas is recorded as paying the rates on a house in Tothill Street, which it seems reasonable to assume he had inherited from his father, who must therefore have died in about 1782. It would thus seem that Thomas moved to his brother's house in Union Street at some time between late 1786 and early 1788. As Paul was born in 1771 the place of his birth appears likely to have been his grandfather's house in Tothill Street, whence his father had doubtless returned on the expiration of his apprenticeship to Romer in about 1764.

The site of Thomas's new property in Horseferry Road was to the south of the Grey Coat Hospital at a point where Horseferry Road bends east and met New Street (now Gillingham Row), Carey Street (now Rutherford Street), and Regency Street. In a list of ratepayers for 1821 the house is given as the last one going north in Carey Street, i.e. on the corner of that street and Horseferry Road.

In 1803 Thomas's landlords, the Dean and Chapter of St. Margaret's, Westminster, agreed to sell him the freehold of his property for the sum of £192. 13s. 4d., but he died on New Year's Eve before the sale could be effected; the amount due was paid out of his estate on 22 January 1804. Under his will, made on 5 October 1803 and proved on 27 January 1804, Thomas made Paul his sole executor and residuary legatee, leaving his property (which included a house in Oxford Street and a freehold in the

2. Held by Westminster Abbey (Lease Book 50, fol. 401); Penzer, p. 40.

City of London) on trust to his wife for life, and then to Paul and his two sisters, Ann (Mrs. Amplelet) and Sarah (Mrs. Bishop).

From 1803 to 1822 the ratepayers of Horseferry Road are listed as Paul's mother, his sister Sarah and a third unnamed Storr. By 1823 the house was unoccupied, and it seems likely that it had by this time been sold, as in an indenture transferring the property to Paul, dated 2 June 1820 (presumably shortly after the death of his mother), Paul is described as 'of Harrison Street, Gray's Inn Lane, Co: Middlesex, Gentleman'.[3]

Having thus traced, so far as is possible, the ancestry of Paul Storr, we come to the life and work of the man himself.

He was born, as we have already seen, in 1771, probably in his grandfather's house in Tothill Street, the eldest child of Thomas and his wife, whose Christian and maiden names are both unfortunately unknown. Having grown up literally to the sound of the goldsmith's hammer (for it will be remembered that at the time of his birth his father was still working as a silver-chaser), it is hardly surprising to find that Paul was apprenticed in 1785 at the age of fourteen to a goldsmith named Andrew Fogelberg, a 'Plateworker' of 30 Church Street, Soho.

Fogelberg was born in Sweden in about 1732, and became apprenticed to one Berenk Harck of Halmstad in 1746, rising to the position of journeyman six years later; he is generally supposed to have reached England some time during the 1760s. Strangely, he never became a member of the Worshipful Company of Goldsmiths, which may perhaps explain why his pupil Paul Storr never became a member either. From about 1770 to 1793 Fogelberg worked in his premises in Church Street, Soho, where in 1780 he was joined by a partner, Stephen Gilbert, who in May 1752 had been apprenticed to Edward Wakelin of Panton Street (whose business is now owned by Garrards). Gilbert was made Free of the Goldsmiths' Company by Service on 1 February 1764, but returned to work in Panton Street as an employee until 1771; what he did during the next nine years is unknown, but as already mentioned he became Fogelberg's partner in 1780; the two goldsmiths registered their joint mark on 17 July of that year.

Such of Fogelberg's work as is extant shows him to have been an enthusiastic proponent of the neo-classical style popularized by Robert Adam. This is exemplified by his predilection for the oval, especially in

3. Lease Book 60, fol. 206; Penzer, p. 41.

the form of vase or urn, decorated with bold bands of oval cartouches, laurel swags hanging from circular rosettes, and tall reeded handles terminating in further oval decorations; lanceolate leaves, narrow reeded legs, acanthus and anthemion foliage, and the oval silver cameo (borrowed from James Tassie (1735–99) the distinguished reproducer of antique jewellery and cameos, near whom Fogelberg worked), are further indications of his love for and support of the neo-classic.

Having completed his apprenticeship in 1792, Storr joined one William Frisbee, a silver-plate worker of 5 Cock Lane, Snow Hill, to the south of Smithfield Market. Frisbee, whose father John was a Tallow Chandler, had been apprenticed in October 1774 to John Crouch of Giltspur Street, becoming Free by Service on 6 February 1782. He entered his own mark early in 1792, and the partners Frisbee and Storr entered their joint mark

(WF over PS) on 2 May of the same year. The partnership was not, however, of long duration, and in 1795 Frisbee moved to other premises in nearby Cow Lane, also off Snow Hill: he was elected to the Livery of the Goldsmiths' Company in October 1806, and died on 9 December fourteen years later.

Meanwhile Storr (incidentally still giving as his address 30 Church Street, Soho, which he may well have taken over from Fogelberg after the latter's retirement) had entered his own first maker's mark (an uppercase P.S. within a rectangular punch separated by a pellet) on 12 January 1793; a second mark, similar to the first but within a lobed punch, followed on 27 April, and a third closely resembling the second on 8 August 1794; on the same page in the Register in Goldsmiths' Hall is a note to the effect that on 8 October 1796 Storr 'removed to No. 20 Aire [Air] Street, St. James', a narrow lane which joins Piccadilly to Glasshouse Street via Regent's Street, a few yards west of Piccadilly Circus; here Storr was to remain for the next eleven years, and it was here that he was to establish himself as one of London's leading goldsmiths.

It was in his workshops in Air Street that Storr produced what is perhaps the first really important piece of his career, a large gold font (dated 1797–8) commissioned by the Duke of Portland for the christening of his son William Henry, Marquess of Titchfield (1796–1824); weighing 245 oz. and standing on a podium 13¾ in. square, it is described by Penzer as being:

Formed of a circular bowl, plain in the lower part and enriched above by a broad classical border in relief and acanthus foliage at the bottom. The border is surmounted by a plain narrow shelf from the inner edge of which rises the vertical rim with a running floral frieze. The bowl is supported by four winged cherubs' feet. On the square pedestal, with beaded edges, stand figures of Faith, Hope and Charity, said to have been made from designs by John Flaxman R.A.[4]

Shortly after entering a fourth maker's mark on 29 November 1799, Storr was entrusted with the manufacture of the 'Battle of the Nile Cup', made as a presentation to Nelson; bearing the date-letter for 1799–1800, weighing 238 oz. and standing 24 in. high, this important *oeuvre* (now in the National Maritime Museum at Greenwich) is described by Penzer as being an:

Urn-shaped, two-handled cup with elaborate Neptune finial. The lower part of the body is decorated with large, broad water-leaves intersected by acanthus foliage on rope stems. The greater portion is plain, with an inscription on one side and the Arms of Nelson, surmounted by the Chelengk crest, on the other. Running round the top, like a frieze, above a narrow oak-leaf border, are ten laurel wreaths circling the names of the defeated French ships. The handles, which extend to the full height of the main body of the cup, consist of winged sphinxes issuant from narrow cornucopia. The gently sloping lid is surmounted by a large central pedestal consisting in its lower part of inverted lotus leaves between beaded borders, and in its upper part of a slightly overhanging plinth with a gadrooned base on the sides of which are two rectangular panels depicting a Nile crocodile, separated by garlands of oak and laurel leaves. Above this, resting on the topmost of three circular steps, is a finial of Neptune enthroned, trident in hand, with two dolphins in attendance. The plain spreading foot, separated from the body of the urn by a gadrooned collar, is ringed with a band of oak leaves, while the base is enriched above by a band of water-leaves, and below by a cable. The inscription, surmounted by the Arms of the Levant Company, reads as follows:

'Presented to the / Right Honble Rear Admiral / Horatio Baron Nelson of the Nile / by the Governor and Company of Merchants / of England trading into the Levant Seas in commemoration / of the Glorious Victory obtained by his Lordship at the Mouth of the Nile on / the first of August 1798 on which ever Memorial day, by the defeat and / capture of a French Squadron superior to his own, he restored to His / Majesty's Arms the Dominion of the Mediterranean and to the / British Merchants the free enjoyment of their ancient and valuable trade to Turkey.'

4. p. 100.

The ten laurel wreaths contain the following account of the captured French ships:

1. Le Guerrier. 74 guns. 600 men. Taken.
2. Le Spartiate. 74 guns. 700 men. Taken.
3. Le Franklin. 80 guns. 800 men.
     Adm¹ Lanquet. Taken.
4. Le Tonant. 80 guns. 800 men. Taken.
5. L'Aquilon. 74 guns. 700 men. Taken.

     and on the opposite side

6. Le Conquerant. 74 guns. 700 men. Taken.
7. Le Mercure. 74 guns. 700 men. Taken.
8. L'Orient. 120 guns. 1010 men.
     Adm¹ Brueys Comm^r in Chief & Le Timoleon.
     74 guns. 700 men. Burnt.
9. L'Heureux. 74 guns. 700 men. Taken.
10. Le Souverain Peuple. 74 guns. 700 men. Taken.[5]

In 1801 Storr married an old childhood friend, Elizabeth Susanna Beyer, one year his senior, who was to bear him ten children who in turn were to provide him with no fewer than fifty-four grandchildren. Elizabeth was the fourth daughter of Adam and Ann Beyer, her father being a member of a family of pianoforte and organ-makers who had arrived in England from Erfurt in Saxony in about 1759, and now occupied premises in Compton Street, just around the corner from Church Street.

A pair of oil-paintings on wooden panels, 10 in. by 7¼ in., in the collection of Edward Stapleton who married Frances Mary Champneys, granddaughter of Storr's fourth daughter Mary Anne, are reputedly portraits of Paul Storr and Elizabeth Beyer. They were found among other family portraits on the death of Mary Anne's third and last surviving daughter, Mary. According to Mr. James Laver and Mr. Graham Reynolds of the Victoria and Albert Museum and Sir Charles Adams (Director of the National Portrait Gallery 1951–64) the male sitter must have been about fifty years old and his clothes suggest that the portrait was painted between about 1820 and 1830. Storr was fifty in 1821.

Paul and Elizabeth Storr's first child, Elizabeth, was born in 1802; she was followed two years later by a second daughter, Harriet, and in 1805 by a son, Paul; although it is likely that Paul Senr. hoped that the boy

5. p. 106.

would follow him in the trade of goldsmith, he enlisted at the age of fourteen as a cabin-boy in the Merchant Navy; in 1836 he married Susan, daughter of Colonel John Utterton; in 1898 one of their grandchildren, Helen, married Henry Whistler, and became the mother of the painter Rex and engraver Laurence; Paul Junr. died in 1874. A third daughter, Emma (1806–79), was followed in 1808 by a second son, Francis, who entered the Church in 1833; three years later he married Caroline, daughter of Lancelot Holland; after her death in 1856 he married in the following year Cecilia, widow of the Revd. Richard Davies; Francis died in 1888. Paul and Elizabeth Storr's remaining five children were Mary Anne (1809–91); Eleanor (1811–89); Sophia Jessy (1812–1900); John Bridge, born in 1814, who died in infancy; and Anna Maria, born in 1815.

Two years after his marriage Storr's father died. It was at about this time, too, that the notorious Philip Rundell (1743–1827) started to make overtures to Storr, now a well-established and highly respected gold-smith, to work exclusively on his behalf. Rundell had already managed to persuade William Theed, Senr., R.A. (1764–1817; later to become his partner) to design for him, and was soon also able to obtain the services of John Flaxman, R.A. (1755–1826), lately returned from a seven-year sojourn in Rome where he had made an extensive study of classical sculpture. The persuasive Rundell was soon also able to prevail upon Storr to quit Air Street and move to his doubtless more spacious work-rooms at 53 Dean Street, Soho. Storr was clearly no fool, however, and feared that by joining Rundell he ran the danger of having his own identity and individuality submerged by the latter's firm. This risk he avoided by adopting what we today regard as the comparatively modern and sophisticated practice of turning himself into a one-man company, 'Storr & Co.'. He was thus able to work both for Rundell and on his own behalf from Dean Street. The move took place in 1807 (accompanied by the obligatory registration of a new mark on 21 August). A sixth mark was

registered on 18 February 1808, and a very small seventh mark (suitable for using on jewellery) on 15 December in the same year. Within three or four years Storr had become a partner in the firm of 'Rundell, Bridge & Rundell', with whom he was to remain for a total of twelve years; the other partners were Philip Rundell, his nephew Edmund, John Bridge and William Theed. That Storr's fear mentioned above was to prove justified, we shall see later.

Orders for presentation and ceremonial silver plate from corporations and distinguished families soon began to flood into Rundell's workshop in Ludgate Hill: the Committee of Lloyd's commissioned two services of plate as a token of the country's gratitude to Nelson for his victories at the Nile and Copenhagen; the British Embassy in Paris ordered a huge silver-gilt table-service for the Duke of Wellington, who was appointed ambassador to France on 5 July 1814; Storr himself made 102 items, consisting of two fruit-bowls and stands, seventy-two dessert-plates, twelve coasters, eight ice-spades, four sugar ladles and four cream ladles, totalling in all 1,768 oz. 15 dwt. Work on the remaining 554 items was put 'out' to such well-known goldsmiths as Robert Hennell (36 soup-plates), Robert Garrard (2 table-spoons), and Benjamin Smith (4 salvers and fruit-baskets). Of the pieces made by Storr the most important are the fruit-bowls, dated 1810–11, and described by Penzer thus:

Both sub-base and base are of triangular form with concave sides and chamfered corners. The sub-base, perfectly plain, is supported on three feet in the form of voluted capitals cast and chased with acanthus foliage and floral helices. The base is of similar shape to the sub-base, but smaller, with a guilloche moulding on the lower edge and a leaf-and-dart moulding on the upper chamfered edge. It stands on three broad volute feet, resting on the sub-base, each of which is cast and chased with the mask of a bearded man with ram's horns, surmounted by a shell. Between the feet depend heavy swags of fruit and flowers. On each angle of the base stands a female figure, of caryatid type, sculptured in the round, clad in semi-transparent classical draperies and shod in sandals. In each hand the figures hold a thyrsus, the wand or sceptre of Dionysus (Bacchus) and his votaries – one surmounted by a pine-cone . . . the other by ivy leaves and berries. . . . The figures face outwards, their downward-stretched arms forming a criss-cross pattern with the thyrsi which are crossed and tied near the top with bows of ribbon. At a point on the base equidistant from the heels of the three figures is a large round floral boss, cast and chased. Resting lightly on the heads of the figures is a circular stand decorated with a *rinceau* frieze of foliage and flowers. Fitting into this is a large concave-sided bowl of open basket-work, the grouped and crossing osiers of which rise from a closely woven base to a double-plaited edge, resembling gadrooning. From this edge an inner border of grape-vine foliage and fruit clusters is attached. Glass liners fit into the basket-work bowls.

. . . They are engraved with the Royal Crest, and the crest of Wellesley within the garter surmounted by a ducal coronet.

Signed on the sub-base: RUNDELL BRIDGE ET RUNDELL AURIFICES REGIS ET PRINCIPIS WALLIAE LONDINI.[6]

These two bowls, standing 13¾ in. high and weighing 136 oz. each, are in the Wellington Museum at Apsley House in London. As with several of Storr's most popular works a number of these fruit-bowls (without the engraving) were reproduced, one of which may be seen in the Victoria and Albert Museum. Although the execution of these bowls is a *tour de force* their composition is not entirely satisfying, as sub-base, base and bowl seem to bear little relation to each other.

Also at Apsley House are two splendid parcel-gilt centrepieces, made by Storr in 1810 and 1811. The earlier one, 33 in. high, commemorates the battles of Vimiera and Reliça of 1808; it consists of a square plinth with mouldings of acanthus, bay-leaves and ovolo; at each corner stand three piled rifles and a standard; on the plinth is a shallow two-handled cup on spreading foot, surmounted by a figure of Victory holding aloft a wreath. The later one stands 21 in. in height; it consists of a similar cup with wreath finial supported by four draped and winged 'angels' standing, with bowed heads and bearing wreaths in their hands, on a circular base guarded by four lions couchant.

In 1973 two soup-tureens by Storr from the Campbell Museum, Camden, New Jersey were exhibited at the Victoria and Albert Museum. The earlier one, marked for 1810–11 and weighing 102 oz. is of oval *bombé* shape (recalling the fashion of the 1750s) with a deeply concave section below the undulating gadrooned rim; the finial of the cover is formed of a rose and bud rising from a bed of leaves. It is interesting to note that Trinity College, Cambridge, possesses a vertical-sided tureen of 1819–20 with scrolling feet and handles apparently made from the same moulds as those of this tureen. The second tureen from the Campbell collection was made in 1816–17 for Robert Hamilton, 8th Baron Belhaven and Stenton and his wife, who had been married in the previous year; their impaled arms are engraved on each side of the circular bowl and matching stand. The reeded handles are joined to the bowl by lions' masks which are repeated as terminals to the handle of the low domed and stepped cover. The bowl, 16½ in. in diameter, and stand together weigh 239 oz.

Shortly after completion of the Wellington plate, Rundell, Bridge & Rundell received a commission, which was entrusted to Storr's hands, from the Lord Mayor and Corporation of the City of London, for the repair

6. p. 144.

of a great silver-gilt candelabrum and epergne or centrepiece and stand, the main body of which had been made by Paul De Lamerie in 1738–9. The six candle-sockets, which have fluted edges with a decoration of foliage in relief, and the octagonal plinth on which the whole piece stands, are by Storr and are marked for 1811–12. The plinth bears the arms of the City of London in relief on each side with four dragons (part of the City arms) supporting the corners; on the top are cornucopia and caducei, on the edge laurel leaves, all in relief: it stands on four large claw feet, with scrolls, foliage and rosettes. The base is inscribed: 'This PLINTH was made during the MAYORALTY of the Rt. Honble. Sir Charles Flower, Bart., by RUNDELL, BRIDGE & RUNDELL, Goldsmiths and Jewellers to their Majesties, H.R.H. the Prince of Wales and Royal Family.' The overall weight of this piece is 779 oz. 11 dwt., of which Storr's base amounts to 418 oz. 15 dwt.

During the decade between 1806 and 1816 Storr was engaged in making a magnificent silver-gilt dessert service, consisting of more than fifty pieces, for Edward Lascelles, created Lord Harewood in 1812. Storr's work of this period is also well represented in the Royal collection at Windsor Castle, largely formed by the Prince Regent: the collection includes what is possibly Storr's most celebrated *oeuvre*, the 'Theocritus Cup', described by Penzer as follows:

This famous cup was designed by John Flaxman, R.A., from the description of a cup in the First Idyll of Theocritus (*c.* 300 B.C.–*c.* 260 B.C.). Its form is based on that of the Krater, a wide-mouthed Greek vessel used for mixing wine and water ... The subjects represented each side of the cup are framed above and laterally by vine branches and grapes. The torus-shaped base is decorated with acanthus and water-leaves in relief. There are two handles of twisted vine stems, placed low down each side of the cup. The circular foot is plain. The cipher of Queen Charlotte and the badge of George IV as Prince of Wales are engraved on the cup.[7]

The 'Theocritus Cup' bears the date-letter for 1812–13, stands 9¼ in. high, and weighs 90 oz. 15 dwt.

Storr is also represented at Windsor by a splendid circular silver-gilt charger, 31 in. in diameter, weighing 374 oz. 15 dwt., bearing the date-

7. p. 158.

letter for 1814–15 and Storr's eighth mark entered on 21 October 1813. To quote Penzer again:

The subject represented in this dish is the triumph of Dionysus (Bacchus) and Ariadne. They stand side by side in an ornamental chariot drawn by four prancing centaurs who respectively play the double-pipe, the harp, the tambourine or wield the cone-tipped thyrsus. In her right hand Ariadne holds a two-handled vase and in her left, which rests lightly on her husband's right shoulder, a long-shafted be-ribboned thyrsus. Dionysus embraces his wife's waist with his right arm, and with his left, in which is a thyrsus, presses a young faun (their son?) to his side. Above hover two winged *putti* – one holding a torch, the other a *pedum*. The whole scene is surrounded by a circle of vine leaves and grapes. The broad flat rim has a reeded edge enriched also with vine leaves and grapes, while the wide surface is covered with Bacchic emblems of every description – the syrinx, thyrsus, *pedum*, tambourine and various kinds of masks, many of which remind us of those on the Warwick Vase. They all rest on a ground of trellis-work. The Royal Arms of George IV are engraved below the main subject represented.

The design for the dish was made by Thomas Stothard, R.A. According to Rundell, Bridge & Rundell's bill of 1815 the main cost was £479. 7. 7., to which was added 18/–d. for engraving the Royal Arms and £118 for the gilding.[8]

Also contained in the Royal collection are a magnificent set of twelve silver-gilt ice-pails, marked for 1812–14, made for the Prince Regent at a cost of £3,470, their design being based on the 'Warwick Vase', a large two-handled white-marble vase brought from Italy to England, where in 1774 it was acquired by the Earl of Warwick, from whom it took its name. The form of the vase, coupled with the classical masks and Bacchic emblems with which it is embellished, suggested endless possibilities to goldsmiths: Storr produced a number of pieces, among them ice-pails, soup-tureens and epergnes, based on the original.

It had by now become clear that Storr's fear of having his own identity overwhelmed by Rundell's firm was proving to have been fully justified. As more and more orders for silver plate poured into the workshops in Dean Street, Storr found his role becoming increasingly that of manager rather than craftsman. His firm of Storr & Co. became increasingly squeezed by Rundell, Bridge & Rundell, as the cunning Philip Rundell had from the outset doubtless anticipated. As time went by Storr found that

8. p. 178.

almost all his time was spent in passing on to Rundell's workmen his own hard-won knowledge and manufacturing techniques, and he must soon have begun to feel that his craftsmanship and individuality were becoming eroded by such a soulless occupation. In order to avoid this, Storr realized that he must resign his partnership with Rundell, Bridge & Rundell, and start work on his own account once more.

To do this must have required considerable moral courage: when Philip Rundell died he left an estate of £1,500,000 and his nephew Edmund died worth £500,000; Bridge, too, made a fortune large enough to enable him to buy an estate in Dorset on his retirement; had Storr elected to remain for the rest of his working life as Rundell's manager, rather than try to re-establish his own reputation, he too would doubtless have died a rich man. Rundell and Bridge were, moreover, bachelors, while Storr had a wife and ten children to support; the temptation to remain in such a lucrative position must, therefore, have been very strong.

To his great credit, however, Storr resisted the temptation, and after a temporary sojourn at 74 and 75 Dean Street (which may have been owned by Rundell and from where he registered a ninth mark on 12 September 1817) he moved on 4 March 1819 to premises at 18 Harrison Street, off Gray's Inn Lane (Road) in Clerkenwell. Some years later Storr purchased an adjoining house with workrooms and a yard in Francis Street, which links Harrison Street and Sidmouth Street. In 1831 he granted a ten-year lease of these premises to Robert, James and Sebastian Garrard of Panton Street.

Mr. Arthur Grimwade describes what must have been one of the earliest orders received by Storr at his new address, a set of four wine-coolers dated 1817, each 10⅝ in. high, which were made for the 2nd Earl Spencer at Althorp:

The design is clearly derived from details of classical vases, one of which, the lioness' skin chased round the swelling base of the body, is taken from the Warwick Vase. . . . The tooling of the partly cast and partly applied vine trails are of the highest degree of finish, while a pleasing contrast is effected by the use of the Bacchanalian ivy leaves round the inside of the collars.

In a note Mr. Grimwade reveals that:

Paul Storr's use of classical designs was interestingly demonstrated by the presence in his workshop in Harrison Street, Gray's Inn Road (unhappily destroyed in the last war), of numerous engravings by Piranesi of vases and architectural details which I myself inspected about 1938-9. Many of these were signed in the corner 'P. Storr', which one assumes to have been a mark of his approval as a possible source of design in plate production.[9]

Another early order received by Storr at his new address was from Frederick, Duke of York, for a set of silver-gilt altar-plate for use in the recently completed church of St. Pancras; this restrained and dignified set, which originally consisted of sixteen items, was designed to be in keeping with the neo-classical architecture of the new church (designed by William and Henry Inwood), and was presented to the church in 1822. Two cups were subsequently melted down by Storr's successors, Hunt & Roskell, in 1853, and were remade as four smaller cups.

During the Regency period it gradually became apparent that the retail market for silverware was moving steadily westward; Storr accordingly began looking for a retail outlet for his goods in the West End; in 1821 he found what he was searching for when one William Gray, a goldsmith and jeweller who was retiring, approached him with a view to a possible amalgamation with his shop-manager, John Mortimer: the deal was agreed, and in 1822 was formed the firm of 'Storr & Mortimer, Gold and Silver Smiths, 13 New Bond Street'.

In 1824 Storr's younger son, Francis, who had recently left Harrow, became apprenticed to his father in order to assist him in the running of this new venture: in 1829, however, he was released from his apprenticeship as described in the following extract from the unpublished *Reminiscences of Francis Storr*:

It was for me a memorable day when my father came into the room where luncheon was laid in Bond St., and said 'It is open to you now Frank, to go to College, if you will.' I had left Harrow five years previous to this time at the earnest desire of my father, who had entered on a business of some magnitude and at some risk, and wanted such help as he might receive from me – at any rate for a few years – in bearing with him the anxieties necessarily accompanying new and untried experiences. I never regretted the sacrifices which I then made. It cost me something to give up the career which I had pictured to myself and the associations with which I was surrounded at Harrow. But it cemented into an indissoluble friendship the love which my father bore me. . . . For about five years I put energetically my shoulder to the wheel in Bond St., when the announcement which doubtless spoilt my appetite for luncheon, while it filled my heart with joy and thankfullness [sic] set me free to follow the bent of my desires, and brought me, as it were, into a new world.[10]

9. 'Silver at Althorp: IV. The Rococo and Regency Periods', in *The Connoisseur*, December 1963, by A. G. Grimwade, F.S.A.

10. Penzer, p. 44.

'Storr & Mortimer' appears to have prospered until 1826, when over-buying of stock by Mortimer brought it to the verge of bankruptcy: from this it was saved by a successful appeal to John Samuel Hunt, son of Richard Hunt and Catherine Beyer, Storr's sister-in-law, who accepted a partnership in the firm in exchange for the sum of £5,000. This evidently sufficed to put the business once more on a sound financial footing, and it continued to trade at 13 New Bond Street until 1838, when it removed to a better site at 156 New Bond Street, on the corner of Grafton Street, where it was described as 'Storr & Mortimer, Goldsmiths & Jewellers to Her Majesty, 156 New Bond St., & Silversmiths and Goldsmiths to Her Majesty, 26 Harrison St., Gray's Inn road' (the firm had moved from 18 Harrison Street in 1834).

On 2 September 1833 Storr registered a tenth maker's mark; he entered

an eleventh and final mark on 17 December of the following year. In 1833 he made one of his most interesting pieces of silver, the famous 'Horse's Head Ewer', described by Penzer as follows:

The body of this large ewer [height 17¼ in., weight 80 oz. 7½ dwt.] is an inverted pyriform resting in a calyx of overlapping lanceolate leaves. Above, with an undulating frilling at the juncture, rises a deep helmet collar or neck, while the rim and spout are decorated by a gadrooned moulding. Below the calyx, and separated from it by a narrow scotia, is a gadrooned convex projecting member. The plain spreading concave, or trumpet-shaped, foot has a round moulded base. The handle consists of two reversed C-shaped scrolls, the upper, and larger, one of which meets a small acanthus scroll projecting from the back of the rim. On one side of the body is applied a square shield bearing the cipher of Ekaterina II – Catherine the Great – of Russia, surmounted by the Russian crown. The date 1787 occupies a prominent place in the centre of the shield. On the opposite side is a wreath of laurel leaves encircling a medallion which has since been lost or purposely removed. The most striking and unusual feature, however, is the finely modelled demi-horse which projects through an embattled opening in the broadest part of the body midway between the shield and medallion.[11]

The history of this fascinating piece is unfortunately unknown, though it is rumoured to have belonged at one time to the Galitzine family. The

11. p. 228.

style is obviously mid-eighteenth century – the handles especially being typical of the period of high rococo – and it seems probable that Storr was commissioned to make a copy of an existing piece of that period, which had perhaps become badly damaged. The date 1787 on the shield is of particular significance, for it was in that year that Catherine made her celebrated 'Tauric Journey' to southern Russia, a trip made largely by horse-drawn sleigh (Catherine's contained four separate rooms), of which there were no fewer than 178, each drawn by teams of up to thirty horses; at every stopping-place 560 fresh horses were waiting. It thus seems not unreasonable to suppose that the 'Horse's Head Ewer' was made as a copy of one originally presented to Catherine to commemorate this epic equine journey.

In the same year (1833) Storr made a splendidly proportioned pair of silver-gilt standing cups and covers (in the possession of the Worshipful Company of Goldsmiths), which combine imaginative design with super-lative craftsmanship. Each one stands 14 in. high and weighs 40 oz. 15 dwt.: they are described by Carrington and Hughes in their catalogue of the Company's plate, as follows:

The bowl of each cup is cylindrical in form with wide lip, and base in two stages. The drum is chased in flat relief with plain curving flutes alternating with Renaissance panels. The under part of the lip is composed of lobes with matted surrounds, the edge being of scroll and diaper work. The lower portion of the bowl has six masks and six plain bosses. The vase-shaped stem is formed with three masks and brackets leading up to a leafage disk on which the body rests. The foot, domed in two stages with hollow between, has broad convex flutes on a matted ground corresponding with those on the bottom of the bowl. The cover, slightly domed and with the same ornamentation as on the drum of the body, is surmounted by a winged boy.

Arms on covers. 1. The first crest, that of 'A swan's head erased issuant from an annulet and holding in the beak an annulet', was the crest granted in 1894 to Viscount Alverstone, then Sir Richard Everard Webster. 2. The other crest, that of Fortescue, Baron Carlingford (1874–98), is 'an heraldic tiger supporting in the forepaw a plain shield argent'.

Inscription: 'To the Worshipful Company of Goldsmiths the gift of the Rt. Hon. Lord Alverston, G.C.M.G., Lord Chief Justice of England, Prime Warden 1893 and 1899'.[12]

Three years later, in 1837, Storr was employed to repair and partially re-make another most interesting item, a silver-gilt reliquary (now at

12. pp. 126–7.

Lambeth Palace) which had originally been made in Lisbon in about 1670. Penzer describes it as being:

Of ciborium form. The bowl is round and shallow, and rests in a calyx of applied acanthus foliage, the main decoration being of small sheaves of corn arranged laterally on a matted ground – the stalks hidden by foliage. The upper edge is unevenly scalloped and stops short of the rim, which is reeded, and into which fits an ornate and elaborate lid. The sloping lower part is embossed with acanthus leaves, above which is a high dome enriched with massed floral decoration from which project four small cherubs' heads. From the top of this is an open vase-shaped member with scrolls attached. This is surmounted by a somewhat large cross with a circular stepped base. Below the bowl, and separated from it by a flattened reel-like member, is a highly ornate knop enriched with foliage and cherubs' heads as before. The stem is of baluster form, the pear-shaped section ornamented with cherubs' heads above and foliage below. An ovolo collar surmounts a spool-shaped section which is surrounded by four small female torso brackets. The domical foot, embossed with acanthus foliage, has an upper member of flowers and foliage from which again cherubs' heads project. A torus of oak leaves forms the base, below which runs ... [an inscription in Portuguese] the literal translation ... of this is as follows:

'This Relic of the most precious Blood of Christ our Lord was (the property) of a Cardinal and came (in) to the hand(s) of (the) Father Brother Sebastian Soto Maior who gave it to this Royal Monastery of St. Maria of Alcobaça in the year 1690.'[13]

Like that of the 'Horse's Head Ewer', the history of this romantic piece is sadly unknown: it has been at Lambeth for almost a hundred years, but there is no certain record of how it came there. However that may be, by 1836 it had reached such a state of disrepair that Storr was called in as 'doctor'. He re-made the whole of the bowl and the sloping portion of the lid, stamped it with his mark and the date-letter for 1836–7 and scratched on the inside of the lid the following words:

'7 Jany 1837. This rim weighing 4 oz. 8 dwt. made to receive a chased top of unknown assay weighing 5 oz. 9 dwt.'

It can thus be seen that the whole bowl and the lower part of the cover are the work of Storr. Whether there was anything remaining of the original design left for him to copy or whether the design of the bowl and cover is Storr's original conception is, of course, uncertain; the overall effect of the complete article, however, is highly satisfactory.

13. p. 240.

The partnership between Storr, Mortimer and Hunt cannot have been an entirely happy one, as by the end of 1838 an action (ultimately apparently settled out of court) between the partners was due for hearing in Chancery. No doubt partly as a result of this dispute Storr, now aged sixty-seven, decided to retire. But before he did so it was agreed that John Samuel Hunt's son John should join the firm as junior partner: this resulted in a change of name to Mortimer & Hunt and the registration of a new mark (IM above ISH, crowned) at Goldsmiths' Hall in 1839. In 1842 Mortimer retired and the Hunts took on Robert Roskell of Liverpool as their new partner, at the same time changing the firm's name to Hunt & Roskell, and dropping the IM from their mark. John Samuel Hunt died in 1865, resulting in yet another change of mark to IH above RR, crowned, which remained unaltered until 1882. John Hunt, who died in 1879, had a son, John Mortimer Hunt, who entered the business after the death of his father, thus reviving the previous name of the firm. Robert Roskell's son, Allen, also joined the firm in about 1880, which resulted in the complicated mark of RR over AR over IMH, crowned, between 1882 and 1889. By the latter date neither a Roskell nor a Hunt remained in the business, and in that year it was acquired by J. W. Benson Ltd., who registered a new mark AB (Alfred Benson) over HHW (H. H. Wintle), crowned, which lasted until 1895. From 1895 to 1897 the mark consisted of AB above AHB (Arthur Henry Benson), crowned. Between 1842 and 1897 the name of the firm had remained Hunt & Roskell; in the latter year a limited liability company was formed and the mark was changed to H & R Ltd., crowned. In 1901 the crown, which had been incorporated in every mark since 1839, and was the sign of a Royal goldsmith, was finally abandoned.

In 1839 Storr went with his wife to live at Hill House, Tooting, where he died on 18 March 1844, Elizabeth having predeceased him on 4 November the previous year. His will, dated curiously on the day of his wife's death, was proved on 3 April 1844 by 'the oaths of Paul Storr Esquire and the Reverend Francis Storr Clerk [in Holy Orders] the sons the Reverend William Weldon Champneys Clerk [ditto] and the Reverend Robert Chapman Savage Clerk [ditto] the Executors to whom Admo[n] was granted. ...' The meagre value of his estate (£3,000), which he left entirely to his executors, is made especially distressing when it is compared with the immense sums accumulated by his partners in Rundell, Bridge & Rundell. One can but hope that he was able to provide in some measure for the various members of his family before his death.

8

Paul and Elizabeth Storr both lie buried in the cemetery of Tooting parish church, together with their grandson Montague Storr Champneys, who died at the tragically early age of twenty-seven in 1868. The simple inscription on their grave reads as follows:

PAUL STORR OF HILL HOUSE TOOTING

DIED MARCH 18 1844

ELIZABETH SUSANNAH STORR

DIED NOV 4 1843

MONTAGUE STORR CHAMPNEYS THEIR GRANDSON

DIED JULY 28 1868 AGED 27

Having thus far traced the ancestry and career of Paul Storr, the time has come to try to assess his work as artist and craftsman. By the early 1790s, at the start of his career, the attractive but slender neo-classical designs of the Adam brothers had begun to give way to a somewhat heavier and more 'masculine' style. In 1773 Walpole had written that 'from Kent's mahogany we are dwindled to Adam's filigree', and had followed this by referring scathingly in 1785 to 'Mr. Adam's gingerbread and sippets of embroidery'; in 1800 George III remarked that 'I am a little of an architect and think that the old school is not enough attended to – the Adams have introduced too much of neatness and prettiness. . . .'

One of the pioneers of the new Age of Romanticism was Charles Heathcote Tatham (1772–1842), who in 1799 published his *Ancient Ornamental Architecture at Rome and in Italy*, and in 1806 *Designs for Ornamental Plate*; in the preface to the latter work he wrote:

To encourage and facilitate the study of the Antique, in its application to that species of Ornament commonly called Plate, has been my principal motive for this publication. It has been lamented by Persons high in Rank, and eminent for Taste, that modern Plate had much fallen off both in design and execution from that formerly produced in this Country. Indeed, the truth of this remark is obvious, for instead of *Massiveness*, the principal characteristic of good Plate, light and insignificant forms have prevailed, to the utter exclusion of all good Ornament whatever. If we consult the Works of the celebrated Italian Chasers, we find that richness of design was a principle ever regarded by them; in Skilfulness of Execution they indeed stand unrivalled. . . . Good Chasing may be considered as a branch of Sculpture, and as it is well known that excellence in this Art is only to be obtained by indefatigable study and labour, so it is constant application to Modelling alone that will form a good Chaser; when this is not steadily regarded, the Art must inevitably decline, and instead of Objects fitted to excite the admiration of Persons of real taste, nothing is to be expected but Sconces, Girandoles, and Candlesticks, fit only for the dazzle of an Assembly House, or of a County Ball-Room.

Tatham and Storr were exact contemporaries, and lauding as it does the work of the silver-chaser (Storr's father, it will be remembered, was a silver-chaser) *Designs for Ornamental Plate* must have provided Storr with ideas for much of his work.

During the Regency period the Graeco-Roman style, for ceremonial and presentation plate, was almost totally abandoned in favour of the heavier and more elaborate Imperial Roman designs, which were some-times used in conjunction with motifs drawn from ancient Egypt: flutes, fans, palm- and lotus-leaves, caryatids, snakes, vines, shells and sphinxes are characteristic decorations of this period in the production of English silver; the techniques of casting and embossing achieved a higher standard of naturalism than at any time since the Italian Renaissance.

Most domestic plate of the first fifteen years or so of the nineteenth century is comparatively plain, and its decoration consists largely of repeti-tive moulded patterns, horizontal bands of chased scrolling foliage, Greek key patterns, and bay-leaf garlands: the anthemion is perhaps the most common single decorative motif.

Towards the end of the Napoleonic wars there was a revival of interest in the rococo style of the eighteenth century, with all that that entailed: asymmetrical scrolls, rock-work and flowers, generally flat-chased or applied but somewhat shapeless and heavy compared with their graceful counterparts of earlier times, began to re-appear on much of the English silver of that period.

The early years of the nineteenth century are regarded by many as among Storr's greatest: during this period, before he joined Philip Rundell, he made some of the finest domestic plate of the day in a style which evolved from the 'feminine' yet somewhat austere simplicity of Adam, using as ornament flat festoons and other decoration in low relief, which served to enhance and not overwhelm the graceful line of his silver.

The revival of the fashion for applied ornament, however, suited Storr admirably, for he was well able to combine form with function and fantasy with simplicity. Some of his designs of this period are out-standingly pure with only the simplest of applied ornamentation, such as a beaded rim or a reeded handle; an example is a tray of 1806 surrounded by gadrooning, but for the two handles which scroll outwards in a boldly reeded pattern.

Storr's leaning towards fantasy, which he nearly always coupled with a quiet and formal (though at times humorous) dignity, is well illustrated in a kettle dated 1802: its body, circular in shape, is chased around the base with a design of palm-leaves, while the top bears a broad band of fluting between feathered borders: the handle, in complete and surprising contrast, consists of two coiled snakes, whose scales are repeated on the spout which has a dolphin-headed terminal.

As we have already seen, Storr joined Philip Rundell in 1807, and at first continued to make at least some items in his previous style. A soup-tureen and cover of 1808 are typical of this period: the gadrooned rim and foot, the reeded handles of the tureen with foliate caps and lion-mask bases, repeated on the handle on the cover, and the bold band of shell and anthemion chasing, are examples of Storr at his elegant best.

Between about 1810 and 1819 (when he finally severed his connection with Rundell) Storr was, as we have seen, largely occupied with over-seeing the production of vast quantities of presentation and ceremonial silver-plate, the design of which seems sometimes rather pompous and on occasion even vulgar by today's austere standard. But it must be realized that this was by no means entirely Storr's fault: Rundell was able to com-mission artists and employ designers for many of his most important orders, and Storr was called upon to interpret in silver the drawings of men who were primarily architects, sculptors, or painters, whose medium was stone, marble, pottery, porcelain and paint, and to whom the nature of silver and gold was virtually unknown. Among the designers and artists used by Rundell were the sculptor Frances Chantrey (1781–1841), Charles Catton (1756–1819), and the Italian medallist and gem-engraver Benedetto Pistrucci (1784–1855). That Storr was able to transfer their designs into silver with such outstanding success speaks volumes for his technical skill and craftsmanship. The way in which, for example, he has created the Greek caryatids in their diaphanous gowns in the Wellington fruit-bowls in Apsley House, is little short of superb.

The Greek and Roman vase and urn shapes were, however, readily adaptable to the production of silver, and Storr used them on many occasions for ice-buckets, cups, vases and epergnes. Many are based on the 'Warwick Vase' and incorporate bands of interlacing vine-leaves, one of Storr's favourite designs; other decorations used by him on 'Warwick Vases' and urns include applied classical and lion masks, entwined handles, cast figures, chasing in high relief, shells, acanthus leaves, and even lobsters and cauliflowers.

From about 1810 some of Storr's silver began to reveal a return to the rococo influence of the eighteenth century. A low pear-shaped kettle of 1817 is a typical example; the body is richly chased with roses, diapered panels and scrollwork; the spout has a petal tap and dolphin mouth; the scrolling handle is chased with flowers and leafage, and the centre is of simulated basketwork.

The designs of foliage on a set of vase-shaped ice-pails made in 1816-17, and their scroll and shell feet, also echo the theme of a previous era; so too does an ornate suite of three centrepieces weighing together 2,117 oz. made in 1816, which in July 1968 sold at Sotheby's for £20,000. An oval tray of 1816 (five years after Storr had repaired Paul De Lamerie's great epergne of 1738) uses scroll, shell and trelliswork designs of flat chasing in the manner of De Lamerie.

Having established himself in Harrison Street, Storr was once again able to re-assert his artistic abilities. Although he continued at times to produce lavish items enriched overall with embossing and chasing, he also returned to the manufacture of simpler and more elegant pieces with a dignity and formality of their own, exemplified by the neo-classical plate for the church of St. Pancras which he produced in 1821-2. Simple gadrooned rims, and foliate, reeded, shell or plain ring handles on pieces of silver standing on round ball feet are typical of Storr at this time. Sometimes, by way of contrast, scrolls of acanthus foliage can still be seen rising from claw feet, and lion-masks re-appear above the plain handles, while on the occasional piece beautifully modelled dolphins or tritons bear dishes of shells and *rocaille*. Each of a set of four salts, made in 1853, has a pair of shell-shaped bowls supported by stems in the form of branch-coral rising from a spreading seaweed base; the set sold for £2,100 at Christie's in 1972.

A man can only be as great as circumstances allow, and it is interesting to speculate on how great a craftsman and artist Storr would have become had there been no Philip Rundell to provide him with important commissions and supply him, through the drawings of his designers, with ideas for their execution. On the other hand, if Rundell had not been available with ready-made designs to offer Storr, the latter might have developed as an artist even further than he did. All things considered it is a wonder that Storr managed to retain such a high standard of craftsmanship when his enforced method of work with Rundell must sometimes almost have

STORR PEDIGREE

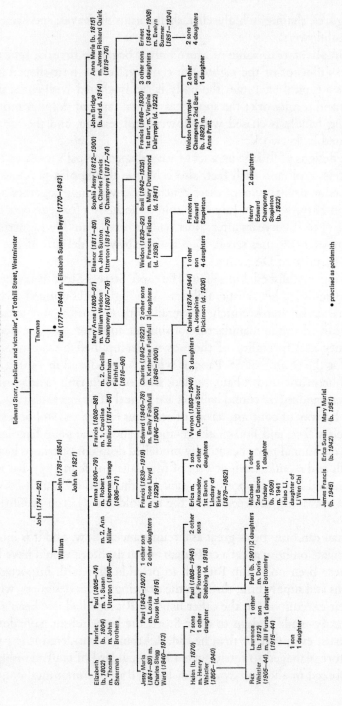

Edward Storr, 'publican and victualler', of Tothill Street, Westminster

● practised as goldsmith

approached mass-production. The design, proportion and elaboration of detail of some of Storr's silver may displease us, but it is well-nigh impossible to criticize any piece made by him for faulty workmanship. If Storr's domestic products are taken into consideration (as of course they must be in any assessment of his true worth), together with his 'important' pieces, we see both the skilled technician *and* the creative artist; as Penzer has rightly said, 'Paul Storr was the last of the great goldsmiths.'

Philip Rundell

No account of the life and work of Paul Storr would be complete without some mention of the man and firm with whom he spent the most productive period of his working life.

Philip Rundell (variously Rundal and Rundall) was born in the village of Widcombe near Bath in 1743, where his father Thomas was a doctor. The leading Bath jeweller of the day, John Wicksteed, had workrooms in Widcombe, and it seems likely that young Rundell spent much of his early life watching Wicksteed at work. In 1760 Rundell was apprenticed, for a premium of £20, to William Rogers who had probably been Wicksteed's foreman before the latter's death in 1754. After the completion of his apprenticeship Rundell travelled to London, where in 1767 or 1769 he was engaged as a shop-assistant by Theed & Pickett, goldsmiths and jewellers at the sign of the 'Golden Salmon' in Ludgate Hill, at a salary of £20 p.a., with a garret-bedroom over the shop.

The history of Theed & Pickett can be traced back to a small shop to the north of St. Paul's Churchyard, where in the early 1700s one Henry Hurt dealt in toys and fishing-tackle (hence the sign of the 'Golden Salmon'). In 1744 Hurt sold the lease of this shop to a certain John Brown, and moved to larger premises (later to be numbered 32) in Ludgate Hill, where he continued to trade (still under the sign of the 'Golden Salmon') in fishing-tackle, to which he added cheap jewellery, trinkets and other knick-knacks. In 1750 Hurt engaged an assistant named William Theed, who assumed the running of the business after the former's death in about 1758, at the same time taking into partnership a relation-by-marriage named William Pickett. The two partners expanded the scope of the business to include a higher grade of jewellery and also silver plate, before Theed retired in 1768; he died four years later.

In the same year (1772) Rundell was taken into partnership by Pickett, who was thus able to enter into semi-retirement and fulfil a long-standing ambition by entering politics, in which he achieved some success. He became an Alderman of Cornhill Ward in 1782, and was elected a Sheriff in 1784, becoming Lord Mayor in 1789; he was a Liveryman of the Worshipful Company of Goldsmiths, but was never elected to the Court of Assistants; nor was he successful in his attempts to enter Parliament, being defeated (as a Whig) in both 1790 and in 1796, the year of his death. In the meantime the scheming Rundell, now left virtually in sole charge of the business, was looking for a way in which he could acquire full control for himself. The unfortunate Pickett suffered from chronic melancholia, originally induced by the death of his daughter Elizabeth in 1781, who was tragically burnt to death while changing to accompany her father to a *soirée*. Rundell, with Machiavellian cunning, took advantage of Pickett's misfortune one evening in 1785 by telling him that business was so bad that there was hardly enough trade to provide a living for both of them; if Pickett cared to sell him his share, Rundell would take on the full responsibility of the business, thus relieving Pickett of all further worry. According to Fox 'He played his part so well that before they parted that evening both of them had signed a Memorandum of Agreement in which they mutually agreed – the one to sell and the other to purchase the share of the business. During the night Mr. Pickett considered what he had done and sincerely repented the bargain he had made, and the next morning wished Mr. Rundell to set the former evening's work aside, but Mr. Rundell with an Oath refused to allow him so to do, and thus placed himself at the head of the House which afterwards was to become the object of envy to all the Trade and the wonder almost of the World.' (The funds for the purchase of Pickett's share of the firm were provided by the wife of Rundell's elder brother, Thomas, an heiress named Miss Ketelby.) Pickett's daughter, Mary, however held a substantial number of shares in the firm, and it was only after her father's death in 1796, when Rundell bought her out in exchange for an annuity of £1,000, that the latter became sole proprietor of the business.

George Fox was a senior employee of Rundell's from July 1806 to March 1833; between 1843 and his death three years later he wrote an (unpublished) account of the history of Rundell, Bridge & Rundell, which is the principal source of our knowledge of Philip Rundell and his firm. The manuscript eventually came into the hands of Fox's great-granddaughter Mrs. Lydia Burgess Brownson, who presented it to the Baker Library of the Graduate School of Business Administration at Harvard University. A photostated copy of this interesting and amusing document is in the library of the Victoria and Albert Museum. A second, though less important source, is the so-called *Memoirs of Philip Rundell* . . . (see Bibliography) published in 1827 (the year of his death) in which the anonymous author gives a brief account of Rundell's life and the history of the firm, interspersed with various anecdotes: it also contains a complete copy of Rundell's will.

Fox gives the following thumb-nail sketch of Philip Rundell:

He was naturally what the world calls a Gay Fellow, and he might often be seen at his shop door early of a morning with his jockey cap, scarlet coat, buckskin smalls, booted and spurred waiting the arrival of his groom with the horses that he might go and follow the chase to settle himself down a little after a night spent over the Bottle or the Card Table.

If this *vignette* be true it was doubtless fortunate that in 1777 the industrious John Bridge joined the firm; Bridge was born on 21 January 1755 at Piddletrenthide in Dorset, and in 1769 became apprenticed for a premium of forty guineas to Rundell's old master, William Rogers, who probably gave him an introduction to Pickett & Rundell on the expiration of his articles. Bridge was fortunate in having a cousin two years his junior, also named John, who was a prosperous and successful farmer at Wynford Eagle, near Bridport, from whom in 1788 he was able to borrow enough money to buy himself a partnership in the firm. In addition John Bridge Junr., having in 1789 met 'Farmer' George III through their mutual interest in agriculture, was able successfully to solicit the King on behalf of his cousin's firm. John Bridge Senr. was commanded to Buckingham House, where he created such a favourable impression that in March 1797 George III caused Messrs. Rundell & Bridge (as the firm had become in 1788) to be appointed by warrant 'Jewellers, Gold & Silversmiths to the Crown': this is the usually accepted version of how Rundell's acquired their Royal Appointment; a possible alternative, however, is that the appointment which was subsequently re-confirmed on the accession of the Prince of Wales as George IV in 1820, came with a business taken over by Rundell. The firm was also granted a similar warrant from the Prince of Wales, the Duke of York and other members of the Royal family.

Such a change in their social status made necessary the acquisition by Rundell & Bridge of an entirely different and better class of stock which would appeal to their new aristocratic customers. Since they were as yet only retailers and not manufacturers, this new stock was obtained mainly from the better wholesalers and individual working goldsmiths. In addition Rundell & Bridge were fortunate in being able to obtain (doubtless through their Royal connections) quantities of jewellery and silver and gold-plate from those refugees of the French Revolution who sought sanctuary in England: they were thus soon able to offer to their patrons examples of the rococo style of Meissonier and François-Thomas Germain, items from the workshop of Jacques Roettiers (b. 1707, retired 1772) pioneer of the neo-classical style in France, and sets of grandiose dinner-services by Henri Auguste (1759–1816).

By the early 1800s important commissions for presentation plate (and for expensive items of jewellery) were daily pouring in to the offices of Rundell & Bridge in Ludgate Hill. Edward Waller Rundell, son of Philip's brother Thomas, joined the firm, bringing with him further capital which reinforced the company's already satisfactory financial position; one of his sisters, Maria, had married one Thomas Bigge, and in 1807 he too joined Rundells: in 1804 John Bridge's nephew, John Gawler Bridge, commenced work as his uncle's (unpaid) assistant, becoming a partner in 1817.

In 1805 the name of the company was changed to Rundell, Bridge & Rundell and two years later Rundell managed to persuade Paul Storr to join him in Dean Street, taking him into partnership in 1811. Agencies were set up in Paris, Vienna, St. Petersburg (Leningrad), Constantinople (Istanbul), Smyrna, Baghdad, Calcutta, Bombay and South America, and from Fox we learn that the company despatched annual consignments of jewels (probably mostly diamonds) to the 'Celestial Empire' (China).

We have now traced the history of Rundell, Bridge & Rundell from its inception to the point where it occupied a pre-eminent position in the trade. The time has come to hear what Fox, who was with them daily from 1806 until Rundell died in 1827 and Bridge in 1834, and who was moreover clearly a shrewd judge of character, has to say about the company's two senior partners:

No two men could have been more opposite in temper and disposition than were Mr. Rundell and Mr. Bridge – indeed so opposite were they that many designated them by the names of Oil and Vinegar. Mr. Rundell was naturally of a violent disposition, very sly and cunning, and suspicious in the extreme. Avarice, covetousness and meanness were so deeply rooted in him that it affected every feature of his face and entered into every action of his life! Not but that he would often perform deeds which would have entitled any other man to the character of a generous person, but when performed by him they seemed to lose all their value in the manner they were performed, seeing that if he bene-fitted any individual it was with the intent of wounding the feelings of some others or not infrequently with the hope of exalting the person benefitted on a pedestal from which he might in some unexpected moment hurl him down again lower than he was before he raised him up. In his shop he was ever the petty despotic King, not only over his servants, but also over his partners, and all the trades-people he employed, and swearing, scolding and noise were the order of the day, and of every day. . . . Mr. Bridge was quite a different man. He was naturally of a timid quiet disposition, and had philosophically learnt to keep down any Violent temper he might have had, and he would hear any insults or brook any imposition rather than he would contend against his more violent Partner, and this he did not more from the love of peace and quietness than from a strong desire to carry on the business in such a manner as eventually to produce for him the large Fortune which he in the process of time obtained. He could perform well on his own stage or amongst his Customers out of doors, for although he possessed as much Pride as any Person need have yet to any one and to every one by whom he expected to gain any thing he was apparently the most humble and obedient Person that could well be imagined, his back was exceedingly flexible and no man in London could bow lower or oftener than could Mr. Bridge. In fact he was a complete Courtier and was highly respected both in the Palaces of Princes, and the Halls of Servants, for his great humility in the former, and his great condescension in the latter. He well knew it was of great importance to him to stand well with all the Servants in a great House and he had learnt (as he often confessed it) that the nearest way to My Lady's Boudoir was down the Area Steps through the Servants Hall and from thence to the Housekeepers Room and so up stairs to My Lady!

The anonymous author of the *Memoirs* confirms Fox's opinion: Philip Rundell was dirty in both his personal habits and in his dress, and was miserly both to himself and his firm. He was mean and petty minded, and pretended to be deaf in order to overhear other people's conversations; he used to pry into his workmen's ledgers and lockers during the night in order to be able to upbraid them over some insignificant lapse the following morning.

On one occasion Rundell visited Buckingham House, where his

ignorance of court etiquette and slovenly behaviour soon made it clear that all such visits must in future be left to Bridge, who was much better fitted than his uncouth partner to obtain valuable commissions from royalty and the nobility, 'beating the bush to drive the game to Ludgate Hill', as Fox described it.

Bridge, in order to circumvent his partner's prying eyes, was forced into inventing a private shorthand code for his own private papers, since even these were not sacrosanct to the 'Old Gentleman', as his partner was known. Yet Bridge was the one person with whom Rundell could ill afford to quarrel, both because of the capital which he had brought into the firm, and because of his cousin's friendship with George III and his own personal success at Court.

Rundell lived in Bridge Street, Blackfriars, in order to save himself the expense of the upkeep of a coach in which to travel to Ludgate Hill, and frequently stayed for lengthy periods with one or other of his innumerable relations. He never married, but kept a mistress, a Mrs. Wartridge by whom he had two sons, on a pittance, and it was in her house that he died on 13 February 1827. In his will he left the major part of his estate, over £900,000, to his great-nephew Joseph Neeld (who in the following year, possibly as a result of his inheritance, commissioned from Bridge a sumptuous silver-gilt soup-tureen and stand which in 1973 was exhibited at the Victoria and Albert Museum from the Campbell Museum collection at Camden, New Jersey); Mrs. Wartridge was only mentioned, together with his servants, in the Codicil.

Small wonder is it, then, that Paul Storr eventually decided to seek fresh pastures, finally severing his connection with the firm in 1819. Three years later Philip Rundell retired, and thereafter the company's decline commenced. A new partnership was formed, breaking up after seven years following some disastrous speculations in South American mining stock, and the retirement of Edmund Rundell. A new company named Rundell, Bridge & Co. was formed by John Bridge and his nephew Thomas Bigge, but came to an end in 1834 on the death of Bridge. On 13 July 1842 began a ten-day sale of the company's stock at Christie's rooms in King Street, St. James's; according to the catalogue there were no fewer than 1,671 lots (many of which were 'bought-in'), the remainder fetching a total of some £20,000. In a final bid to keep the firm going George Fox and two of his fellow workmen were offered the opportunity of acquiring the property, but the price was too high, and they knew full well that trade was moving west. This, then, was the sad end of the firm with which

Paul Storr spent the twelve most productive years of his working life.[14]

14. According to F. J. Britten in *Old Clocks and Watches and their Makers* the business of Rundell, Bridge & Co. was subsequently purchased by Francis Lambert (d. 1841), and transferred to 11 and 12 Coventry Street. Sir Ambrose Heal in his *London Goldsmiths*, and a number of more recent authors, repeat Britten's statement. However, in view of the fact that, as Penzer points out, Lambert's successors, Harman & Lambert of 177 New Bond Street, have lost their complete archives, it is impossible to know whether or not Britten's statement is correct.

Augustine Courtauld

(1685/6-1751)

and his Family

THE Huguenot family of Courtauld (derived from the French derogatory *courtaud*, the name is the English equivalent of Short) are able to trace their pedigree back to one Christophe Courtauld born in about 1516 in the town of St. Pierre, on the Ile d'Oleron in the province of Saintonge in western France. During the sixteenth and seventeenth centuries they multiplied exceedingly, and as mariners and merchants built up a considerable family fortune. In common with other French Protestants the family suffered grievously after the Revocation of the Edict of Nantes in 1685, and in late 1686 or early 1687 the then representative of the family, Augustin, emigrated with many of his unfortunate compatriots to England.

Augustin Courtauld was born on 11 May 1655, the second son of Pierre and his wife Judith Gribaud, and the great-great-grandson of Christophe. He was baptized on 27 May in the Protestant church at Marennes on the mainland of France, as is shown by the following extract from the Marennes Protestant Registers preserved in the *Archives départmentales de la Rochelle*:

Du Jeudy 27 Mai 1655 par Monsieur Bastid. Augustin Gourtaux. – Ogustin fils de Pierre Gourtaux et de Judith Guibaud est né le onzième du présent mois présenté au bapteme par Jean Chaillollieau et Jeanne de la Jaille.

On 19 August 1677 Augustin married Julie, daughter of Daniel Giraud of Marennes and his wife Jeanne, *née* Sauteron, who bore him four children, only one of whom, named Augustin after his father, survived infancy. The exact date of the boy's birth is uncertain, but would appear to have been between late 1685 and early 1686. His mother died shortly after his birth.

On 28 September 1685 Augustin, in order to escape the worst excesses meted out to those of his faith under the notorious *dragonnades*, signed at St. Pierre, in company with three hundred and fifty of his fellow Protestants, a document abjuring their beliefs.[1] Late in 1686 or early in the following year Augustin, by now a widower, sailed from France to start a new life in England.

The first mention of Augustin in this country is to be found in the marriage register of the French church in Glasshouse Street (where, it will be recalled, the great Paul De Lamerie was himself married twenty-eight years later):

Le dimanche 10ᵉ Mars 1688/9 à l'assemblé du Matin le mariage de Augustin Courtaux et Esther Poitier de la province de Sante Onge et de la Rochelle.

Esther was the daughter of Abel and his wife Elizabeth (Fredonnet) and was born on 26 September 1656 in La Rochelle. On 10 January 1689/90 she bore her husband a son Peter, who was baptized in the church in Glasshouse Street eight days later, when his father's occupation was given as that of 'merchant'.

As a prelude to being joined in this country in 1697 by the son of his first marriage, Augustin Junr. now aged about eleven or twelve (who had been left behind in St. Pierre d'Oleron in the care of his grandfather Pierre when his father fled to England), Augustin took out papers of denization as an English citizen in 1696.

In common with a number of other Huguenot refugees, and because it was one of the few socially acceptable trades for a gentleman to engage in, Augustin chose for his son the career of a goldsmith. In the registers at Goldsmiths' Hall may be seen the following entry:

1701 August ye 9th: Memorand' that I Augustin Courtauld son of Augustine Courtauld of the p'ish of St. Annes Westm' in the County of Midd'x Wine Cooper doe put myself Appr' to Simon Pontaine Citizen and Goldsmith of London for the term of seven years from this day.

Made a Denizen [referring to the father] as appeared by a Certificate from Nich. Hayward Not. Publ. dat 20th July 96.

Simon Pontaine (anglicized as Pantin) was a noted Huguenot goldsmith

1. In the *Archives de la Mairie de Saint-Pierre, Registre Paroissial*, 1678–92.

who had himself been apprenticed to another fine Huguenot crafts-man, Pierre Harache, who worked in Suffolk Street from 1675 until his death in 1700. Pantin was first established in 1699 at the sign of the 'Peacock' (French *paon*, a punning allusion to his name) in St. Martin's Lane. He became Free and entered his mark at Goldsmiths' Hall in 1701; eleven years later he was admitted to the Livery of the Company. In 1717 he moved his home and workrooms to Castle Street, Leicester Fields, where still under the sign of the 'Peacock', he died in 1728. He was suc-ceeded by his son and apprentice, Simon Junr. who died in 1733, who was in turn followed by his widow Mary, at Green Street, Leicester Fields, until 1735. Lewis Pantin, probably a brother, carried on the business until 1744. His son, Lewis Junr. became a member of the Livery of the Gold-smiths' Company in 1776, and died between 1802 and 1811. As we shall see, Judith, daughter of Esaie Pantin, born in 1690, married in 1709 Peter Courtauld.

From the following extract taken from the registers at Goldsmiths' Hall, it seems safe to assume that Augustine (as his name is now usually spelt) was an industrious pupil, and that he and his family retained friendly relations with his master, Simon Pantin:

1705 March 28th: Memorandum that I Peter Courtauld son of Augustin Courtauld of St. Annes Westm' in the County of Midd'x Vintner doe put my selfe Apprentice to Simon Pantin Citizen and Goldsmith of London for the terme of seven yeares from this day. Mem'd' Letters of Denizason of the sd. Augustin Courtauld under the hand and seale of Nich. Hayward Notary publ' dated 20th July 1696.

A little over a year after seeing his younger son safely launched on his career, Augustin died, aged fifty-one, on 26 September 1706. In his will, dated 5 September of the year of his death, he is described as 'Mr. Augus-tine Courtaud born in St. Peter in the Ile d'Oleron in France, residing in the parish of St. Anne in Soho in the Liberty of Westminster.' He named as his executors his wife Esther, who died in 1732 aged seventy-five and was buried in St. Anne's Church, Soho, and his brother Pierre, a lawyer by profession, who had arrived in England at some unknown date.

Most unusually, while still not qualified and at the early age of twenty, Augustin's younger son Peter married, on 5 February 1709, at the French church known as 'Le Tabernacle', Judith, daughter of Esaie Pantin, 'Gold-smith of St. James's', and doubtless a relation of his master, Simon. Peter became Free of the Goldsmiths' Company in 1712, but did not register his marks – CO on 15 June and PC on 21 July both surmounted by a crown, one for each standard of silver – until 1721, when he was working in Litchfield Street, Soho. One can only assume that between obtaining his Freedom and entering his marks he worked as a 'journeyman', quite possibly for his elder brother Augustine. In 1723 he accepted an apprentice, Thomas Bonnett of Stepney, whose father Anthony (most suitably a 'hatter' by trade) paid him a premium of £17. No known plate bearing his mark is extant and he died in 1729, being buried at St. Martin's-in-the-Fields on 8 March.

Augustine Courtauld, the most important goldsmith member of the family, became Free of the Worshipful Company of Goldsmiths by Service on 20 October 1708, in the same year taking workrooms in Church Street (or Court), St. Martin's Lane, from which address he entered his first mark, the first two letters of his surname surmounted by a *fleur-de-lis* (a device much favoured by Huguenots) within a three-lobed punch.

In the following year (1709) Augustine married Anne Bardin, by whom he had eight children: Anne, born in about 1710, married on 21 December 1738 John Jacob, a goldsmith of Heming's Row, St. Martin's-in-the-Fields; Esther, born in 1711, married on 21 May 1729 Stephen Goujou; Judith, born on 1 July 1714, died unmarried; Julia, born on 12 November 1712; Catherine, born on 13 June 1715; Peter, born on 2 August 1716; Augustine, born in 1718 who on 19 March 1749 married his cousin Jane Bardin at St. Luke's Church, Chelsea; and Samuel, born on 10 September 1720, who was baptized three days later at the same church as his brothers and sisters had been, namely the French church in Leicester Fields.

As with Paul De Lamerie, the working life of Augustine Courtauld can be divided into halves: during the first, from 1708 to 1729 he worked in Church Street, St. Martin's Lane, using the higher 'Britannia' standard of silver. In the latter year he moved to what were presumably larger and better premises in nearby Chandos Street, where he was to stay for the remaining twenty-two years of his life, and from where in 1729 he entered his third mark, A C surmounted by a *fleur-de-lis*. After that date he em-

ployed primarily sterling silver, although on occasion he reverted to the use of the higher 'Britannia' standard. In Chandos Street, Augustine accepted at least three apprentices, all, be it noted, of Huguenot extraction; Isaac, the son of Hopken Ribouleau, a 'distiller' of Hammersmith, in 1716 at a premium of £10; Louis Ouvry of Jersey in 1730, and Francis David, son of Charles Quenouault of St. James's, Westminster, for £25 in 1739. In this year he also entered a fourth and final mark, a *fleur-de-lis* surmounted by A C in script.

Augustine and Anne Courtauld both died within a few weeks of each other, the former, his death perhaps hastened by that of his wife, in April, the latter in March, 1751 – the same year, it will be remembered, as that in which Paul De Lamerie died. Augustine was buried on 14 April in St. Luke's Church, Chelsea. His will, dated 13 March 1750, was proved by his executors, his son Samuel and his son-in-law Stephen Goujou, on the day preceding his funeral. Each of his five surviving children received the sum of £400 and an equal share in the residue of his estate; to Samuel were left his goldsmith's patterns and tools of the trade which, as we have seen, were among a craftsman's most prized possessions. Among other beneficiaries were his various nephews and neices and his cousins Augustine and Peter Courtauld.

Two portraits of Augustine Courtauld are known, in one of which he is shown resting his left hand gently on the shoulder of a little girl aged perhaps five or six, probably either Esther or Mary. He has a fine aristocratic face, with dark, deep-set eyes below heavy brows, a long nose, firm chin and generous mouth: he gives the impression of being a man able to work with both mind and hands; both portraits are by unknown artists. A painting of his wife, Anne Bardin, also by an unknown hand, shows her with her hair drawn back from her oval face, with large dark eyes and a somewhat prominent aquiline nose.

Augustine was the finest and most prolific of the Courtauld family of goldsmiths. Although he was in no sense an innovator or experimenter, he produced work of a consistently high standard of design and execution, basing much of his early plate on the style of the man with whom he had learnt his craft, Simon Pantin. Most of his work is in the English 'Queen Anne' taste rather than in the French Louis XIV style favoured by the majority of his fellow Huguenots. From the many pieces which are extant, the following are a few examples: a plain pear-shaped tea-kettle with stand and burner, with a domed and moulded cover and moulded shoulder and spout, weighing 89 oz. 12 dwt. and dated 1719; this is remarkably similar to one made by Pantin six years previously. Another tea-kettle, of compressed spherical form made by Augustine in 1732 bears the following inscription: 'Presented to Mr. Robert Brooke by the Turkey Comp^y for his sarvice in saveing their ship the *Euphrates* – a ground on the Woolpack Sand – Feby 1732' – an unusual and enterprising form of presentation. Also made in 1719 is a plain tankard with a domed and moulded cover standing on a low moulded foot, weighing 51 oz. 9 dwt., contemporarily engraved with the arms of Atherton. A chocolate-pot of 1721, 9½ in. high, has a tapering body and swan's-neck spout. A large tray measuring 20½ in. by 16 in., finely engraved in the centre with a coat-of-arms within a cartouche was made in the same year. During this early period of his working life Augustine also produced a number of candlesticks and sugar-casters standing on the octagonal base then much in vogue.

As pointed out by both Mr. Arthur Grimwade and Mr. John Hayward, the 'toy' silver formerly attributed to Augustine Courtauld was actually made by David Clayton, whose mark was misread by Jackson. Occasionally Augustine departed from the basic simplicity of his early pieces, as when he produced in 1723 a most attractive pear-shaped chocolate-pot standing on a spreading moulded base.

Among the more important items made by Augustine are a number of two-handled cups and covers, many made as presentation gifts: one such, made in 1723, bears the arms of Francis, 2nd Earl of Godolphin (1678–1766), but is otherwise quite plain. A somewhat similar cup made in the same year is in the collection of the Inner Temple. Three other cups of 1724 and 1725 are remarkably similar in design, and although well executed demonstrate a certain lack of originality; the earliest, in silver-gilt, weighs 99 oz. 15 dwt. and stands 13 in. high. The plain top half, which is superbly engraved with on one side an elaborate coat-of-arms within a most unusual cartouche, and on the other with a crest, is divided from the lower half by a moulded band; two versions of applied lanceolate straps rise from the base (which rests on a moulded foot) and are repeated on the cover. The straps on all three cups are widely spaced and the handles lack the boldly scrolling outline seen on much Huguenot silver. Other cups made by Augustine include one of 1729 in the collection of Trinity House.

A large salver made by Augustine in 1732, 19⅝ in. in diameter and weighing over 100 oz., is engraved in the centre with a coat-of-arms within an elaborate contemporary cartouche, consisting of two vases of flowers, two human figures, two demi-figures and a bust; inside the moulded edge is a beautifully chased and engraved border containing six busts and six vases of flowers, placed alternately. From the quality of the engraving, it has been suggested that this border might be the work of Hogarth, who at the time was coming to the end of his career as a silver-engraver.

Although Augustine did not contribute to the immense service of plate (totalling in all 365 pieces) made for the Empress Catherine I of Russia, and which was largely supplied by Huguenot goldsmiths working in London, he is represented in the Kremlin by a large tea-table (1742), the top of which is engraved with elaborate baroque borders, and in the Hermitage by a somewhat ordinary and uninspired standish, made in 1730.

In 1725 Augustine, working in collaboration with his Huguenot *confrère* David Willaume, made a fine toilet service equal in style and execution to that made the previous year for George Treby by Paul De Lamerie. The design of the panels which decorate the pomade pots are the same in both services; it thus appears probable that De Lamerie lent his moulds to Courtauld and Willaume.

Mr. Arthur Grimwade has pointed out to me a set of three fine salvers of 1727, one 12½ in. and two 12 in. in diameter, owned by Earl Spencer at Althorp. 'These are distinguished by exceptionally fine flat-chased borders of masks, shells and strapwork and are engraved with the arms of Poyntz incorporating many quarterings. They were undoubtedly made for Stephen Poyntz, who . . . served in a succession of diplomatic posts in Europe at this period and whose daughter was the 1st Countess Spencer . . . the salvers however did not reach Althorp until 1840 when they . . . were inherited by Elizabeth, the first wife of the 4th Earl, from the Poyntz home at Cowdray. In the valuation made at the time they were valued at seven shillings per oz. – or £25. 11s. od. for the large one of 73 oz. and £26. 6s. 9d. for the pair weighing 75 oz. 5 dwt.'[2]

Undoubtedly the most important surviving piece of silver bearing Augustine's mark is the State Salt of the Corporation of the City of London at the Mansion House. This superb example of the goldsmith's craft was made in 1730 as a private commission, but was presented in 1741 to the Sword Bearer of the Corporation and 'to his successors for the use of their table at the Lord Mayor's'; this impressive item was the last of the great ceremonial central standing salts to be made in England, and is thus of historic importance and interest. It is also the only known piece bearing Augustine's mark to show any real originality of design. The bowl of the salt rests on four dolphin feet, in the manner of Nicholas Sprimont, presumably an allusion to sea-salt.[3] The bowl is ornamented with applied lambrequins cast and chased with strapwork and shells – a typical Huguenot form of embellishment. Above the bowl rise four curious scrolls with human-head terminals, which on seventeenth-century salts were intended to support a napkin to keep the salt clean at the start of a meal, and at the end to hold a dessert-dish, but which by the mid-eighteenth century were totally obsolete.

Towards the end of Augustine's career the new fashion of the rococo was sweeping England, and was quickly developed by the majority of Huguenot craftsmen working here. Almost alone among his countrymen Augustine to the last kept aloof from this new style, preferring to remain faithful to the kind of unadorned silver on which his success had been founded. Few pieces are of plate bearing his mark are known in the rococo style; an example is a fine oval cake-basket measuring 14 in. by 12 in. standing on four paw feet. The border is decorated with a rococo band of scrolls, flowers, fruit and leaves. The everted sides are finely pierced and the base is nicely engraved with a coat-of-arms within the usual surround. The swing handle is joined to the basket by dolphin-head terminals resting on stylized shells. Although bearing Augustine's mark and the date-letter for 1745 (the year before he retired) this piece may well have been fashioned in the workshop of his son, Samuel.

2. 'Silver at Althorp: III. The Huguenot Period', in *The Connoisseur*, June 1963, p. 94, by A. G. Grimwade, F.S.A.

3. Cf. Paul Crespin's centrepiece at Windsor Castle, p. 194. This magnificent example of the rococo style was once incorrectly attributed to Augustine Courtauld, who could never have produced anything so uninhibited and flamboyant.

Although we do not know whether Augustine's two eldest sons, Peter and Augustine, ever worked in their father's business, the third son Samuel became apprenticed to his father in Chandos Street in 1734. After completing his apprenticeship in 1741 he continued to work with his father as a journeyman until 1746, in which year, as no pieces are known bearing his mark later than 1745, Augustine appears to have retired. In 1746, therefore, Samuel began to work on his own account from Chandos Street, at the same time entering two marks at Goldsmiths' Hall: the first and larger mark consists of his initials SC separated by a pellet and

surmounted by a sun, within a three-lobed punch; the second and smaller mark, which was designed for use on minor domestic pieces, consists of his initials divided by a pellet in a plain rectangular punch. He was received as a Freeman in 1747. His first trade-card depicts a rising sun behind a rocky shore-line, with beneath the inscription 'Samuel Courtauld / Goldsmith / & Jeweller / At the Rising Sun / in Shandois Street / St. Martin's-Lane / London'.

On 31 August 1749 Samuel married Louisa Perina Ogier at St. Luke's Church, Old Street. His wife was the youngest of the nine children of Pierre Ogier and Catherine (*née* Rabaud) of Sigournay in Poitou; soon after 1730 the family emigrated from France to England; Pierre died in 1740 leaving in his will, in which he is described as a 'silkweaver', each of his children £250 and a ninth share in the residue of his estate. To Samuel and Louisa Perina were born eight children, of whom only four survived infancy: Augustine, born on 26 August and died September 1750; Samuel, born in London on 20 October 1752, married Sarah Norris Wharton in Philadelphia, United States, and died near Wilmington, Delaware, in 1821; Louis, born on 5 August 1758; George, born in London on 19 September 1761; he married Ruth Minton of Co. Cork on 10 July 1789 in New York State, and died on 13 August 1823 at Pittsburg; Louisa, born on 9 March 1754, died in 1756; Esther, born on 16 February 1757; Catherine, born on 7 April 1760, married on 27 January 1783 William Taylor; she died on 17 June 1826; and Sophia (1763–1850).

Following the death of his mother and father, in March and April respectively 1751 (the same year, incidentally, in which Paul De Lamerie died) and the resulting legacy, Samuel removed to what we can assume were better workrooms and a larger house at 21 Cornhill, in which to accommodate his growing family. Here he issued a second and much grander trade-card surmounted by a crown in which he stated within an elaborate cartouche that 'Samuel Courtauld / Goldsmith & Jeweller / at the Crown in Cornhill / facing the Royal Exchange / London. / Makes & Sells all sorts of Plate, Jewels, / Watches & all other Curious Work in Gold & Silver / at the most Reasonable Rates. / N.B. Likewise Buys & Sells all sorts of / Second-hand Plate, Watches, Jewels, &c.' Whether Samuel ever dealt in 'running-cashes', i.e. acted as a banker, which as we have seen in the Introduction a number of eighteenth-century manufacturing and retailing goldsmiths were accustomed to do, is unknown; but had he wished to do so he would have been ideally situated, for then as now Cornhill was in the financial heart of the City of London.

In 1753 Samuel took as an apprentice, Stephen Dupont, son of Louis Dupont, late of St. Anne's, Westminster, but then a merchant in San Domingo, at a premium of thirty-five guineas. In 1763 he was elected to the Livery of the Worshipful Company of Goldsmiths, dying in February 1765 at the sadly early age of forty-five; in his will, which he made only a few days before his death and which was proved on 24 February, the same day as his funeral, Samuel left all his worldly goods to his widow, Louisa.

Whether or not Samuel was the maker of the rococo cake-basket of 1744 which bears his father's mark, he soon became an enthusiastic exponent of the new style. As early as 1747 he produced a pair of small oval sauce-boats, each with an outsize dolphin handle, standing on three scrolling rococo feet. Another large sauce-boat, weighing 34½ oz. which he made three years later, shows distinct signs of De Lamerie in the cherubs' head terminals to the scrolling feet. Also in the manner of De Lamerie is a waiter of 1752, with a pierced border of grapes and vine-leaves and scrolls, enclosing beautifully executed cherubs' heads. A tea-caddy of the same year is covered with swirling rococo scrolls on the bulging body, on the domed lid, and on the gently spreading foot. A finely pierced and chased epergne of 1751, weighing 220 oz. 18 dwt., its central basket surrounded by eight smaller baskets on two different levels, standing on four scrolling legs, is also a fine example of work in the rococo taste. Yet Samuel also produced many basically simple pieces; a pear-shaped coffee-pot of 1757, for example, is unadorned apart from spiral gadrooning and fluting around the cover, base and neck. A splendid pear-shaped, two-handled tea-urn of 1760, again in the rococo manner, was sold at Christie's in February 1974.

Samuel's most celebrated extant pieces of work are three surviving items from what was presumably a complete toilet-service, probably made for a member of the Russian Court. These fine pieces include a silver-gilt jewel case, 11 in. by 7¾ in. by 5½ in., weighing 120 oz. Mr. S. L. Courtauld records that the box was purchased from the State Antiquary Shop, Torqsin in Leningrad in 1933 by a Mr. Svend E. Carlsen who wrote that 'during the years 1933–5 the Russian State bought gold and silver from the population, paying with Torqsin roubles, giving the possessor the right to buy food, cloth, etc., in shops otherwise reserved for foreigners with foreign currency. The gold and silver pieces were delivered to the State Antiquary Shop, where the sorting-out took place; by chance I was present one day the shop received some sacks of silver, saw the box, and bought it on the spot.'

This box, which stands on four scrolling legs, is magnificently embossed on the sides with floral swags, foliage, husks and trophies. On the cover, within a scrolling frame, is a fine representation of the 'Toilet of Venus'. The matching circular toilet-boxes, 3½ in. in diameter, stand on three scrolling feet, the bodies encircled with embossed floral swags. The handle on the lid of each is formed of a reclining cupid. According to Mr. Courtauld these two boxes 'were acquired between the wars by an English diplomat in Warsaw, and were said to have come from Riga'. These three fine pieces, which are dated 1763, have a distinctly Continental flavour in the style of Louis XV.

Had Samuel not died at such a tragically early age he would almost certainly, from examples of his work extant, have gone on to emulate his father Augustine. In design and quality of craftsmanship he was fully his father's equal, and being clearly of a more adventurous nature, far surpassed him in originality of both design and form.

After the death of her husband, Louisa lost no time in taking over the management of the family business, entering her mark LC within the customary diamond-shaped widow's shield in 1766. On her invoices she described herself as 'Lᵃ· Pᵃ· Courtauld / Jeweller, Goldsmith, &c. – / At the Crown, in Cornhill, opposite the Royal Exchange. No. 21.'

An admirable portrait of Louisa by Zoffany shows her wearing a green dress over which is a yellow silk cape edged with fur, leaning her hands, with long delicate fingers, on a large book lying on a table. Around her throat she wears a double string 'choker' necklace of pearls; her greying hair is drawn back from her face, and is decorated above the forehead with a bow from which hangs a large pearl surrounded by a circle of smaller pearls; she wears in her ears rings of the same pattern. Her dark eyes regard the viewer with a steady gaze – the view of a kindly but resolute woman.

As with Hester Bateman, it would be naïve and absurd to imagine that Louisa was involved in the actual fashioning of the wrought plate which bears her mark; rather was she concerned with running the business and, probably, with dealing direct with the influential patrons who came to place with her commissions for silver-plate.

Two nice rococo cups and covers bearing the mark of Louisa, one 14½ in. high, the other 16 in. high, were made respectively in 1765 and 1766. The cover and foot of the former are embossed with vines, the body being further embossed with vines and scrolls; around the foot and rim is a border of heavy gadrooning; the handles are generously double-scrolled: above the high domed cover is a fruit finial. The cover, body and foot of the second cup are embossed with foliated scrolls and beading: again there are double-scrolled handles, now embellished with scrolls, beading and foliage, and again a high domed cover, this time with a twisting finial.

Possibly finding that the combination of managing a busy and time-consuming business and a growing and noisy family was more than she could reasonably cope with, Louisa took on in 1768 a partner, George Cowles. In the same year he became her nephew-by-marriage, by marrying Judith Jacob, the daughter of her late husband's sister, Anne.

During the years of her partnership with George Cowles, Louisa's workship produced silver in both the rococo and neo-classical taste. An example of the former bearing their joint mark, LC surmounting GC within a square, is a pierced cake-basket with swing-handle of 1771; that of the latter a two-handled cup and cover made a year earlier with unusual inset squares containing classical subjects, good bright-cut engraving and drop-ring handles – a most original conception.

In 1777 Cowles dissolved the partnership by moving to another address in Cornhill where, and in nearby Winchester Street, he carried on business by himself until his death in 1811.

To replace Cowles, Louisa took into partnership her son Samuel, then aged twenty-five. Two portraits of Samuel Junr. exist, both by unknown artists: in one he appears in uniform wearing a tricorn hat; in both he is portrayed as having a sensitive, aesthetic face, with a long thin and rather pointed nose. Whether Samuel had been apprenticed or had received any other training is unknown; however that may be, he and his mother registered their joint-mark, LC over SC, in 1777.

The best-known piece of plate bearing the mark of Louisa and her son Samuel is the 17 in. high silver-gilt FitzGibbon Cup made in 1778 for John FitzGibbon (1748–1802), who as Baron FitzGibbon became Lord Chancellor of Ireland from 1789 until his death; he was created Viscount FitzGibbon in 1793 and Earl of Clare in 1795. The ovoid body of this cup is embossed with festoons of foliage depending in swags from ribbon-bows, with paterae between. Below a guilloche band, fluting rises from the foot, which is itself decorated with complementary festoons. The high-domed cover is decorated above with fluting and below with embossed acanthus leaves. The finial is in the form of a fruit.

The partnership between mother and son lasted for only three years, for in 1780 No. 21 Cornhill was sold, lock, stock and barrel, to John Henderson, a fine jeweller/goldsmith who in 1809 was elected to the Prime Wardenship of the Worshipful Company of Goldsmiths; he died in 1824. Louisa Perina died at Clapton in Middlesex on 12 January 1807, aged seventy-seven, and was buried at Spitalfields eight days later. Samuel, as noted above, emigrated to the United States where he became a prosperous West India merchant; he died in 1821.

Thus ended the connection between the old and respected family of Courtauld with the even more ancient and equally respected craft of goldsmithery – a connection which had lasted for several generations over a span of almost eighty years, during the most successful period of the history of the craft in England.

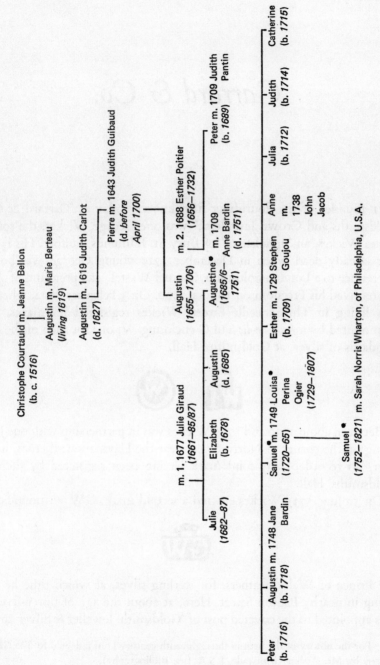

COURTAULD PEDIGREE

Christophe Courtauld m. Jeanne Bellon
(b. c. 1516)

Augustin m. Marie Berteau
(living 1619)

Augustin m. 1619 Judith Carlot
(d. 1627)

Pierre m. 1643 Judith Guibaud
(d. before
April 1700)

Augustin
(1655–1706)

Augustine ●
(1685/6–
1751)

m. 1709
Anne Bardin
(d. 1751)

m. 2. 1688 Esther Poitier
(1656–1732)

Peter m. 1709 Judith
(b. 1689)   Pantin

Elizabeth
(b. 1678)

Augustin
(d. 1685)

m. 1. 1677 Julie Giraud
(1661–85/87)

Esther m. 1729 Stephen
(b. 1709)   Goujou

Anne
m.
1738
John
Jacob

Julia
(b. 1712)

Judith
(b. 1714)

Catherine
(b. 1715)

Julie
(1682–87)

Samuel ● m. 1749 Louisa ●
(1720–65)   Perina
                   Ogier
                   (1729–1807)

Samuel ●
(1752–1821) m. Sarah Norris Wharton, of Philadelphia, U.S.A.

Augustin m. 1748 Jane
(b. 1718)   Bardin

Peter
(b. 1716)

● practised as goldsmith

Garrard & Co.

THE founder of the flourishing firm known today as 'Garrard & Co., Goldsmiths and Crown Jewellers',[1] was one George Wickes, the son of James Wickes, an 'upholsterer' of Bury St. Edmunds, Suffolk. His father was already dead when in December 1712 young George was bound apprentice to a London goldsmith, Samuel Wastell, at a premium of £30. He received his Freedom on 16 June 1720. On 3 February 1722, when he was living in Threadneedle Street, Wickes registered his marks, WI surmounted by a *fleur-de-lis* and G enclosing W, one for each of the two standards of silver, at Goldsmiths' Hall.

Between about 1730 and 1735 Wickes was in partnership with one John Craig on the corner of Norris Street near the Haymarket; there is, however, no record of any joint mark having been registered by them at Goldsmiths' Hall.

On 30 June 1735 Wickes entered a second mark, G W surmounted by

the Prince of Wales' feathers, for sterling silver, at which time he was living in nearby Panton Street. Here, at about the age of thirty-five, he was appointed to the coveted post of 'Goldsmith, Jeweller & Silver-smith'

1. For the history of the firm in the eighteenth century I am indebted to *The Garrard Ledgers* by Mr. Arthur Grimwade, F.S.A. (see Bibliography).

to Frederick, Prince of Wales, and here he issued his first trade-card on which, beneath the Royal Arms, he informed the public in both English and French, that he supplied 'all sorts of jewells and curious Work in Gold and Silver, made after ye Best and Newest fashion, and at Reasonable Prices'. He stated that he was to be found 'a deux Portes du Marché au Foin', which may have somewhat surprised some of his French customers.

To quote Mr. Grimwade:

The ledgers of the firm which . . . came finally to be known as Garrard & Co. . . . form what is probably the most complete set of goldsmiths' business records extant. With the exception of the first two volumes, dating from 1735 to 1747, still preserved by the firm, the remainder are housed in the Library of the Victoria and Albert Museum, where they were sent in 1952 [having been saved from probably pulping by the timely intervention of Mr. Grimwade]. . . . The volumes number forty-two down to 1820 and almost as many again down to the present day. They fall into several groups. The first and largest is that containing private clients' accounts which begin in 1735. The second is a sporadic series entitled 'Workmen's Ledger's', which commence in 1766 and detail all purchases made by the firm from other goldsmiths and jewellers. . . . The third is an extremely interesting group of accounts for the work carried out by Sebastian and James Crespell for Parker and Wakelin and for Wakelin and Garrard from 1778 till 1806. Lastly there is a small group of Day-books from 1795 to 1801 and again from 1815 onwards.

The earliest ledger is dated 23 June 1735: on the following day, under the heading 'My House', we find, among amounts due to 'Brigs painter: Wooton Joyner; Gabb Smith; Burden Plummer; Young Bricklyer and Cobbett Glasher', the sum of £14. 3s. 6d. due for 'The King's Arms and feather': clearly Wickes lost no time in erecting his 'By Appointment' signboard.

The first entry in his Royal client's ledger was a shrewd gesture:

Mar 24 1735/6. To a black Eboney Handle for a tea kettle and a Button for a teapott . . . 0s. 0d.

This move clearly paid off, for only five weeks later Wickes entered in the Prince's ledger:

1 May 1735–6. To a fine Cup & cover 124 oz. 17 dwt. ... ... £80.
To a fine Bread Baskett 87 oz. 9 dwt. ... ... £50.

On 10 September 1737 George II banished his high-living and extravagant heir from Court, and two days later the latter retired in dudgeon and disgrace with his retinue to Kew. Here, in an attempt to improve his finances, Frederick instituted a number of economies which resulted in Wickes writing in his ledger on 20 September:

To the Damadge and Loss to me in a Large Parcell of Plate
Bespoke and ordered by the Prince which was in such for-
wardness when countermand as amounts to more than   ... £500.

In a later, but undated, entry he records that he: 'Sold Six Doun of plates and twelf Dishes which I allow att Six pence per oz. . . . 2000 . . . £50'; i.e. the plate-tax charge of 6d. per oz., introduced in 1720.
   Immediately below this entry Wickes wrote:

The Damadge on the other side being Reduced by executing
part of the work intended and I have now taken of token of
the whol Damadge altho' I have not Recd it any other wise
than by the profitt of work made   ...   . £450.

In other words, he decided to cut his losses and write off the amount as a 'bad debt'.
   In spite of the foregoing unfortunate experience, Wickes appears to have been willing to accept future Royal commissions, as for instance in February 1738 for '18 chased Sconces' weighing 426 oz. which cost £126. 1s. 6d. (5s. 11d. per oz.) plus a charge of five guineas each for fashioning, an additional £94. 10s. 0d., totalling £220. 11s. 6d. On 3 March of the same year he made '3 pairs of fine candlesticks' weighing 132 oz. for £69. 7s. 6d. at the inclusive cost of 10s. 6d. per oz.
   In 1739 Wickes registered a fourth and final mark, GW surmounted by the Prince of Wales' feathers.
   Another entry for the Prince reads:

April 14 1744. To 2 Breadbaskets, 120 oz. 12 dwts. at 9s. 2d.   £55. 5. 7.

One of these finely pierced baskets weighing 59 oz. 5 dwt., 14⅜ in. wide, made by Wickes for the Prince of Wales in 1743 and engraved in the centre with his Arms, is now in a private collection in the United States. Also made for the Prince of Wales at this time were:

2 Silver gilt Tureens and covers, 2 Lynings, 2 Dishes and
2 Ladles, 633 oz. 15 d. ...   . £448. 18. 0.

Most important, however, of the Royal silver made by Wickes is a silver-gilt epergne, designed by William Kent, which, extensively altered by Paul Storr's firm, Rundell & Bridge, is still in the Royal collection:

in 1954 it was exhibited at the Victoria and Albert Museum. The entry
in the ledger reads:

Nov. 11. 1745. To a silver gilt Epergne a Table 4 Saucers,
    4 Casters, 8 Branch Lights and Pegs, 845 oz. 9 d. at 15s. 8d.   £662. 5. 2.
To Graving the Table 4 Saucers and Caster ...   . £ 23. 16. 0.
To 6 Glass Saucers   ...   . £ 3. 3. 0.
To 2 Wainscot Cases   ...   . £ 6. 10. 0.

After the death of the Prince in 1751 his widow continued to patronize
Wickes, who also received a fresh warrant from the succeeding Prince of
Wales; this was continued when the Prince came to the throne as
George III in 1760.

The work carried out by Wickes for his Royal patron was, of course, only
the jam on his bread-and-butter: to supply the latter he looked for commissions to the nobility and gentry; among customers recorded in the
first ledger are the Dukes of Chandos and Devonshire; the Duchess of
Gordon and the Dowager Duchess of Norfolk; the Marquess of
Caernarvon; the Earls of Winchelsea, Nottingham and Inchquin, the
Bishops of Norwich and Ely, and Lord Cornwallis.

    The second ledger, commencing in 1741, includes the names of the
Dukes of Bridgwater, Kingston (twenty-six silver coat buttons in 1742
for £2. 15s. 6d. and two years later a further five dozen for £16. 18s. 8d.),
Montrose and Roxburgh ('2 silver backs for Spunges 1 oz. 3 dwts.
13s. 0d.'); the Earls of Kildare ('a Pudding Trowle 4 oz. 18 dwts. 6s. 2d.
per oz. £1. 10. 2.') and Scarborough, and the Rt. Honble. Arthur Onslow,
Speaker of the House of Commons, who in 1744 bought 'a Large Cistern,
2008 oz. 5s. 8d. per oz. £568. 18. 9d. Contra By an old Cistern 1495 oz.
5s. 4d. per oz. £398. 13. 4.', which Wickes clearly took in part exchange;
Mr. Onslow also bought in 1749 '6 lark spits 2 oz. 13 dwts. £1. 11. 0.'.

    The third ledger, which begins in February 1747, includes the Dukes of
Richmond and Somerset, the Marquess of Granby, and the Earls of Jersey,
Traquair, Northesk and Macclesfield.

    Among the commoners for whom Wickes provided plate in the 1730s
and 1740s were Mr. Everard Fawkener who in September 1735 purchased
'A Surtoit a Table [epergne] Casters, Cruett & Complat' weighing altogether 590 oz. 3 dwt. which cost him £239. 15s. 0d. (8s. 1½d. per oz.),
and a Mrs. Fuller, who in 1741 bought for £82. 7s. 0d. 'A Sett of Dressing

plate' weighing 253 oz. 10 dwt. (6s. 6d. per oz.). On 25 September 1742
Sir Lister Holte, Bart., was debited:

To a Tureen & Cover 135 oz. 4 dwts. @ 4s. 8½d.   ...   ...   £55. 4. 3.
To a Soup Ladle 12 oz. 5 dwts. @ 6s. 2d.   ...   .   £ 3. 15. 6.
To Graving 2 Coats and 2 Crests with coat mantng. on ye
  Tureen and cover   ...   .   £ 2. 2. 0.
To Graving a Crest on the Soup Ladle ...   .   £ -. 1. 0.

The tureen, which measures 13¾ in. long and has finely scrolling handles,
stands on four claw-and-ball feet with lion-mask knees.

In 1745 a Mrs. Elton bought 'a square Coffeepot 21 oz. 8 dwts. 8s. 3d.
per ounce £8. 16. 0.'. Mr. Grimwade records that 'This unusual piece
has been identified with one ... bearing the arms of Sir Abraham Elton,
3rd Baronet of Clevedon Court, Somerset, Sheriff of Bristol 1728, and
Mayor of that city 1742. He was unmarried and the piece may have been
a gift from a sister, Mrs. being the usual 18th century courtesy title, or
from a sister-in-law.'

On 2 November 1747 the ledger records the transfer of 'a Moiety of the
Stock in Trade' by Wickes to a new partner, Edward Wakelin, the son
of Edward Wakelin, a 'baker' of Uttoxeter, Staffordshire, who was dead
by the time his son became apprenticed in 1730 to the famous Huguenot
goldsmith, John Le Sage. On 17 November Wakelin registered his first
mark, E W under the Prince's feathers, at Goldsmiths' Hall; from that

date he appears more or less to have taken over the running (at any rate
the goldsmith's side) of the business, as little, if any, plate by Wickes is
known after 1747.

In about 1750 Wickes and Wakelin took into partnership one Samuel
Netherton, who, since he appears not to have entered a mark either on his
own account or jointly with Wickes and/or Wakelin, was probably
concerned primarily with the jewellery side of the business.

On 7 July 1751 Wickes took on an apprentice, John Parker, the son of
'Thomas Parker, Gent.', of Longdon, Worcestershire, for a premium of
£50, a figure which he no doubt felt justified in asking in view of his

position as 'Royal Goldsmith'. Parker entered his joint mark with Wakelin, the Prince's feathers over IP over EW, in which somewhat surprisingly his initials appear above those of Wakelin as if he were the senior partner; the precise date on which this joint mark was entered is unknown, as the register of 'Large Plateworkers' from 1758 to 1773 is missing at Goldsmiths' Hall.

Parker and Wakelin lost no time in issuing a new trade-card (on which, be it noted, Parker's name again precedes that of Wakelin) where, under the Royal Arms, they stated that: 'John Parker & Edward Wakelin / Goldsmiths & Jewellers / in Panton Street near St. James's / Haymarket / make and sell all sorts of Jewellery, Watches, Plate / and all other curious Work in Gold, Silver Variety / of Falsestone Work in Aigrettes, Earrings, Buckles &c. / All manner of Seals in Stone, Steel & Silver Engraved in / the Newest Taste at the most Reasonable Rates / Neat Mourning Rings of all Kinds / N.B. Likewise Buy & Sell all sorts of second- / -hand Plate, Jewels and Watches.'

On 8 May 1752 Wakelin took on as an apprentice Stephen Gilbert, who had been working as a boy in his workshop since 1749 at the munificent salary of between £5 and £6 per annum. Gilbert became Free of the Goldsmiths' Company by Service on 1 February 1764 and returned to Panton Street where he worked as a journeyman for two years; he then joined forces with another ex-employee of Parker and Wakelin, James Ansill; between 1766 and 1773 they supplied a considerable quantity of goods to their old masters. Gilbert, it will be remembered, was in 1780 taken on as a partner by Andrew Fogelberg who some five years later became the master of Paul Storr.

A number of interesting entries for this period are to be found in the firm's ledgers:

Dec. 31. 1756. To 2 Terrines and dishes 500 oz. 14 dwts.
at 11s. 1d. ... ... £277. 9. 6.
To 2 Souplades 23 oz. 18 dwts. at 9s. 1d. ... ... £ 10. 17. 0.
To graving 2 coats of Supps and 6 Crests and Corts ... ... £ 2. 8. 0.

These soup-tureens and covers, which bear the maker's mark of Wakelin and the date-letter for 1755, stand on dishes engraved with the

arms of Cecil with Townshend in pretence for Brownlow, 9th Earl of
Exeter. In July 1959 they were sold at Christie's by Lord Exeter, appearing
at Sotheby's in 1970 in the sale of the Plohn collection, and at Christie's
again in 1972 in the Engelhard sale. In 1758 the Archbishop of Canterbury
received an account for:

2 Terrines and Covers 238 oz. 8 dwt. 8s. 6d. per oz.	£101.	7. 0.
To engraving 2 coats and crests with ornaments and mitres ...	£ 2.	0. 0.
2 Red Leather cases	£ 1.	14. 0.

In 1761 an account with Parker and Wakelin was opened by William,
Duke of Cumberland (1721–65) and his nephew, Prince Henry (1745–90),
who was later to succeed his uncle in the dukedom. In 1762 the Queen's
brother, the Prince of Mecklenburg, made his first purchases from Parker
and Wakelin; in the following year the Countess of Holderness bought
from them some 'gold needles'; a year later the King's brother, the Duke
of Gloucester, is recorded in the ledgers as having made his first purchase;
also in 1764, the Earl of Rosebery bought 'a pair of pearl night cloaths
earings' for £3, and later on gave £800. 18s. 6d. for 'a brilliant
[presumably diamond] necklace'. In 1770 Lord Yarborough paid £4,000
for a large service of plate; a year later the Duke of Newcastle gave
£3,900 for a similar set. In 1772, and again in 1774, the Duke of
Cumberland bought gold race-cups and some silver slippers.

Four shaped oval pie-dishes with gadrooned borders, made by Parker
and Wakelin in 1772, sold at Christie's in November 1973 for £2,100:
they are engraved with the arms of Clinton with Pelham in pretence, for
Henry, 9th Earl of Lincoln and later 2nd Duke of Newcastle, K.G. (born
1720), who married in 1746 his cousin, Catherine, eldest daughter of the
Rt. Hon. Henry Pelham, younger brother of Thomas Pelham Holles,
1st Duke of Newcastle. In the appropriate ledger for 1773 is the following
entry:

Jan. 4. To 26 Oval 18 Round Gadroon'd Dishes 1656 ozs. 4 at 6/11	£572/15/6.
To Engraving 140 Coats, Supporters, Garters & Corts. on ye Com. Dishes & Plates @ 5/-	£35

Also in 1772, Parker and Wakelin made for the Honble. John Smith
Barry of Marbury, county Chester, son of James, 4th Earl of Barrymore,
probably as a racing trophy, a very fine 22 carat gold two-handled cup

and cover standing 9½ in. high and weighing 40 oz.: the entry in the ledger reads:

Oct. 8. To a fine Chased Gold Cup & Cover ... 40.9.0.
    at £3.18.9.   ...   .   £157. 15. 0.
To Making   ...   .   £ 50. 0. 0.
To Graving 2 Coats & 2 Crests 8/– a Red Leather Case &
    Deal Box 15/6. ...   .   £ 1. 3. 6.

From 1766 the firm kept accounts with nearly seventy manufacturing goldsmiths, each of whom appears to have specialized in the production of a different article. From 1766 to 1775, to quote Mr. Grimwade:

the firm bought candlesticks and waiters from Ebenezer Coker, salt and tea-spoons from James Tookey, spoons from William and Thomas Chawner, salt cellars from David and later David and Robert Hennell, miscellaneous plate from Daniel Smith and Robert Sharp, cruets from Robert Piercey, sugar and cream baskets from Emick Romer, papboats, mugs and cream jugs from Walter Brind, dishes and plates from S. and J. Crespell ... miscellaneous plate from Charles Wright and Aldridge and Co., and candlesticks and waiters from John Carter ... epergnes from Thomas Pitts ... there are accounts with Jewellers, Ringmakers, Watchmakers, Pearl Stringers, Plated goods makers and the makers of such accessories as Plate chests, knife boxes, Pocket books, and also Bullion dealers.

In March 1766 Edward Wakelin's son, John, became apprenticed to his father: ten years later he registered a joint mark, I W over W T

surmounted by the Prince of Wales' feathers, with one William Taylor (about whom nothing can be learnt either from the ledgers or the registers at Goldsmiths' Hall), at which date it would appear that both Parker and Edward Wakelin retired.

John Wakelin and Taylor issued a new trade-card in which, describing themselves as 'successors to Parker and Wakelin', they offered to the public a 'Variety of useful and Ornamental Plate, Jewells, &c. .... Mourning Rings, Seals and Rich Toys in Gold and Silver'. In 1776 the new partners sold some tea-pots to Sir Joshua Reynolds (1723–92), then living in nearby Leicester Fields (Square), and mended the locks on his tea-chests. In the same year they sold a cup with a yacht on the cover to the Duke of Cumberland. In 1783 Josiah Wedgwood bought for a hundred guineas 'a fine chased tureen and cover, with a dish, according to a drawing, the bas-reliefs and figures by Flaxman'. Queen Charlotte purchased, in April 1788, two gold toothpicks, a pair of pearl and diamond bracelets and a ring with a 'diamond knott'.

The ledgers show various payments and transactions on behalf of Mrs. George Wickes between 1771 and 1774, so it seems reasonable to assume that the founder of the firm died in about 1770. Edward Wakelin died at Mitcham in Surrey in 1784 (an item of £31. 15s. od. appears in the ledger on 24 April for his funeral expenses), and John Parker at Stockwell in 1792.

In the ledger of 1793, to quote Mr. Grimwade again:

We find the firm of Pitts and Preedy continuing the connection begun by William Pitts's father . . . the rising firm of Matthew Boulton of Birmingham supply plated goods as well as Roberts, Cadman and Co. of Sheffield. . . . William Edey and William Fearn supply tongs [and] buckles. . . . Walter Brind continues with papboats and pannikins . . . and the Chawner establishment with knives. . . . In a succeeding volume which extends to 1806 Robert Hennell and sons re-appear, Richard Cooke supplies tea-services, and Joseph Preedy . . . epergnes. . . . Paul Storr . . . sells one or two bee-hive honey-pots to the firm in 1802.

In addition there is a long list of firms supplying other miscellaneous items connected with the goldsmiths' trade.

From 1769 the names of Sebastian and James Crespell, who had work-shops in Whitcomb Street, Leicester Fields, close by Panton Street, appear in the ledgers. From 1778 they were producing such quantities of plate for Wakelin and Taylor as to justify having a ledger to themselves. By 1782 the Crespells appear to have been what today would be called a 'wholly owned subsidiary' of Wakelin and Taylor. From 1788 only James' name appears in the Wakelin and Taylor ledger, so it seems likely that Sebastian died early in that year. James continued to produce enough plate to justify having his own ledger until October 1806, after which his name disappears.

An entry in the ledgers for 1792 for the Earl of Chesterfield reads:

Feb. 24.

To a fine chased epergne bason & table 86.18 @ 10/6	£ 35.	12.	6.
To 2 small -do-do- 101.13 @ 10/6	£ 53.	7.	4.
To Duty 94/3. Case 50/-	£ 7.	4.	3.
To 2 large glass basons @ 27/- each 4 small @ 14/- and for			4.
divided 7/- each	£ 8.	6.	–.
To engraving Coats supp: & Crests	£ 3.	–.	–.
To a large glass bason broke/broke by the servant/ ...	£ –.	–.	–.

In June 1973 Christie's sold these pieces for £3,400; they were described in the catalogue as follows:

. . . the baskets each on four laurel bud feet, the sides applied and chased with alternate plain and husk panels and with pierced arches above, each with two ram's mask dropring handles, the centres of the sides applied with a circular cartouche pendant from a ribbon and engraved with a coat-of-arms, [Stanhope for Philip Stanhope, 5th. Earl of Chesterfield, K.G. (1755–1815), Master of the Mint, 1789–90, and Master of the Horse 1798–1804)] with pierced continuous scrollwork rim, the stands similarly engraved and with pierced centres.

In 1792 Taylor appears to have left the firm; as a result Wakelin took as his new partner Robert Garrard (1758–1818) who entered a joint mark with Wakelin, I W over R G, at Goldsmiths' Hall on 20 October of the same year (1792). Ten years later Wakelin retired or died, and on 11 August 1802 Garrard registered his own mark, a cursive R G; from that

date the firm, founded by George Wickes in 1722, remained for one hundred and fifty-four years in the hands of members of the Garrard family.

Robert Garrard's grandfather, who came from Newbury, Berkshire, died early in life, leaving two young sons and a widow who married secondly one Ellis a 'clothier' of Stroud, Gloucestershire. The younger boy entered the Church while the elder, Robert Haslefoot, was sent to his step-father's brother, Stephen, a 'merchant' in Cheapside who lived in Crouch End Lane, Hornsey. Robert Haslefoot became a 'linendraper' in Cheapside, and married in about 1756 Miriam, daughter of Captain Richards, Royal Artillery, of the Isle of Wight and of Biggin Farm,

Norwood, Surrey; they had four children: Samuel, born in 1757; Robert, born 'at one quarter of an hour past 10 o'clock in the morning' on 15 November 1758; George, born in 1760, who later achieved distinction as an artist, becoming an A.R.A; he married Matilda, daughter of Sawrey Gilpin, R.A. (1733–1807); and Miriam, born in 1762. Robert Haslefoot died on 29 March 1785, and his wife in 1801.

Robert Garrard was apprenticed on 7 October 1773 to Stephen Unwin, 'hardwareman', of Cheapside, a member of the Grocers' Company. Robert obtained his Freedom of that Company in 1780, when he was described as the 'late apprentice to Stephen Unwin now with Messrs. Wakelin & Co. Goldsmiths, Panton Street, Haymarket'.

It appears possible that Robert Garrard was a descendant of Sir William Garrard, Lord Mayor of London in 1555; Sir John Garrard, 1st baronet, Lord Mayor in 1601; and Sir Samuel Garrard, Bt. (1650–1724), Master of the Worshipful Company of Grocers and Lord Mayor in 1709, when the notorious Dr. Henry Sacheverell (1674–1724) preached his seditious sermon with the text 'In Peril, Amongst False Bretheren' on Guy Fawkes Day to the Lord Mayor's congregation in St. Paul's Cathedral. Garrard was subsequently involved in Sacheverell's trial in 1710 before the House of Lords in Westminster Hall.[2]

Robert Garrard clearly never received any training as a goldsmith, apart from what he was able to pick up in the course of his daily work with Wakelin & Co., and must have achieved control of the firm solely through his business acumen; he died on 26 March 1818 and was succeeded in the firm by his three eldest sons, Robert, James (born 13 June 1795; Free by Redemption 1 June 1825; Liveryman 1829; Assistant 1842; Prime Warden of the Worshipful Company of Goldsmiths 1847–8 and 1850–1; died at No. 1 Broad Sanctuary, Westminster, on 3 November 1870), and Sebastian (1798–1870). After his father's death Robert appears to have assumed control of the firm, a position which he maintained until his death sixty-three years later.

Robert Garrard II was born on 13 August 1793; he was apprenticed to his father, 'Citizen and Grocer' on 1 June 1809, becoming Free in July 1816. He became a Liveryman in 1818 (the year of his father's death) and on 18 April of that year registered his first mark, a cursive RG. His second

2. See *The Trial of Doctor Sacheverell*, Geoffrey Holmes (London, 1973).

mark, RG crowned, was entered on 17 January 1822 from St. Martin's, Panton Street. In February 1836 Robert moved to No. 29 Panton Street, from where he entered his third mark, again RG crowned, on 29 June 1847. He was elected to the Court in 1843, and became a Warden in 1844, 1845 and 1852, before becoming Master of the Worshipful Company of Grocers in 1853. On 11 June 1825 Robert married at St. George's, Hanover Square, Esther Whippy (died 1848), of North Audley Street, W.1. Robert died on 26 September 1881.

Under Robert's guiding hand the nineteenth century saw the rise of Garrards to a pre-eminent position in their trade. In 1817 the Queen presented to the Duke of Sussex a fine service of Garrard table-plate engraved with his coronet and cypher. In 1819 the Duke of Kent bought a pap-boat for the future Queen Victoria (who was born in that year), probably as a christening-present. Between 1817 and 1820 Garrards made a number of cups which were used as racing trophies at Bodmin, Derby, Lincoln, Northampton, Richmond, and Stamford. Shortly after his accession in 1820 George IV commissioned from Garrards a cup to be raced for at Brighton.

The coronation year of 1821 resulted in a considerable amount of work for the firm. The sum of £2,000 was paid to the Royal Mint for a quantity of gold, silver and bronze commemorative medals, which were sold to the public by Garrards for six guineas, one pound and ten shillings respectively. The Duke of Wellington (who had opened an account with the firm in 1816) paid £26 for a ducal coronet, presumably to wear in Westminster Abbey. Twenty years later he bought from Garrards a gold mug as a christening-present for the new Prince of Wales, later Edward VII.

In 1825 the Liverpool Committee bought from Garrards for £3,489. 12s. od. a service of plate for a Mr. Huskisson – later to gain fame as the first man to be killed by a railway-train. In the following year a service of plate was ordered for the Duke of Devonshire, and the Lord Chamberlain's office was debited £88. 15s. od. for 'two complete sets of silver-gilt Waterman's badges prepared in the usual manner'. These silver-gilt and enamel badges, bearing the rose, shamrock, thistle and cypher of the reigning sovereign, are worn by the crew of the Royal Barge.

In 1824 the firm produced a splendid silver soup-tureen, now in the collection of the Campbell Museum, Camden, New Jersey, which in 1973 was exhibited at the Victoria and Albert Museum. The bowl, which rests on the tails of four dolphins rising from a stand decorated with simulated waves which has shell-encrusted scrolling handles, is engraved on each side with the arms of Norton of Ripon. The rim of the bowl is decorated with a pattern of shells and limpets; a triton blowing a conch-shell and a mermaid form the handles. The cover is surmounted by a finial formed as a crayfish amidst shells and foliage rising from embossed acanthus leaves. The circular bowl, 21 in. in diameter, and stand together weigh 507 oz. and stand nearly 16 in. high.

In 1827 Garrards made the first of a number of cups which were used as racing-trophies by the Royal Yacht Club (Squadron). George IV's last purchase from Garrards was 'a large table diamond' with a miniature of the Duke of Marlborough set in pearls, made up as a bracelet.

On the accession of William IV in 1830 Garrards succeeded Paul Storr's firm, Rundell & Bridge, as 'Goldsmiths and Crown Jewellers', an appointment which resulted in the addition of a galaxy of new and illustrious names to their books: among these were the Duke of Buccleuch, the Marquesses of Anglesey (the hero of Waterloo), Abercorn and Wellesley; the Earls of Brownlow, Dudley, Haddington and Kilmory, and Lord Charles Townsend. In the following year the firm supplied, for a fee of £541. 11s. 0d., the regalia for the Garter King at Arms and nine heralds at the coronation of William IV, who a few years later bought from Garrards 'a very fine brilliant Jerusalem cross' and a pair of gold dog-couples. In 1832 the name of Edwin Landseer appears for the first time in the firm's ledgers: from 1834 to 1841 Garrards were employed by the War Office to supply a number of inkstands; between 1833 and 1839 they provided several cups for use as racing-trophies at Ascot. In the last year of William IV's reign they received an order from the Marquess of Exeter to make for him silver models of some of his prize-winning bulls at Burghley.

31 Self-portrait of George Garrard, A.R.A.
(*Photo: courtesy of Spink & Son.*)

32 George Wickes: silver-gilt epergne, 1745.
The Royal Collection. (*Reproduced by gracious
permission of Her Majesty the Queen.*)

3 Garrard & Co.: gilt table-centre,
designed by Prince Albert, 1842.
The Royal Collection. (*Reproduced by
gracious permission of Her Majesty the
Queen.*)

4 Robert Garrard: one of a set of four
gilt shell salts, 1867. From the collection
of the late Miss Eva Goldman.
(*Photo: courtesy of Christie's.*)

5 Garrard & Co.: soup-tureen, 1824.
The Campbell Museum, Camden,
New Jersey.

36 Portrait of David Hennell; artist unknown. (*Photo: Percy Hennell.*)

37 Portrait of Robert Hennell III; artist unknown. (*Photo: Percy Hennell.*)

37a Portrait of Robert Hennell IV; artist unknown. (*Photo: Percy Hennell.*)

37b Portrait of James Barclay Hennell; artist unknown. (*Photo: Percy Hennell.*)

38 Robert and David Hennell: coffee-pot made for Lord Nelson, 1799. National Maritime Museum, Greenwich.

39 Robert Hennell: wheatear basket, 1850. The Worshipful Company of Goldsmiths.

40 Hennell Ltd.: pair of gilt and silver rosewater bowls, designed by Anthony Elson, 1970. The Saddlers' Company.

41 Anthony Nelme: one of a pair of silver-gilt altar-candlesticks, 1694. St George's Chapel, Windsor Castle. (*Reproduced by gracious permission of Her Majesty the Queen.*)

42 Anthony Nelme: 'Pilgrim' wine-bottle, 1715. The Devonshire Collection. (*Courtesy of the Trustees of the Chatsworth Settlement.*)

43 'The Ancestor', a presumed portrait of Paul Crespin, 1720–40. From the collection of the late Miss E. M. Barraud. (*Photo: courtesy of Miss Judith Banister.*)

44 Paul Crespin: tureen-centrepiece, 1741. The Royal Collection. (*Reproduced by gracious permission of Her Majesty the Queen.*)

On 13 February 1843, six years after Queen Victoria came to the throne, Garrards were reappointed to the coveted position of 'Crown Jewellers', a post which the firm still holds today. According to General Sitwell 'This seems to have been first used as a title by Rundell & Bridge; only two firms have used it, Rundell & Bridge and Garrards. Apparently the title implies the responsibility for the preparation of the Regalia and Crown Jewels for Coronations, and their maintenance generally.'

From 1833 until his death in 1860 the head of Garrard's designing department was Edmund Cotterill, a sculptor who had been trained at the Academy School, and who 'deservedly stands at the head of the class of artists who model for silversmiths and his productions, annually exhibited at Messrs. Garrards, have earned for that house a celebrity which no other can equal'.[3] Most of the large sculptural groups, then much in vogue, made by Garrards during this period were to the design of Cotterill.

The firm exhibited a number of important and impressive pieces at the Great Exhibition of 1851, among them 'Arabs of the Desert tracking travellers by their footmarks in the sand'; 'The Arab disdains all inducements of the Turkish merchant to barter for his mare and foal'; 'John, Duke of Marlborough writing the despatch of the Victory of Blenheim' (made as part of a table-service for the Duke and bearing Robert Garrard's mark and the date-letter for 1846; now in the collection of the Duke at Blenheim Palace); 'Lucy Ashton at the death of the Stag', and 'Thomas the Rhymer and the Fairey Queen'. A magnificent gilt table-centre designed by Prince Albert has ornamental motifs based on those of sixteenth-century Germany and Italy, and incorporates models of four of the Queen's favourite dogs; punched with Robert Garrard's mark and the date-letter for 1842, it is in the collection of the Queen – on loan to the Victoria and Albert Museum. Also in the Exhibition of 1851 were a number of the then popular hunting scenes. The most elaborate pieces on show, in the baroque style, were a cup in the form of a nautilus shell, ornamented with Neptune attended by nymphs; and ewers depicting the story of 'Perseus and Andromeda' and the 'Labours of Hercules'.

In the year following the Great Exhibition, Garrards were awarded a prize of £200 presented by the Worshipful Company of Goldsmiths for the best piece of plate exhibited – a centrepiece incorporating a candelabrum in the 'Moorish' style, depicting a scene from Sir Walter Scott's

3. *Illustrated London News*, Vol. 1, p. 73 (1842).

Talisman. 'The style of ornament of the centrepiece is that of the early Arabs or Alhambraic. The ever varying lines of which this style admits, its great variety of beautiful ornament, and the novelty of its adaptions to works in gold and silver, render it likely in some measure to supersede the scroll ornamentation of Louis Quatorze. . . .'[4]

Other important pieces made by Garrards during the 1840s include a centrepiece, with branches for eight candles, depicting a scene at the Battle of Lansdowne during the Civil War, designed by Cotterill and made by Garrards in 1840; in 1851 a pair of four-branch candelabra were made *en suite*: these pieces are now in the collection of the Marquess of Bath at Longleat.

In 1849 the firm exhibited at the Society of Arts a soup-tureen, made for Mr. H. T. Hope, based on metal work of the Italian Renaissance: 'this splendid piece of plate . . . is sensible and simple in its structure . . . it is a really beautiful vessel, admirably adapted for its purpose.'[5]

To designs by Cotterill were made the Doncaster Cup of 1847, depicting Richard Coeur de Lion at the Battle of Ascalon; the Ascot Cup of 1842 with a scene taken from the Battle of Crecy; that of 1847, showing Queen Elizabeth I being offered a stag by a hunter; and the Queen's Cup at Ascot (1848) depicting a Mexican roping a horse. The baroque Chesterfield Cup of 1849, with decoration of strapwork on the bulging lower part of the body and on the baluster-stem, has, on the upper part which curves inwards, Sioux Indians hunting bison: the group are after a drawing by Cotterill, the cup itself by W. F. Spencer, who was to succeed Cotterill on the latter's death.

In 1848 the 1st Marquess of Anglesey presented to the Royal Yacht Squadron a silver ewer by Garrards as a racing trophy: the first winner at Cowes on 22 August 1851 was the United States schooner *America*; since then the 'America's Cup' has been the 'Holy Grail' of English yachting, but has yet to be wrested from the hands of the New York Yacht Club; even the most patriotic American, however, would be unlikely to claim that this ugly cup was one of Garrards more inspired designs.

Made to a design by Cotterill was the Emperor's Vase at Ascot for 1850, showing the 'Labours of Hercules'; the rocks and flowing water on the base represent the cleansing of the Augean stables; on the body of the cup is a lifelike group of Hercules striking the horses of Diomedes; the lower

4. *Illustrated London News*, Vol. 21, p. 10 (1852).
5. *Journal of Design*, Vol. 1, p. 81.

part of the cup is ornamented with horses' heads; the birds of Stymphalus encircle the neck of the cup, whose handles are formed of Hydra.

Also designed by Cotterill for Garrards was the Emperor's Vase of the following year, in the form of an oval-bodied wine cooler. The everted top forms a shell-shaped lip decorated with scrolled strapwork. The whole piece is embellished with waves and acanthus foliage from which two dragons rise, their feet resting on the side of the cistern. At the back the shell-lip rises higher than in the front, and curls over in a succession of flowing waves which support a rocky plateau, on which a horse-drawn sleigh is being attacked by a pack of wolves in a forest.

In the early 1850s Cotterill paid a visit to the East where he 'had many opportunities of seeing Oriental scenery and costume'; from this trip originate his designs in the 'Moorish' style as, for instance the 1858 Queen's Vase at Ascot, showing a Pasha under a palm-tree; and the Good-wood Cup of 1854 depicting a group of Arab horsemen at an oasis.

Garrards also carried out early essays into the use of enamels to decorate silver-plate: an example is the 'Great Railway Salver', embellished with enamel portraits of famous railroad engineers together with examples of their work, contained within a cartouche of Elizabethan-style strapwork. The border of the salver consists of rococo scrolls, foliage and flowers. Whether the marriage between enamel and silver is more or less successful than between enamel and wood is a matter of taste.

A magnificent table-centre made by Garrards in 1852 is of a hybrid design; the main portion is the work of E. Lorenzo Percy, working from a sketch provided by the Prince Consort; the horses are by Cotterill; this co-operative piece was shown at the International Exhibition in 1862.

On 16 July 1852 the Duke of Wellington ceremonially cut the first facet of the Koh-i-Noor (Mountain of Light) diamond at Garrard's workshops in Panton Street. This famous eight-hundred-year-old stone came into the possession of the East India Company on the annexation of the Punjab in 1849. In the following year it was presented by Lord Dalhousie to Queen Victoria to commemorate the 250th anniversary of the granting of a Charter to the East India Company by Queen Elizabeth I. In 1937 it was inserted into the crown – incidentally the only platinum crown in existence – of Queen Elizabeth at the coronation of George VI.

In 1855 the firm received a commission from the Queen to make, from a design by Prince Albert, a jewelled pendant for presentation to Florence Nightingale, 'as a mark of esteem and gratitude': St. George's Cross in red enamel appears on a plain white ground, encircled by a black band on which is the inscription 'Blessed are the merciful'. Superimposed on the cross, from which burst rays of gold, is the Queen's cypher, surmounted by a crown of diamonds; branches of palm in green enamel form a frame for the shield, their stems being bound with a blue enamel ribbon (the colour of the Crimean Medal), on which is the single word 'Crimea'; above, between the palm-branches, are three brilliant stars of diamonds. This splendid jewel, measuring some 3 in. by 2½ in., was intended to be worn not as a brooch but as the badge of an order.

W. F. Spencer, who succeeded Cotterill as chief designer for Garrards in 1860, was rather more pedestrian than his predecessor. Among his better-known pieces are a racing trophy cup which was entirely oxidized (then a comparatively new process) giving it a greyish matt finish. When shown at the International Exhibition at Dublin in 1853 it was said that 'of the execution it is sufficient to say that it is the result of the skill, judgement and experience of the very famous establishment from which it issues, to become one of the ornaments of a Palace. . . . Moors attending upon Arab horses are arranged beside the pillar, which stands on a base of antique fragments, in keeping with the composition and foliage characteristic of the scene.'[6]

In the International Exhibition of 1862 Garrards, whose work was considered by the Jury to be 'especially distinguished by the excellence of its manufacture', showed three table-ornaments designed by Spencer for the Maharajah Duleep Singh; the catalogue relates that 'the principal group of the centre ornament represents the late Maharajah Runjeet Singh seated in his houdah on an elephant, receiving a famous horse which he desired to possess'. Also in the exhibition was an elaborate cup and cover in the Renaissance style, commissioned by the Queen for her grandson, the infant Prince of Prussia: the cover is decorated with figures of angels and birds; St. George and the Dragon appear on the base.

In 1860, the year of his death, Cotterill produced his last two designs for the firm with which he had spent most of his working life; these were the Ascot Cup and Goodwood Cup of that year, taking the form respectively of a statue of Richard Coeur de Lion, and a fine model of a racehorse.

In 1862 Garrards were commissioned to make a suite of diamonds and pearls for presentation by the City of London to Queen Alexandra on her

6. Art Journal of the Catalogue of the Dublin Exhibition 1853, p. 64.

marriage; on the Queen's silver wedding the firm created a beautiful diamond tiara (chosen by the Marchionesses of Ailesbury and Salisbury and the Countesses of Cork and Spencer) on behalf of the peeresses of the United Kingdom. By the Queen's special request the shape of the tiara was that of a Russian peasant's head-dress.

In 1881, at the advanced age of eighty-eight, Robert Garrard II died at his home, the White House, Wokingham, Berkshire – he also owned a London house in Onslow Gardens – and was subsequently buried in the family vault in Streatham. One of his sons, Robert (1831–96), a Captain in the 5th Dragoon Guards, became Free by Service in 1852 and was elected a Liveryman in 1853.

Robert was succeeded in the firm by his nephew, James Mortimer (1834–1900), then living at Pinner Place, Middlesex (which he inherited through his wife) who registered his mark, IG crowned, in 1881. James Mortimer was the eldest son of Henry Garrard (1808–62) who on 24 February 1831 married in New South Wales, Australia, Mary Mortimer. Their four eldest children returned to England, where they were adopted by their uncle Sebastian (1798–1870) and his wife Harriet, who were childless. James Mortimer was apprenticed on 6 March 1850 to George Withers of No. 32 Panton Street; he became Free on 1 April 1857 and was elected to the Livery in 1860, becoming Prime Warden of the Worshipful Company of Goldsmiths in 1897. On 3 August 1865 James Mortimer, describing himself as 'Captain, Honourable Artillery Company & Goldsmith', married Mary, daughter of Marseille Middleton Holloway, 'Publisher'. After his death in 1900 James Mortimer was succeeded by his elder son, Sebastian Henry (doubtless named after his great-uncle and grandfather) who was born at 13 St. George's Road, W.1, in 1868; he became Free by Patrimony on 4 December 1889 and was elected to the Livery in 1895. Sebastian Henry married on 2 June 1894 at the church of St. Michael the Archangel, Warfield, Berkshire, May Eleanor, second daughter of Frederick and Gertrude Cazenove of Warfield Grove. After the demolition of Pinner Place, Sebastian Henry purchased Welton Place, Daventry; following the death of his father in 1900 he registered his maker's mark, S G crowned, later in the same year, re-registering it without the crown in the following year. This change is explained by the inscription on a heavy silver-gilt salt, marked with S G crowned and decorated with applied acanthus leaves on the bowl and base, in the possession of Mr. Frederick H. Eyles, head silver buyer and valuer of Garrards from 1927–1952: the inscription around the inside of the bowl reads: 'This is the last piece of plate marked at Goldsmiths' Hall, London, with the crown over maker's mark, that emblem being abandoned by Garrard & Co. April 18th 1901 in deference to the objection of the Sheffield Assay Office.' (It will be remembered that a crown was, and until the end of 1974 will remain, the Sheffield town mark).[7] Sebastian Henry Garrard died in 1946. His younger brother, James Robert Lindsay, who was born, also at 13 St. George's Road, on 12 June 1871, became Free by Patrimony on 5 July 1892, was elected to the Livery in 1897, and died on 11 July 1935.

In 1889 the Duke of Fife gave his bride, the Princess Royal, as a wedding-present a diamond tiara by Garrards with a row of swinging drops. Four years later the girls of Great Britain presented to Queen Mary, on her marriage to George V, a Garrard diamond and pearl tiara.

As they had done many times before, Garrards made, in 1907, the famous Ascot Cup which was stolen from the Royal Enclosure, and never recovered. By an unfortunate juxtaposition of headlines a daily newspaper announced: 'Mark Twain arrives in England'; 'Ascot Cup stolen.'

As Crown Jewellers and Goldsmiths Garrards were responsible for the plate and regalia at the coronation of Edward VII and Queen Alexandra in August 1902; they carried out a number of modifications to the regalia, and in addition, undertook the preparation of the 'Royal Offerings', or 'Oblations', consisting of ingots of fine gold.

In 1911 Garrards moved from the premises in Panton Street and the Haymarket, which they had occupied since 1735, to a new home at No. 24 Albemarle Street and 17 Grafton Street, a few yards from where Paul Storr had worked nearly a hundred years earlier. At the same time they opened a workshop in Avery Row off Grosvenor Street.

For the coronation of George V on 22 June 1911 the firm were entrusted with the insertion of portions of the famous 'Cullinan' diamond comprising the 530 carat drop-shaped 'Star of Africa' and a 317 carat cushion-shaped stone, into the Sovereign's Sceptre and the Imperial State Crown. The Cullinan was discovered on 25 January 1905 in the Premier Diamond Mine, Pretoria, Transvaal, after whose chairman, Sir Thomas Cullinan, it was named. In its rough state it weighed 3,106 metric carats,

7. But see chapter on Matthew Boulton, p. 82.

or over 1⅓ lb. It is of superb colour and is the largest diamond ever discovered. It was purchased for £150,000 by the Government of the Transvaal, who presented it to Edward VII.

As a present to Queen Mary on this occasion, the 'Marys' of the Empire banded together to give her the insignia of the Most Noble Order of the Garter, comprising garter, star, shoulder-brooch, and badge, or Lesser George, containing a cameo of St. George and the Dragon in carved sardonyx, set with diamonds and rubies, all prepared by Garrards. On 13 July of the same year the firm provided the insignia, designed by Sir Goscombe John, R.A., consisting of chaplet, verge, amethyst ring, sword and clasp, for the investiture of the Prince of Wales at Carnarvon Castle; the gold used was mined in the area of Carnarvon. Later still in 1911 Garrards designed and made the Imperial Crown of India for the Delhi Durbar, containing some 6,000 diamonds, emeralds, rubies and sapphires of unusually fine colour.

In 1937 Garrards were once again involved in refurbishing the jewels and regalia for a coronation, this time for that of George VI.

After the death of Sebastian Henry Garrard in 1946 there were no male members of the family to succeed him in the firm as he and his brother, James Robert Lindsay, produced between them eight daughters but no sons. This brought to an end one hundred and fifty-four years of control by members of the Garrard family. In 1952 the firm was acquired by the Goldsmiths and Silversmiths Company – founded as the 'Goldsmiths' Alliance' by Mr. William Gibson and Mr. (later Sir) John Langman – which became a limited liability company on 27 May 1898. After the acquisition the firm moved to the Goldsmiths and Silversmiths address at 112 Regent Street, the name of Garrards being retained. Mr. Alex Styles, who had joined the Goldsmiths and Silversmiths Company in 1947, became head-designer of Garrard & Co., a position which he still holds today.

Soon after the change of ownership and address, Garrard & Co., as 'Goldsmiths and Crown Jewellers',[8] were once again involved in preparing the Crown Jewels and regalia for a coronation, this time of our present Queen in 1953. Among their more interesting commissions were

8. The Royal Warrant of Appointment is granted not to a firm but to an individual: the present grantee at Garrards is Mr. Eric Hodges; the Crown Jeweller is Mr. W. H. Summers.

a pair of 22 carat gold armills (bracelets) presented to the Queen by the countries of the Commonwealth.

During the post-war period the pattern of patronage has changed from that of private individuals to that of public corporations, companies, universities, and institutions. For them Garrards have produced maces, mayoral badges and chains-of-office, and services of table silver.

Continuing their nineteenth-century tradition of providing sporting trophies, Garrards have made in recent years the Gillette Cricket Cup; the Massey Ferguson Trophy; the Agfa-Gevaert 'Iris' Trophy; the Rugby Union Football Centenary Trophy, and the Greyhound Derby Trophy.

In 1971 the firm made a cup and cover in gilded 'woven' silver – the finial on the cover bearing a modern stylized version of the coat-of-arms of the Worshipful Company of Goldsmiths – designed by Mr. Alex Styles for presentation by Mr. J. W. Isaac (managing director of Garrards from 1949 to 1966) to the Company following his term of office as their Prime Warden in 1968.

To commemorate the silver-wedding in 1972 of the Queen and the Duke of Edinburgh, Garrards produced a limited edition of twenty-five statuettes in the 'Britannia' standard of silver, each some 9 in. tall. Two years later, to mark the centenary of the birth of Sir Winston Churchill, Mr. Alex Styles in collaboration with Sir Winston's nephew, Mr. John Spencer-Churchill, designed a set of sterling silver in a limited edition decorated with gilded Churchillian motifs – fine examples of the silver made today by 'Garrard & Co., Goldsmiths and Crown Jewellers'.

LINE OF DESCENT

Name	Mark	Date of Registration
George Wickes	W I surmounted by *fleur-de-lis*	1722
George Wickes	W enclosed by G	1722
George Wickes	G W surmounted by Prince of Wales feathers	1735
George Wickes	G W surmounted by Prince of Wales feathers	1739
Edward Wakelin	E W surmounted by Prince of Wales feathers	1747
John Parker and Edward Wakelin	I P E W surmounted by Prince of Wales feathers	?
John Wakelin and William Taylor	I W W T surmounted by Prince of Wales feathers	1776
John Wakelin and William Taylor	I W W T crowned	1777

Name	Mark	Date of Registration
John Wakelin and Robert Garrard	I W R G	1792
Robert Garrard	R G in script	1802
Robert Garrard	R G in script	1818
Robert Garrard	R G in script crowned	1822
Robert Garrard	R G in script crowned.	1847
James Garrard	I G in script crowned	1881
Sebastian Garrard	S G in script crowned	1900
Sebastian Garrard	S G in script	1901

GARRARD PEDIGREE

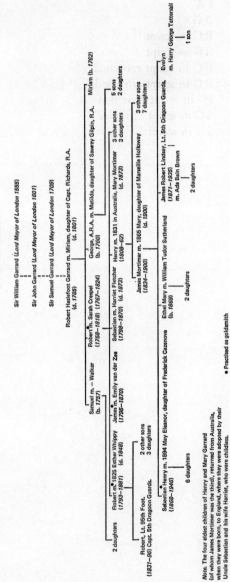

Sir William Garrard (*Lord Mayor of London 1555*)

Sir John Garrard (*Lord Mayor of London 1601*)

Sir Samuel Garrard (*Lord Mayor of London 1709*)

Robert Haslefoot Garrard m. Miriam, daughter of Capt. Richards, R.A.
(d. 1765)   (d. 1801)

Samuel m. — Walker   Robert ● m. Sarah Crespel   George, A.R.A. m. Matilda, daughter of Sawrey Gilpin, R.A.   Miriam (b. 1762)
(b. 1757)   (1758–1818) (1767–1824)   (b. 1760)

Robert m. 1825 Esther Whippy   James ● m. Emily van der Zee   Sebastian m. Harriet Fletcher   Henry m. 1831 in Australia, Mary Mortimer   3 other sons   5 sons
(1793–1881)   (d. 1848)   (1795–1870)   (1798–1870) (d. 1873)   (1808–62)   (d. 1873)   3 daughters   2 daughters

2 daughters   2 other sons
               3 daughters

Robert, Lt. 95th Foot.   Sebastian Henry m. 1894 May Eleanor, daughter of Frederick Cazenove   James Mortimer m. 1865 Mary, daughter of Marseille Holloway   3 other sons
(1831–96) Capt. 5th Dragoon Guards,   (1868–1946)   (1834–1900)   (d. 1900)   7 daughters

6 daughters   Ethel Mary m. William Tudor Sutherland   James Robert Lindsay, Lt. 5th Dragoon Guards,   Evelyn
               (b. 1869)   (1871–1935)   m. Harry George Tattersall
                                                         m. Ada Bain Brown
               2 daughters   2 daughters   1 son

● Practised as goldsmith

Note. The four eldest children of Henry and Mary Garrard
(of whom James Mortimer was the third), returned from Australia,
when they were born, to England, where they were adopted by their
Uncle Sebastian and his wife Harriet, who were childless.

The Hennell Family

THE books of Apprenticeship and Freedom of the Worshipful Company of Goldsmiths in the City of London contain the names of no fewer than twenty-two members of the Hennell family between 1735 and 1956; it is thus hardly surprising to learn that the Hennells are probably the largest single family ever recorded at Goldsmiths' Hall.

The family tree begins with one Robert Hanwell or Hennell (seven or eight variations of the spelling of the family name occur in Buckinghamshire, and several more in the City of London), a framework knitter of Newport Pagnell, Buckinghamshire, where he founded a drapery business which was later transferred to Kettering. According to Bull's *History of Newport Pagnell* (1900) Robert, having previously acted as a lay preacher, became pastor of the Newport Pagnell reformed church in 1707; he appears to have been the first member of the family to settle in Newport Pagnell, as there are no entries for Hanwell (or Hennell) in the church registers prior to the birth of his children. The family were ardent Baptists and a member of a later generation, the Revd. David Hennell, was a co-founder, with William Wilberforce (1759–1833), of the Sierra Leone Company, formed in 1791 to assist in the repatriation and resettlement of freed slaves.

The birth of Robert's second child, David (1712–85) (the first was a daughter), appears in the register of Newport Pagnell church on 8 December. In November 1728, at the age of sixteen, David was sent to London and apprenticed to Edward Wood, a salt-maker in Gutter Lane next to Goldsmiths' Hall; he received his Freedom on 4 December 1735, and registered his first maker's mark (No. 1) at Goldsmiths' Hall on 23 June of the following year, at the same time moving into premises almost next door to the Hall under the sign of the 'Flower de Lis and Star'. Although the *fleur-de-lis* was a sign usually adopted by immigrant Huguenots, it is certain that the Hennells are not of Huguenot origin. David may well have acquired his workrooms from a Huguenot, in which case he would doubtless have adopted for himself the previous owner's sign. It was here that he made his earliest recorded pieces of silver; an interesting and unusual wine-taster dated 1736, weighing 3·7 oz. and contemporarily engraved 'Robert Cooper Cannon Street, 1737'; and a severely plain but classically elegant pair of cast octagonal oblong trencher-salts, each with a shallow well and moulded base, made in the same year; he was to repeat this form as late as 1749. David, like Edward Wood, his master, appears to have specialized as a 'salt-maker'; in 1737 he produced a set of four circular gadrooned salts, the knees decorated with lions' masks, which are almost identical to some produced by Paul De Lamerie; possibly both Hennell and De Lamerie used the same mould. In 1761 he made a pair of circular salts the knees of which are, most unusually, formed of cast and chased Chinese men's heads wearing cabbage-leaf hats.

On 4 April 1737 David's young half-brother, William, was apprenticed to him for the usual period of seven years; although William never registered a mark of his own, he probably remained with David for some time after the expiration of his articles of apprenticeship; he became Free by Service on 12 June 1745.

In spite of the fact that goldsmiths often made use of new marks for some time before entering them at Goldsmiths' Hall, there is no evidence to show that David registered another mark (as after 1739 he was legally obliged to do) until he and his son Robert II registered a joint mark (No. 4) after the latter had completed his apprenticeship with his father in 1763. However, the initials DH in Gothic lettering surmounted by a *fleur-de-lis*, appear on a number of salts in the 1740s; this mark is similar (except, of course, for the different letters) to the mark registered by David's late master, Edward Wood, in 1740. Now in 1735 Wood, then working in Cary (or Carey) Lane, had registered a mark consisting of a circle enclosing a Roman EW surmounted by a star with a *fleur-de-lis* beneath; since David's trade-card tells us that he worked 'in Gutter Lane, ye corner of Cary Lane, near Cheapside', it seems likely that David worked from the same address and adopted the same sign as Wood. This, coupled with the similarity in design and workmanship between salts made by master and former pupil, makes it almost certain that the pre-1740 mark

(No. 2) belongs to David. A variation of David's first mark with a pellet between the initials appears after 1740 (No. 3), but was also never entered at Goldsmiths' Hall.

In common with most other families, of whatever social class, David's children suffered from the appalling infant mortality rate prevalent at the time: of his fifteen children only five reached maturity, and nine died before reaching their third birthday; no fewer than four sons were christened David, but it was not until the tenth child had been born that a boy lived long enough to survive his father.

The eldest son, John (1739–1809), became a Freeman of the Goldsmiths' Company by Patrimony (the legitimate sons of a Freeman could receive the Freedom of their father's Company without serving any apprenticeship) on 3 June 1772, but instead of entering the trade he went into his grandfather's drapery business in Newport Pagnell. The fifth child, Robert II (1741–1811), became apprenticed to his father on 4 April 1756 and on 9 June 1763, the day after receiving his Freedom, father and son registered a joint mark (No. 4, which was re-registered on 9 July 1768);

later in the same month David was elected to the Livery of the Worshipful Company of Goldsmiths. Father and son continued to work together (now in Foster Lane close to where Anthony Nelme owned a shop from 1691) for a number of years, still mostly making salts: in 1771 they supplied two dozen circular salts, with gadroon borders and standing on three feet decorated with shells, to Goldsmiths' Hall; a further dozen were added by Robert's son Samuel in 1811.

At some date between 1770 and 1773 David retired from business; in the latter year, when he was Deputy or 'Touch' Warden in charge of Assay Office business, he was one of the signatories of a petition presented to Parliament by the 'Goldsmiths, Silversmiths and Plateworkers of the City of London', against the establishment of Assay Offices at Birmingham and Sheffield; he died in 1785.

On 9 October 1773 Robert II, describing himself as a 'Salt Maker of 16 Foster Lane' registered his own mark (No. 5). During the 1770s he produced large numbers of oval salts in the 'Adam' taste, some decorated with swags depending from ribbon-ties, others finely pierced with a pattern of perching birds, to show off their blue-glass liners. Although calling himself a 'salt-maker' Robert soon began to extend his range of products to include wine-coasters, and later tea-pots, sauce-boats, cake-, sugar- and sweetmeat-baskets, cream-pails, mustard-pots, epergnes and other pieces of domestic and decorative plate in the neo-classic design associated with this period, and with the names of its chief exponents in England, the brothers Adam.

A fine example of 'Adam' silver by Robert is a 14 in. high coffee-urn of 1788, standing on an octagonal base resting on three ball feet. The body of the urn, which is finely engraved with swags and foliage, has a band of guilloche decoration above the spigot and as a frieze around the rim; on top of the cover is an urn-shaped finial. Two especially fine epergnes were made by Robert in 1780 and 1786, the former now owned by Eton College.

An interesting item made by Robert in 1782 is a glass-lined cream-pail of cylindrical openwork design with beaded borders, embossed and chased with a rustic landscape consisting of a windmill with a bridge leading over a stream to a house; a dovecote; a grazing cow, and a stork flying overhead, all surrounded by trees in full foliage. The design and decoration of this piece are reminiscent of the work of Charles Chesterman, a contemporary of Robert Hennell, who specialized in such ornamentation. From 1752 to 1766 Chesterman was working in Carey Lane, just around the corner from Hennell in Foster Lane. Robert is today undoubtedly the most famous of the Hennell family of goldsmiths, and is indeed one of the finest craftsmen of the eighteenth century, whose work is currently much sought-after in the sale-rooms.

On 8 April 1778 Robert's brother John, now a successful and prosperous draper in Newport Pagnell, apprenticed his son, also called Robert (III) (1763–1832), to the boy's uncle in Foster Lane; unusually, two days later Robert III also signed articles of indenture to a silver-engraver, John Houle; both apprenticeships, presumably by mutual arrangement, were to run concurrently. It was normal practice for a goldsmith to send his plate away to be engraved by an 'outworking' engraver; this John doubtless hoped to enable his son to avoid by having him trained for a dual role.

On 7 June 1780 Robert III's younger brother, William, also became apprenticed to his uncle, being turned over on the same day to David Cooper of Holywell Street, Strand, a 'Mercer, Citizen and Tallow Chandler'.

On 6 February 1782 Robert II's son, David II (1767–1829), became apprenticed to his father in Foster Lane, and was followed on 5 April 1786 by his younger brother Robert IV (1773–1832), and in 1800 by the youngest, Samuel (1778–1837), who did not, however, serve out his apprenticeship but became Free by Patrimony on 2 December of that year. After receiving their Freedoms (David on 5 August 1789), Robert II's three sons continued to work with their father in Foster Lane, while his nephew Robert III left to start in business on his own. Thus the family of Hennell became divided into two separate lines, both of whom were directly descended from Robert and David of Newport Pagnell; we shall consider these two lines separately.

After completing his apprenticeships on 1 June 1785, to his uncle as gold-smith and to John Houle as engraver (the receipt for the balance of £30 paid as premium to Houle by John Hennell for 1783 to 1785 is still extant), Robert III left Foster Lane and moved into his own premises in Windmill Court, near Smithfield Market. As he did not register a mark at Gold-smiths' Hall during the following twenty-three years, it seems likely that he worked solely as an engraver; this supposition is confirmed by the fact that in 1799 (when he was working in Noble Street) one Henry Kinder became apprenticed to him as a 'silver-engraver'. On 17 June 1808 Robert III at last entered his first (joint) mark as a manufacturing goldsmith (No. 9), with Henry Nutting (Free 6 January 1790), giving as his address '38 Noble Street'. The partnership did not, however, endure and in 1809 we find that Robert moved to 35 Noble Street, from where he registered his first (individual) mark (No. 10) on 3 November. It was at this address that in 1814 Robert III received a commission for three dozen soup-plates from the Crown Goldsmiths, Rundell, Bridge & Rundell (of which Paul Storr was at the time a partner) as part of the ambassadorial service presented to the Duke of Wellington on his appointment to the Court of Louis XIV. In 1817 Robert moved from 35 Noble Street to the Strand where, on 11 August 1820, he registered a new mark (No. 13). An interesting item punched with this new mark (although bearing the hall-mark of 1819–20) is the coffin-plate, measuring 12 in. by 9½ in., of George III: the inscription on which reads as follows:

DEPOSITUM
SERENISSIMI POTENTISSIMI ET EXCELLENTISSIMI
MONARCHAE
GEORGII TERTII

DEI GRATIA BRITANNIARUM REGIS
FIDEI DEFENSORIS,
REGIS HANOVERAE AC BRUNSVICI ET LUNEBURGI DUCIS
OBIIT XXIX DIE JANUARII
ANNO DOMINI MDCCCXX,
AETATIS SUAE LXXXII,
REGNIQUE SUI LX.

As the plate states that 'Gilbert Goldsmith to His Majesty fecit', it seems probable that Gilbert, having designed the plate himself, sub-contracted the engraving to Robert, in view of the latter's training and reputation in this branch of the trade.

Since Wellington was the last ambassador to be permitted to keep his presentation service after retirement, a new set had to be commissioned for his successor, Lord Granville, in 1824: this task was entrusted to Robert Hennell, who produced a complete service comprising eight wine-buckets, four soup-tureens, a quantity of table-silver, a fine circular charger with a heavy cast border and engraved with a decorative cartouche surrounding the Royal arms, and a set of Communion plate, much of which is still in use today in the British Embassy in Paris.

On 23 January 1826 Robert entered a new mark (No. 14), and two years later moved to 14 Northumberland Street off the Strand: here he remained until his retirement on 25 May 1833, announced in the 4 June edition of the *London Gazette* as follows:

Take notice, the Partnership between Robert Hennell, sen. and Robert Hennell, Jun. [V: 1794–1868] Silversmiths, carried on at No. 14 Northumberland-Street, Strand, under the firm of Robert Hennell and Son, has been dissolved; and the business will in future be carried on by the said Robert Hennell, jun. alone; Robert Hennell, sen. retired.

Robert V, who adopted his father's mark, obtained his Freedom by Patrimony in the year following his father's retirement, and registered his own mark (No. 15; in three sizes) on 30 June of that year (1834).

In 1842 the Design Registry was established, and among the earliest firms to take advantage of it were Hennells. A number of their designs are stamped with the Registry mark, the discrepancies between the date of the mark and that of the hallmark indicating that the same designs were often used for several years in succession.

In 1849 Robert V's elder son, Robert VI (1826–92), who had been apprenticed to his father, became Free by Service. In the following year Robert V made an interesting and unusual piece of plate which is now in the collection of the Worshipful Company of Goldsmiths: this is a silver ortolan- or wheatear-basket made in simulated woven wicker-work with ropework borders, and a twisted 'wicker' swing handle divided at the top by a coronet. The basket, 9¼ in. long, contains eleven small oval 'nests' chased with ears of wheat, designed to hold an ortolan or wheatear, a small bird of respectively the bunting and thrush family, much esteemed as delicacies in the nineteenth century.

After the death of Robert V in 1868 his son, Robert VI, registered his mark (No. 17) on New Year's Day 1869, re-registering it on 2 February 1870 (No. 18). In January 1973 an unusual lemonade-jug, entwined with a writhing Chinese dragon, made by him in 1875, was sold at Sotheby's for £420. Robert VI must have been an interesting and entertaining man, and a number of the amusing entries in the diary which he was in the habit of keeping shed a fascinating light on some of the fashions of his trade. He relates how, in the absence of cosmetic surgery, his products included silver noses for enamelling. In addition, 'we once had an order for a tankard into which were introduced the diseased bones of a favourite horse, with the leg bone forming the handle, whilst a very decayed portion formed the button, and another piece made the ornament in front'. In his journal Robert also described his extensive travels in Europe, which he illustrated with fine pen-and-ink drawings.

Robert VI's younger brother, James Barclay (1828–99) was apprenticed to his father on 1 February 1843, became Free by Service on 6 February 1850, was elected to the Livery of the Goldsmiths' Company on 29 April 1859, but did not register his mark (No. 19) until 27 February 1877; after his death in 1899, this branch of the family finally left the trade.

It is now time to turn our attention to the Hennells of Foster Lane, from whom are descended the firm which still today bears their name.

For a period of between sixteen and twenty years after entering his first mark in 1773 (No. 5), Robert II, working alone, produced a quantity of fine silver upon which his reputation today is based. During this time he made a very considerable quantity of plate for Wakelin & Taylor (now Garrards) whose ledgers, now in the Victoria and Albert Museum, detail the quantity of silver issued to three generations of Hennells between

1766 and 1773, and 1797 and 1803, and include a complete inventory of what they fashioned from it, and how much they were paid. An entry in the ledgers on 18 July 1767 for 'David Hennell & Son' reads:

By 2 chaised salts & spoons to match 5 oz. 8 dwts.	...	...	16s.	0d.
By doing up 4 salts and spoons as new ...	...	...	4s.	0d.
By 8 glasses	...	3s.	4d.

Between 29 October 1766 and 3 October 1767 Hennells received from Wakelin & Taylor 230 oz. of silver, from which they fashioned fifty-three salts and some other small pieces; they also supplied 111 white or blue glass liners: for this the firm received a total of £33. 9s. 1d.

Most of the items supplied by Hennells to Wakelin & Taylor were salts: some exceptions, dating from 1797, were 'Roman, fluted, waved, bulged, Wedgwood and engraved tea-pots'. Some of Robert's straight-sided tea-pots, which with their rather severe lines appear disarmingly modern to our eyes, display both his originality of design and also his realization that purity of form is more important than ornamentation: a typical example is a fluted oval tea-pot, one of the finest of its form recorded, engraved with fringed swags and tassels, which he made in 1788. Such pieces as these, and his early essays into the neo-classic style introduced into this country by the Adam brothers, ensure him his place of honour among English goldsmiths of the eighteenth century.

After his nephew Robert III had completed his apprenticeship, Robert II was left with his three sons, David II, Robert IV and Samuel to help him carry on the family business in Foster Lane. In 1795 Robert took his eldest son into partnership, and a joint mark (No. 6) was registered on 15 July. Later in the same year father and son produced a magnificent set of two dozen silver-gilt dessert-plates bearing the arms of George III; these plates, now in the Royal collection at Windsor Castle, are also engraved with the arms of Queen Elizabeth II as Princess Elizabeth, Duchess of Edinburgh. In 1799 Robert and David made a fine barrel-shaped coffee-pot with reeded edges, domed cover and urn finial and tapering swan neck, and lamp and stand *en suite*, for Nelson, engraved with his coat-of-arms, to which the viscount's coronet was added after Nelson's elevation in 1801: this piece is now in the collection of the National Maritime Museum at Greenwich. Other items of silver made by Robert and David for Nelson include four boat-salts (1797), a barrel-shaped tea-pot (1799), and a pair of wine-coasters (1800). Robert's and

David's mark is also found on a number of tea-caddies and pierced coasters and salts which were much in demand towards the end of the eighteenth and in the early nineteenth centuries.

Whether David's young brother, Robert IV, ever completed his apprenticeship is unknown; what is certain, from the handwritten signatures in the registers at Goldsmiths' Hall, is that he never entered his mark, either individually or jointly with one of his brothers, nor took over that of his father. As we have already seen, the youngest brother, Samuel, became Free by Patrimony in 1800, and on 5 January 1802 the mark (No. 7) of Robert II, David and Samuel was entered by the father and his two sons. Most unusual pieces bearing this joint mark are a pair of coffee-cups and saucers and a pair of tea-cups and saucers, with plain everted rims and moulded feet, the cylindrical cups with scrolling foliate handles. They bear the cypher and name of the Rajah of Coorg State, Pakistan, for whom they were almost certainly made as a special commission. For some unknown reason this partnership appears to have lasted only a little over nine months, as on 20 October Robert and Samuel together registered a new mark (No. 8). As mark No. 6 is found only up until 1804, it must be presumed that at about that time, when he was aged only thirty-seven, David, for some reason unknown, retired from business, although he remained a member of the Livery of the Worshipful Company of Goldsmiths from his election on 18 February 1791 until he resigned on 4 December thirty years later.

Together with John Emes and Henry Chawner, and Duncan Urquhart and Napthali Hart, Robert II and Samuel were largely responsible for the introduction of the new fashion of matching services of tea-pot (sometimes with kettle *en suite*), coffee-pot (sometimes with spirit-lamp below), cream-jug and sugar-basin: at first round or oval high-fronted tea-pots were among their most typical designs; these later gave way to larger, squat, square-shaped tea and coffee services, and later still to semi-gadrooned and mandarin-topped hot-water jugs which exemplified the increasing Oriental taste of the Regency. In 1818 Samuel made a magnificent silver-gilt tea and coffee service (now owned by the Londonderry Trust, on loan to the Brighton Pavilion) for the Marquess of Londonderry, totalling altogether ten pieces, consisting of a tea-kettle, burner and stand, two tea-pots, one coffee-pot, a cream-jug, a sugar bowl, a toast-rack and a set of four egg-cups and stands. The shaped pieces are elaborately chased and embossed with flowers, scrollwork and cartouches, with busts of Chinese men as finials, and have cast handles and spouts.

The egg-frame and toast-rack have open shaped rectangular bases with console and paw feet.

In 1823 Samuel made, also for Lord Londonderry, the Durham Race Cup for that year, in the form of a silver-gilt campana-shaped cup and cover, the body chased with a pair of galloping horses within an applied oak-leaf wreath, with acanthus and satyr-mask handles: the stepped domed cover is topped by a flower finial.

In 1811, at the age of seventy, Robert II died; although the joint mark (No. 8) of Robert and Samuel was in use up to the time of the former's death, the style of silver produced afterwards by Samuel alone is indistinguishable from that bearing the mark of father and son. Taking into consideration Robert's earlier designs, it seems likely that he had retired from active work some years previously, and may have permitted his son to continue using his initials only in order that the latter might reap some advantage from his father's reputation. In addition, Robert II doubtless still held a controlling interest in the firm of 'Hennell & Co.', which had been formed in about 1810.

On 22 June 1811 Samuel registered his own individual mark (No. 11, within a deeply indented punch; this mark is sometimes confused with that of Solomon Hougham, a plain SH), and on 6 April 1814 a joint mark (No. 12) with John Terry, who in the previous year had married one of his nieces. A 10 in. silver-mounted tipstaff (Water Bailiff's Staff of Office) made in 1814 by Samuel and Terry although bearing the mark of Robert and Samuel, and inscribed 'HENNELL & Co. FOSTER LANE LONDON', is in the collection of the Worshipful Company of Goldsmiths, to whom it was presented in 1885 by William Ernest Brymer, M.P. The handle is formed of a steel flint-lock pistol; the large silver crown finial is supported by four arches and is designed as a mace; within the pistol is a silver oar for attaching to the top of the crown, around whose bowl are engraved the arms of the City of London, with a crowned rose, thistle and shamrock between; the steel barrel is finely engraved with trophies and wheat-ears.

Whether the partnership between Samuel and Terry was of long duration is uncertain, but Samuel's subsequent changes of address in 1816 (twice), 1817 and 1818 are all recorded under his own individual mark. Samuel's eldest son, Samuel II, did not serve any apprenticeship either to his father or to any other goldsmith; his second son, Robert George, who was born between July 1800 and November 1803 and died in 1884, set himself up in business as a goldsmith and jeweller in 1835 in the fashionable residential neighbourhood of Southampton Street (now Place) on the Duke of Bedford's estate in Holborn.

For the next one hundred and thirty years this side of the family was to concentrate on the production of fine jewellery. In 1860 the second Duke of Wellington commissioned from Robert George a necklace consisting of no fewer than six hundred and sixty matched pearls. In 1901 Walter Lonsdale designed for Hennells a splendidly impressive 18 carat gold and enamel Mayoral Chain and Badge of Office for the Borough of Holborn: it comprises twenty-four links, eight of which contain enamelled emblems relating to the Borough, the parishes of Sts. Giles, George, Andrew, and George the Martyr, Lincoln's and Gray's Inns, and the arms of the donor, the Duke of Bedford, first Mayor of Holborn. The central figure of the badge, whose design is based – in the early Renaissance style – on the Holborn Borough Seal, is a standing figure of St. George, with a figure of St. Giles on his right hand and St. Andrew on his left. Above is a representation of the old houses of the Borough, with the Holbourne issuing from a central arch. This piece is now in the possession of the London Borough of Camden.

Although he never entered a mark at Goldsmiths' Hall, two Communion cups bearing the mark (No. 16) of Robert George and the date-letter for 1844-5 are in the church of St. George, Bloomsbury; after Robert George's death in 1884 the business was continued under the name 'R. G. Hennell & Sons' at No. 4 Southampton Place by his two sons, Edward and Montague (1849-1905).

Between 1808 and 1915 the names of a number of Hennells appear in the registers at Goldsmiths' Hall, but none ever entered the business. On 15 May 1956 Percy Garnett Hennell, who was appointed a Director of Hennell Ltd. (as the firm is now known) in 1966, became Free by Redemption on payment of the required 'fine and fees' to the Goldsmiths' Company, being admitted a Freeman of the City of London on 21 June of the same year. He was born in 1911, the great-great-grandson of Charles (1792-1843), elder brother of Robert III, and is thus the six-greats grandson of Robert Hennell I of Newport Pagnell. It is interesting to note that this descendant of John Hennell of Newport Pagnell is now a member of the firm founded by the other branch of the family in Foster Lane.

Hennell's Stock Books, which are still in use today, date back to 1887: they contain numerous coloured drawings by A. W. Tutt, who was manager for many years until his death in 1947. In 1928 C. L. Bruno, at one time a teacher at the Central School of Arts and Crafts, was appointed chief designer of both jewellery and silver at Hennells. Until his death in 1955 he provided the inspiration from which stems the beauty of much of the firm's present-day silver and jewellery.

In 1966 Hennell Ltd. merged with Frazer & Haws Ltd. (founded in 1868 by an ex-employee of Garrards), and in the following year moved from No. 4 Southampton Place (where they had carried on business since 1835) to a more fashionable address, No. 1 Davies Street, Berkeley Square, from where, on 2 January, they entered a new mark, H over FH separated by a pellet (No. 20). In 1968 the firm of E. Lloyd Lawrence, which had been founded in 1830, was incorporated with Hennell Ltd. Two years later a new tradition was established when the name of Hennell was conjoined with that of Anthony Elson, the fine young goldsmith and designer, to produce the first maker's mark incorporating the names of two separate entities, Hennell Ltd., goldsmiths, and Anthony Elson, designer and manufacturer. The new mark (No. 21), consisting of the initials H over AE separated by a mullet, was not, however, registered at Goldsmiths' Hall. It was succeeded by mark No. 22, H over AE divided by a mullet contained within a *fleur-de-lis* shaped shield, which was entered at Goldsmiths' Hall on 23 June 1971, the 235th anniversary of the registration of David Hennell's mark (No. 1) in 1736. A typical example of Hennell–Elson silver is a set of three light-cast three-branched candelabra, designed, made and assayed in 1971; the tapered stems are delicately fluted, and the hexagonal bases and drip-pans have borders of ribbed ornamentation, which is characteristic of much Hennell–Elson silver.

Mark No. 23, H over FH divided by a mullet within a *fleur-de-lis* shaped shield (for Hennell Ltd. and Frazer & Haws Ltd.) was entered on 24 November 1972.

From 29 March to 29 April 1973 an exhibition was held at the Victoria and Albert Museum, London, of silver and jewellery made by the Hennell family.

The exhibition was in three parts: the first included representative examples of work by the original firm founded by David Hennell in 1736, and of his various successors up to 1882; the second comprised modern silver produced by or for the present firm of Hennell Ltd. between 1952 and 1972; the third was devoted to jewellery dating from 1869 to 1972; pattern- and stock-books and similarly related material were also on view.

Many of the exhibits from the first part (which included thirty-two salts made between 1736 and 1804) have already been described, e.g. the cream-pail made in 1782; the fluted tea-pot of 1788; and the two epergnes of 1780 and 1786 – all by Robert II; Nelson's coffee-pot of 1799 and the Rajah of Coorg's tea- and coffee-cups made by Robert and David in 1801; the tipstaff made by Samuel Hennell and John Terry in 1814; Lord Londonderry's tea-service of 1818 and the Durham Race Cup of 1823, by Samuel; and Robert V's delightful little wheatear-basket made in 1850.

Among other pieces on view made in the first hundred and fifty years of the firm's existence, a silver-gilt rectangular inkstand (1820), heavily encrusted with cast and chased floral decoration, is of particular interest, as its original box bears the label of 'Storr & Mortimer', who, as retailers, ordered the inkstand from Hennells.

The Victoria and Albert Museum lent a charming little silver-gilt travelling Communion set (1823) consisting of chalice, paten and gilt-mounted wine-flask; the chalice is embossed with a calyx of palmettes, and has a foliate knop and a fluted base; the paten, standing on a spreading fluted foot, has a flat-chased frieze and a gadroon border. Another piece of ecclesiastical plate on view was a chalice with a cast bell-shaped bowl with a gilt interior, standing on an embossed (seventeenth-century style) domed foot, from which rises a baluster stem: the bowl and base are decorated with a winding pattern of passion-flowers; in the year that it was made (1830) it was presented to the Chapel of Westminster, and was lent for the exhibition by Westminster Cathedral.

From Temple Newsam House, Leeds, came a shaped hexagonal salver with a gadroon and shell border, standing on three cast and chased scrolling shell feet (1822); and a chamber candlestick of scalloped form with a moulded border, an open scrolling handle, and a conical snuffer (1836).

A silver-gilt circular salver of 1837 with openwork vine frieze and reeded edge, standing on a trumpet foot decorated with an applied acanthus border, is of particular interest, as the design is very similar to that used by craftsmen such as Paul Storr working during the Regency for Rundell, Bridge & Rundell.[1]

1. Cf. the fruit-bowls made in 1810–11 by Storr for the Duke of Wellington (see pp. 104–5).

The City Art Gallery, Bristol, lent a tea-pot of 1838, the body embossed and chased with flowers and fruit within six panels, one containing a wreath enclosing the engraved reversed monogram of Prince Albert. From the Corporation of London came a large typically Victorian ornate parcel-gilt cup and cover of 1868. The Board of Faculty of Dental Surgery, Royal College of Surgeons, lent the 'Saunders Vase' (1870), of amphora form with gadroon border and engraved key-pattern and scrolling decoration; the gilt interior contains a gilt cylinder (1875) which encloses an illuminated scroll.

Finally, from this part of the exhibition, which contained over a hundred items, many of them from private collections, were a number of pieces made in the Victorian 'naturalistic' style by Robert V and his sons, Robert VI and James Barclay. An inkstand of 1845 by Robert V (lent by the Victoria and Albert Museum) is in the shape of a leaf with a twig handle, bearing two ink-pots cast as a pomegranate and an apple, and a bell in the shape of a pear, each on leaf trays; in the middle is a taperstick (with a snuffer) shaped as a tree-stump, with two branches forming a pen-stand. Pieces in this style by Robert VI included a pair of pepper-pots cast and chased as jesters (1868); a 'Punch' mustard-pot, and a 'Judy' ink-pot (1871); and a salt-stand of 1876 cast and chased as a walking bear supporting two panniers with gilt interiors, and a candle-holder, with a seated monkey between. By James Barclay were a pair of pepper-pots (1880) with gilt interiors in the form of children's heads, each wearing a frilled collar, one crying and one laughing; a cast and chased 'begging cat' ink-pot (1879); and a peperette cast and chased as a cat with a lyre (1881).

The second part of the exhibition – that devoted to modern silver – included three examples designed by C. L. Bruno: the earliest of these was a fluted cylindrical water-jug made in 1952, with an everted and scalloped lip and a ribbed and scrolling handle, standing on a lobed and matted base: the jug is engraved with the arms of the University of London and was made for presentation by Sir George Barstow, K.C.B., a Member of the Court from 1931 to 1952. A circular bowl and cover made in 1953 has an everted and scalloped border and a faceted tent-shaped cover; it stands on a low collet foot. A christening-cup and cover made in 1955 has a tall conical body, fluted around the base, which rises from a domed and faceted tent-shaped foot with an annular knopped stem; the handles are formed of cast and chased lions.

In 1967 the Duke of Westminster commissioned from Hennells, for presentation to the Royal Yacht Squadron, the 'Chichester Award'; designed and made by Stuart Devlin in the form of a representation of a plain sail emerging from a tempestuous sea, it symbolizes man's fortitude and solitude in his conflict with the elements. It was made to commemorate the circumnavigation of the globe by Sir Francis Chichester, and is awarded to any British citizen who achieves an outstanding feat of solo navigation. In 1973 the trophy was presented to Commander W. D. King in recognition of his single-handed circumnavigation of the world in his yacht *Galway Blazer*.

A pair of silver-gilt candlesticks, their cylindrical stems embossed and chased with a lozenge pattern, designed and made by Anthony Elson in 1968 and inscribed in memory of Dr. C. A. Alington, Headmaster of Eton from 1917 to 1933, were made for the pulpit of College Chapel.

In 1970 Elson designed a pair of silver and gilt rosewater bowls for presentation by the Grocers' Company to the Saddlers' in gratitude for their hospitality from the time the Grocers' Hall was destroyed by fire in 1966 until it was rebuilt in 1970: each has a high oxidized central boss, representing ashes, mounted with two circlets of gilt and matted 'flames', and bears the arms of the Saddlers' Company; when the bowls are filled with water the 'flames' appear to flicker in the reflection of the polished silver.

In 1971–2 Elson designed and made a table service for presentation to the Council of the Stock Exchange to celebrate the completion of their new building in Threadneedle Street, opened by the Queen in November 1972. Included in the exhibition was a four-light candelabrum, with a fluted column rising from a fluted circular base engraved with the arms of the Stock Exchange; the capitals are cast and chased as a lion passant before a tower, the crest of the Stock Exchange; (one of a set of four): a pair of two-light candelabra, *en suite* with the above: a salt-pourer, pepper-pot and mustard-pot whose design is based on the Stock Exchange crest; (one of a set of ten): an openwork cake-basket: a coffee-pot, cream-jug and sugar-bowl with fluted bases; and a pair of cast and chased silver-gilt decanter labels, one for brandy, one for whisky.

The third section of the exhibition, consisting of jewellery, included two pieces dating from the nineteenth century; a diamond necklace made in

12

1869; and a bangle of 1884 consisting of three diamond flower-heads mounted on a gold bracelet.

The exhibition included the Borough of Holborn Mayoral Chain and Badge, designed by Lonsdale in 1901; and a number of items designed by Bruno between 1925 and 1940, most noteworthy of which was a magnificent diamond tiara of 1935, which can be divided into a necklace, two bracelets, two clips and a brooch. Finally, designed and made in 1972, was a very fine 18 carat gold necklace set with aquamarines and diamonds, with a central detachable emerald-cut aquamarine of some 60 carats – a worthy example of the work currently being produced by Hennell Ltd. of Davies Street.

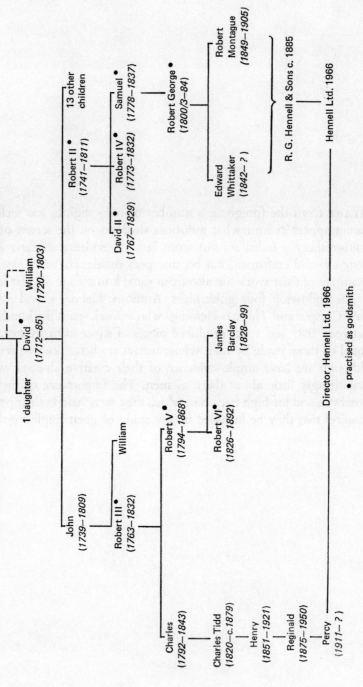

HENNELL PEDIGREE

Robert Hennell of Newport Pagnell, Buckinghamshire. *'framework knitter'*

1 daughter

David
(1712–85) •

William
(1720–1803)

John
(1739–1809)

Robert II •
(1741–1811)

13 other
children

William

Robert III •
(1763–1832)

David II •
(1767–1829)

Robert IV •
(1773–1832)

Samuel •
(1778–1837)

Robert V •
(1794–1868)

Robert George •
(1800/3–84)

Charles
(1792–1843)

Robert VI •
(1826–1892)

James
Barclay
(1828–99)

Edward
Whittaker
(1842– ?)

Robert
Montague
(1849–1905)

Charles Tidd
(1820–c.1879)

R. G. Hennell & Sons c. 1885

Henry
(1851–1921)

Reginald
(1875–1950)

Director, Hennell Ltd. 1966

Hennell Ltd. 1966

Percy
(1911– ?)

• practised as goldsmith

APART from the foregoing a number of only slightly less well-known names appear as somewhat indistinct shadows on the screen of English goldsmithery – indistinct not from lack of evidence of their ability as designers and craftsmen, but because personalities are made not only by examples of their work but also from some knowledge of their lives.

The following four goldsmiths, Anthony Nelme, David Willaume, Paul Crespin and Thomas Heming, whose work spans the hundred years between 1681 and 1782, produced pieces of silver in many instances the equal of those made by men whose names are better known today; yet, although we have ample evidence of their creative abilities, we know tantalizingly little about them as men. The importance of their work, however, and the high esteem in which they were held in their profession, requires that they be included in any study of great English goldsmiths.

Anthony Nelme

(*fl*: 1681 – 1722)

ANTHONY NELME is the best-known native-born English goldsmith working in this country at the time of the arrival of the Huguenot refugees from France.

The son of John Nelme, he was apprenticed on 1 November 1672 to Richard Rowley, later being made over to Isaac Deighton. He became Free of the Goldsmiths' Company on 16 January 1679, was made an Assistant in 1703, Fourth Warden in 1717, and Second Warden in 1722, the year of his death.

One of the earliest extant pieces of silver stamped with Nelme's first presumed mark (a monogram ANE), is a covered cup bearing the date-

letter for 1681; of a type much in vogue during the reign of Charles II some twenty years earlier, it is finely embossed with acanthus leaves around the base and on the finial of the cover, while the handle is decorated with small human heads. According to Fallon this mark was only recorded at Goldsmiths' Hall in 1722 under the name of Anthony's eldest son Francis. Where it is found on silver prior to 1697 (when in April Anthony entered a mark AN) it is presumed to be Anthony's mark

entered but now missing. The design of a set of three casters dated 1683 (now in the Manchester City Art Gallery) also harks back to the 1660s:

so too does that of two pairs of candlesticks (one in the Ashmolean Museum, the other in the Bank of England), which take the form of scantily-clad female figures supporting the branches on their heads. A third pair of candlesticks, dated 1697, are in the form of chained kneeling blackamoors, who support the nozzles above their heads. Made in the same year as the sugar-casters is a fine silver tankard, in the collection of the Honourable Society of the Inner Temple; the top of the lid bears a design of acanthus leaves in cut-card work, and the finial is formed from further acanthus leaves in a 'cabbage' shape; the thumb-piece is modelled as a lion couchant.

In 1685 Nelme was working under the sign of the 'Golden Bottle' in Amen Corner, Ave Maria Lane, in the parish of St. Martin's, Ludgate Hill, in the City of London, where he was to remain for the rest of his life, although in 1691 he acquired a second shop in Foster Lane. By this time it is clear that he had established himself as one of London's leading goldsmiths, as in 1694 he was given an important Royal commission for a pair of large (40 in. tall) silver-gilt altar candlesticks for St. George's Chapel, Windsor Castle. These are without doubt his most important *oeuvre*; the sumptuously balustered stems rise from boldly scrolling, three-footed bases which are decorated with cherubs' heads, the insignia of the Most Noble Order of the Garter (founded by Edward III in 1348), and St. George and the Dragon in relief. The cherub heads are close in style to the work of Grinling Gibbon (1648–1721), who was not only a skilled woodcarver but also a designer of repute.

Nelme was one of the signatories, together with the Royal goldsmiths George and Francis Garthorne, Benjamin Pyne and a number of other leading English-born goldsmiths, to a 'humble petition' presented to the Worshipful Company of Goldsmiths on 11 August 1697, which outlined a number of complaints against the *emigré* Huguenots, whose actions Nelme and his friends considered 'will in all probability lead to the beggary and impoverishment of your petitioners'. This petition complained firstly that some Huguenots used large amounts of solder in their silver (thus falsifying its weight) 'to the detriment of the public and discredit of English workmen in general'; and secondly that a number of Freemen had agreed to have the work of Huguenots assayed or 'touched at the Hall contrary to certain By-laws in the case provided'. In spite of these complaints, which were probably justified, Nelme and his compatriots were not averse to adapting to their own use the French designs of their rivals: an example by Nelme is a wall-sconce of 1704, with a cast back-plate formed as a bracket; the single dignified branch is clearly in the French taste rather than in that of the English baroque. Also of Continental design is a soup-tureen dated 1703, which may be the earliest recorded example of an English-made tureen. Similarly adhering to Huguenot design are a pair of silver 'Pilgrim' wine-bottles made by Nelme in 1715 for the 3rd Earl of Burlington, now owned by the Duke of Devonshire at Chatsworth: they are decorated with cast (rather than embossed) lions' heads, shells and foliage, and lanceolate leaves in cut-card work; a similar but unmarked pair at Windsor Castle weighing 483 oz. are also probably the work of Nelme.

Between 1696 and 1704 Nelme was employed by the Board of Ordnance to supply them with a number of domestic items of silver; among these were a pair of candlesticks and a snuffer-tray, all dated 1696; a hand-bell (1697) (which at one time stood on a standish of 1754 by William Shaw and William Priest on the desk of the Permanent Under-Secretary); and a standish of 1697 with tray, inkwell, sand-caster and bell: in 1972 these pieces were presented by the Army Department of the Ministry of Defence to the National Army Museum. While engaged on this work Nelme secured, after her accession in 1702, the valuable patronage of Queen Anne. He also produced a number of ordinary domestic utensils in silver, e.g. a small brandy saucepan (1695) in the collection of Trinity Hall, Cambridge, and a bread-toaster (1705) of unusual design in Queen's College, Cambridge. A plain tea-kettle, lamp and stand, weighing in all 94 oz. made by Nelme in 1715, sold at Christie's in June 1973 for £4,200; the catalogue described these pieces as follows:

the kettle of pear form and with curved spout, the domed cover with ivory baluster finial and with large ivory and scroll handle above the two-handled stand on three boldly modelled baluster supports and applied between two with an oval cartouche, the central detachable lamp with hinged cap to the cover, each piece engraved with a lozenge-of-arms, the kettle and stand within scalework and shell and foliage surrounds.

Five months later a second tea-kettle, made by Nelme in 1718, was sold in the same auction room for £2,900. Indeed, some of Nelme's simplest creations in the English 'Queen Anne' style are among his most successful works: a square tea-pot of 1708 (one of the few of its shape recorded) with lamp and stand en suite, and an inkstand dated 1717 (in Manchester City Art Gallery), are typical examples of Nelme's work in this taste.

Anthony Nelme had three sons; the eldest, Francis, was apprenticed to his father on 6 March 1711, becoming Free on 9 April 1719; he was elected to the Livery of the Goldsmiths' Company in October 1721; the second son, Younger, was apprenticed to Roger Hudson in 1713; the third son, John, was apprenticed to his father in 1718, becoming Free by Patrimony in 1725.

In 1721 Anthony took Francis into partnership with him; after Anthony's death a year later Francis adopted his father's marks until 19 June 1739, when from Ave Maria Lane he registered his own mark, FN. Francis made use of a number of his father's designs, but is perhaps better known for his more elaborate items, of which a gold cup dated 1731 (enamelled at a later date and now in the Louvre) is a good example. Francis appears to have died shortly after 1759.

David Willaume

(1658–1741)

AMONG Huguenot goldsmiths working in London in the late seventeenth/
early eighteenth centuries was David Willaume – in the opinion of many
the equal as an artist to Paul De Lamerie. The son of Adam Willaume,
he is said to have been born in Metz in Lorraine, although 'the registers of
the church of La Patente in Soho describe him as *marchand orfèvre de la
ville de Mers* – that is to say Mer en Blaisois between Orléans and Blois'.[1]
Willaume appears to have arrived in England at some time between 1674
and 1686, and in order to be able to serve his apprenticeship he took out
letters of Denization in December 1687 at the same time as Jean Harache
(a relation of Pierre) and Daniel Garnier.

According to Heal, Willaume was working under the sign of the
'Windsor Castle' near Charing Cross between 1686 and 1690: in 1693
he married Marie, daughter of Samuel Mettayer, the *curé* of the French
church in Crispin Street, Spitalfields. (Marie's sister, Anne, married the
Huguenot engraver Simon Gribelin.) Louis Mettayer, Samuel's son or
grandson, was later apprenticed to Willaume, and in due course also
became a goldsmith of much repute, producing work of a consistently
high standard between about 1700 and 1720.

On 27 January 1693 Willaume became Free of the Goldsmiths' Company by redemption, being elected to the Livery in 1698 and an assistant in
1724. In 1700 he took on as apprentices Pierre Le Cheaube and Jean Petry
(both presumably of Huguenot extraction), in 1706 his son David Junr.
and in 1708 David Tanqueray, later to become his son-in-law.

From 1697 Willaume carried on business at the sign of the 'Golden
Ball' in St. James's Street, where in addition to acting as a goldsmith he

1. Honour, p. 138.

also engaged in 'running-cashes', i.e. acted as a banker. From St. James's Street, Willaume entered his maker's marks: WI surmounted by two

mullets with a *fleur-de-lis* below in April 1697, which he re-registered in 1718; and D W with mullets and *fleur-de-lis* on 27 July 1720. In the London Assay Office is a copper plate stamped with makers' marks before 1697; at one time strips of parchment giving names and dates hung between each row of stamped marks, but these have long since disappeared. Among these marks is a D W with a pellet over and under, which may well be an earlier mark of David Willaume.

In the matter of style much of Willaume's work was in advance of its time; an example is a two-handled cup bearing the date-letter for 1705, which anticipates the basic design of the 1730s; he also produced a number of highly individualistic pieces of silver: a delicate helmet-ewer with cut-card work and recurved mermaid handle (as also used by Pierre Harache) of 1700 (in the Victoria and Albert Museum), is of a particularly spectacular pattern; and the design of a large tea-pot of 1706 (in the Manchester City Art Gallery), 6⅞ in. high, with three rows of cut-card work on the body is an example of Willaume at his most idiosyncratic.

Among Willaume's more grandiose pieces are a helmet-ewer and basin of 1706, the ewer decorated with cut-card work and beading, the basin having a gadrooned border, which were presented to the Worshipful Company of Fishmongers in 1717; and a large and impressive Queen Anne charger, made in 1711, which was shown by S. J. Phillips Ltd. and Frank Partridge and Sons Ltd. at the 'Fanfare for Europe' exhibition at Christie's in January 1973.

In 1708 Willaume made his two most important pieces of plate, an enormous and impressive wine-cooler and fountain for the 5th Earl of Meath, which were later acquired by George II when Prince of Wales; these especially fine examples of work in the Huguenot taste, with heavily gadrooned borders and splendidly modelled sea-horse handles on the cooler and lions' masks, from which depend ring handles, on the fountain, are now in the collection of the Duke of Brunswick.

In 1721 Willaume produced a nicely proportioned pair of circular *écuelles* (soup bowls or porringers) with gadroon edging, each weighing some 17 oz. and measuring 9½ in. in diameter. The handles are formed of somewhat stylized scallop shells, and the covers each have a bud finial. These bowls, from the Campbell Museum, Camden, New Jersey, were on view at the Victoria and Albert Museum in 1973.

In 1725 Willaume, working in collaboration with Augustine Courtauld, produced a fine toilet set equal in design and workmanship with that produced a year earlier by Paul De Lamerie for George Treby; the design of the cast panels on the pomade pots of both sets are identical, and it therefore seems likely that De Lamerie lent his moulds to Willaume and Courtauld.

Between 1699 and 1727 Willaume carried out a number of commissions for John Hervey, 1st Earl of Bristol, as is shown by the following extracts from the latter's account-book:

1699. Jan 17. Paid David Willaume for the silver borders of 8 glass sconces for the drawing room weighing 231 ounces 13 dwt. £75. 5. od.
Jan. 20. Paid ditto for a pair of the same borders for the chimney weighing 53 ounces 13 dwt. at 6s. 6d. & for a pair of chimney sconces all of silver weighing 90 ounces 3 dwt. at 7 shillings per ounce, in all £47. 6. 0.
Feb. 21. Paid David Willaume for the 8 great silver sconces weighing 491 ounces at 7s. per ounce & for graving etc. in all £175.
1700. July 6. Paid Willaume the French silversmith for 2 pottage & 4 ragout spoons £15. 15. 0.
1727. Apr. 17. Paid David Willaume the silversmith for the case of 12 gilt knives, 12 spoons & 12 forks, weighing 131 ounces at 5s. 8½d. bought at the Duke of Shrewsbury's sale, & for boiling and mending old plate, in all £37. 10. 0.

As the last two entries show, Willaume produced, in addition to his more important commissions, a quantity of simple everyday domestic utensils, such as salvers, trays, waiters and cutlery. He also undertook such commonplace and mundane tasks as engraving, repairing and polishing old plate: a lengthy account (in the archives of Leeds Public Library), dated between 20 August and 11 October 1726, gives details of work of this kind carried out for Lady Irwyn (Irwin) of Temple Newsam, near Leeds (see illustration). It is interesting to note that part of the account (which totalled £70. 6s. 1d.) was settled in kind, by delivering to Willaume 62 oz. of plate for which he allowed Lady Irwyn from 3d. to 6d. an ounce.

As the name of neither Willaume nor any of his family appears on the list of those in receipt of the Royal Bounty, it would seem that he arrived in this country in a rather more prosperous condition than most of his fellow Huguenots: by 1709, at any rate, he had amassed sufficient capital to enable him to purchase a country estate, Tingrith Manor in Bedfordshire, from Sir Pynsent Chernock, Bt., who had run through a fortune by unwisely contesting local elections with the powerful neighbouring Russells of Woburn.

On 6 March 1706 Willaume's son, David Junr., became apprenticed to his father, obtaining his Freedom by Patrimony on 2 May 1723; he was elected a Liveryman in March 1726. In the previous year Willaume Junr. made a set of twelve plain dinner plates which in the second sale of the Plohn collection at Sotheby's in 1971 sold for £13,500; in 1958 they had been purchased for £2,200. On 2 April 1728, when he was working in Hanover Square, he registered two marks, WI and DW, each within an oval punch. In the same year he made a pair of bowls, each 5⅞ in. in diameter and weighing 15 oz., with fluted sides and scalloped rims, standing on a circular moulded base: in November 1973 these bowls sold at Christie's for £4,000. David Junr. accepted at least two apprentices, Aymé Vedeau on 3 May 1723, and William Cripps in 1730. On 19 June 1739 (when in a list of the Court of Assistants and Liveryman of the Worshipful Company of Goldsmiths he gave his address as Tingrith Manor) David Junr. entered a third mark, DW within an indented punch with a pellet over and under.

Willaume Senr. died late in 1740, and his will, drawn up on 13 June 1720, was proved on 22 January 1741 'before the worshipfull John Audley Doctor of Laws . . .'. In it Willaume stated that:

I give to my son in law David Tanquoray [Free 1722; died about 1726, when his business was continued by his widow, Anne] the sum of Twenty pounds and . . . I give to my Daughter Anne Tanquoray his wife the sum of Eighty pounds with the intent following that is to say my Will and desire is and I do so order and direct that the said sum of Eighty pounds which I have given to my said Daughter Anne Tanquoray be paid by my Executor hereafter named into her own hands and for her own separate use . . . to do with as she shall think fitting with which her husband shall not at any time intermeddle neither shall the same be lyable to his fforfoiture. . . . I give to the poor of the parish of Saint Martin's in the ffeilds the sum of ffive pounds to be distributed by my Executor hereafter named in such manner as he shall think fitt and proper. . . . I give to my well beloved son David Willaume whom I likewise constitute make and Ordain the sole Executor of this my last Will and Testament all and Singular my Goods Chattels and Credits. . . .

The witnesses to the will were Wm. Peach, Fran. Pages, and Jn. Wallis.

Paul Crespin

(1694–1770)

THE Crespin family are known to have been established in England by 1687 (when their name appears among the recipients of the Royal Bounty), having fled from France as Huguenot refugees after the Revocation of the Edict of Nantes.

Paul was born in 1694, the son of Daniel Crespin of the parish of St. Giles-in-the-Fields, Westminster. (Miss Barraud suggests that Daniel may have been one of three men of the same name: (i) at Merchant Taylors 1641–2, or (ii) a widower who died in Chelsea in 1743, or (iii) the son of Bernard Crespin and Salome Waidman of Lausanne, naturalized in 1726). Paul was apprenticed on 24 June 1713 to Jean Pons of the Longbow String Makers' Company, whose name appears in 1701 among members of the French church in Castle Street as '*de Fumel Angenois*'.[1] Crespin became Free of the Longbow String Makers' by Redemption on 26 April 1721,[2] and entered his marks, CR and PC, each over a mullet, apparently

between July 1720 and December 1721. (Jackson records Crespin's early mark as being a cursive PC surmounted by two mullets with a *fleur-de-lis* below; he has, however, misread this mark which is in fact IC and is that of Isaac Collard). Crespin, who never became Free of the Goldsmiths' Company, worked under the sign of the 'Golden Ball' on the corner of Old Compton Street and Greek Street in the parish of St. Ann, Soho;

1. Index of Apprenticeship Books of the Society of Genealogists.
2. See Longbow String Makers' Freedom records, now held by the Fletchers' Company.

on 10 February 1728/9 he was granted a sixty-five-year lease on this property by his landlord, the Duke of Portland, who was also one of his principal patrons. On 4 July 1739 Crespin entered a further mark, P C in script within an indented punch; on 7 November 1740 he registered CR in script, also within an indented punch; and on 22 January 1757 P C within an oval punch – all from the same address.

One of the earliest extant pieces, bearing Crespin's mark and the date-letter for 1720, is an extremely fine small octagonal casket: the sides are chased all over in the *Régence* style – the four corner panels with tall vases of flowers set between Corinthian columns; the end panels with male and female busts; the side panels with mythological scenes of Pan playing his pipe, surrounded by animals – all contained within elaborate cartouches with a diapered background, a foretaste of the coming rococo period: the lid bears a coat-of-arms with sea-gods as supporters. Crespin's mark on this casket is overpunched by that of Paul De Lamerie, suggesting that De Lamerie may have submitted it for assaying before Crespin had become fully established. Other early pieces by Crespin are a twin-bottle cruet (1723), which displays fine piercing on the octagonal frame, and a circular dish made in the same year which bears the arms of the 2nd Viscount Howe, suggesting that it was not long before Crespin was a highly-regarded goldsmith in his own right.

On 15 August 1724 *The Weekly Journal or British Gazeteer* carried the following notice: 'Some days ago, Mr. Crispin [*sic*], a silversmith of this city carried the fine silver bathing vessel (made for the King of Portugal [John V]) to His Majesty at Kensington, who was well pleased with so curious a Piece of Workmanship which can scarcely be match'd in all Europe.' This 'curious Silver Vessel for bathing in' weighed about 6,030 oz., but has, incredibly, completely disappeared. Its commission from a Royal Household, however, meant that Crespin was established as a goldsmith of repute.

Two years later, in 1726, Crespin joined with a number of other Huguenot goldsmiths working in London to provide a large set of plate (consisting of 329 items in silver and 36 in gold) to the Empress Catherine of Russia. Crespin's contribution, a large two-handled cup and cover bearing Catherine's cypher and crown, is now in the Hermitage Museum.

In the following year (1727) Crespin made a noble pair of oval soup-tureens (possibly part of an ambassadorial service) with chased and applied strapwork on their bodies, weighing 276 oz. A small ewer (in the Ashmolean Museum) made in the same year shows that in spite of the fact that he had been born and brought up in England, Crespin still felt in sympathy with the Parisian designers; the applied scrollwork moulding under the lip and the flying scroll handle with its bust thumb-piece, are typical examples of the French style of the period.

In 1727 or 1728 Crespin, then aged thirty-three or thirty-four, married Mary Branboeuf, who, as her name suggests, was of French extraction. To them were born five children, of whom only three survived infancy. Their first child, Magdalen Benine, was born on 13 June 1729, and was christened a week later in St. Ann's Church, Soho, where her four brothers and sisters were also baptized. Magdalen married 'Mr. Francis Barraud, Watchmaker', by whom she had three children, the eldest of whom, named Paul Philip after his grandfather, became a celebrated maker of chronometers in Cornhill. (A portrait, painted between about 1720 and 1740, in the possession of the Barraud family in New Zealand since about 1900, depicts a man in a red velvet beret (as was customary indoors when the wig was removed), wearing a shirt open at the neck with his sleeves rolled above the elbow. In his hands he holds an ornate vase, apparently in the French taste and dating from about 1690. This painting is known in the family as the 'Ancestor': family tradition holds that the subject was a goldsmith who made plate for the Emperor [sic] of Russia. Since researches have failed to show any goldsmith other than Crespin among the Barraud ancestors, the portrait may well be that of Paul Crespin.) The Crespin's second child, Lewis Vincent Paul, was born in 1732. Their third child, Elias David, born in 1734, took Holy Orders and eventually became Dean of Guernsey. A son, Paul, was born in 1739. The Crespins' fifth and last child, a daughter, Sarah, was born on the tenth and baptized on 20 February 1743; in 1776 she married an apothecary, John Bacot.

Although none of Paul Crespin's children appear to have followed in their father's footsteps as a goldsmith, one Lewis Crespin was apprenticed to a silversmith, Jean Silberrad (who in 1760 married one Ann Crespin), in 1759. On 13 February 1760 Lewis Crespin married Anne Massey at St. Paul's Church, Covent Garden. A will made between 1795 and 1806 refers to 'Mr. Crespin, Jeweller, of Stephen Street, Rathbone Place'. Crespins are known to have lived in No. 3 Stephen Street between 1776 and 1824; from 1776 to 1795 the ratepayer's name is given as Mary Crespin; from 1795 to 1824 the name appears as Anne Crespin.

In the 1730s and early '40s Crespin proved that, in addition to being a fine craftsman, he was also, so far as design was concerned, a courageous innovator. In 1734 he made a set of candlesticks with a broad octagonal dished base in place of the conventional stepped foot; in the same year he produced a cream-boat with a heavy swag of coral and flowers depending from lions' masks. A bottle-shaped chocolate-pot, dated 1738 and now in the Ashmolean Museum, has a side-handle like that of a saucepan and a long silver-mounted wooden stirrer. A gilt shell-shaped inkstand, made in 1739, in the collection of the Duke of Devonshire at Chatsworth, is covered with coral and sea-shells. The design of a set of four candlesticks, dated 1741, is taken direct from William Kent (1684–1748); their reeded columns rise from foliate scrolls on the bases.

During the 1730s and '40s Crespin produced some of his finest work, and commissions flowed into his workshops from the noblest in the land, among them the Dukes of Portland, Somerset and Devonshire and the Earls of Rockingham and Albemarle.[3] In November 1973 Christies sold for £2,900 a set of twelve shaped circular dinner-plates with gadrooned borders, 9½ in. in diameter and weighing together 207 oz., engraved with the arms of Cavendish impaling Boyle for William, 4th Duke of Devonshire, K.G., who married in 1748 Charlotte, Baroness Clifford, only daughter and heir of Richard, Earl of Burlington: these plates were made by Crespin in 1732 and remained at Chatsworth until 1958. A manuscript 'List of the Plate belonging to the Right Honourable the Lord Viscount Townsend, Made by Paul Crespin' (in the library of the Worshipful Company of Goldsmiths), details 3,650 oz. of plate supplied to Lord Townsend by Crespin: among quantities of dishes and plates with 'guderoone' borders, are a pair of salts 'with 4 Dolphin's feet, chas'd'. 'New plate bot of Paul Crespin, 8 Oct. 1747' appears in the list for that year and 'A new Bread Baskett, Viscs' Arms in a Mantle and Motto, 48 oz. 10 dwt.', on 11 July 1759, the year of Crespin's retirement. Lord Townsend subsequently transferred his patronage to the partnership of Peter Meure and Peter Archambo (one-time apprentice to Paul De Lamerie) who worked under the sign of the 'Golden Cup' in Coventry Street.

In 1740 Crespin made, for the Duke of Somerset, a large and ornate soup-tureen. The shallow oval bowl rests on the backs of a pair of hinds couchant: the lid and base are covered with a profusion of fruits – plums, apples, pears, lemons, oranges, and bunches of grapes; this tureen is given

3. Plate by Crespin at Welbeck Abbey included '181 dinner plates of massive silver; 23 meat dishes; 20 other dishes; 12 butter boats; salts, candlesticks, soup-plates, soup-tureens and other costly things' (E. A. Jones in the *Proceedings of the Huguenot Society*, XVI, 1940, and his catalogue of plate at Welbeck Abbey, seat of the Duke of Portland).

additional interest by the fact that in four separate places Crespin's 'Britannia' mark (a cursive CR re-entered on 7 November 1740) has been overstruck by his old PC mark (re-registered on 4 July 1739); this suggests

that on being 'touched' at the Assay Office this tureen proved to be below the intended 'Britannia' standard. Although the workmanship of this impressive piece (now in the Toledo Museum of Art) is beyond reproach, the incongruity of its component parts produces a somewhat unsatisfactory overall effect.

Possibly as a result of these ducal and other noble commissions Crespin received, in 1741, an order from Frederick, Prince of Wales, for what was to prove his greatest *oeuvre* – a magnificent rococo tureen/centrepiece, weighing some 85 lb. or over 1,000 oz., which is still in the Royal collection at Windsor Castle; in 1965 it was exhibited at the British Antique Dealers' Fair. On the cover of the oval bowl, whose sides are hung with floral swags and masks, sits Neptune with his trident. The whole is supported by a fantasy of dolphins, mermaids, rocks and shells, which rest on a coral base, in the centre of which are the Royal Arms. Charles Oman has suggested that this silver-gilt centrepiece was the work of the Liège-born goldsmith Nicholas Sprimont (1716–71) who lived in the same street (and possibly even in the same house) as Crespin, but who did not enter his mark at Goldsmiths' Hall until 1742. Since the design of the base bears a close relationship to Sprimont's naturalistic *stil rustique*[4] models of crab, whelk, and other shells, coral and insects (which, having founded the Chelsea Porcelain Factory in about 1743, he subsequently employed in that medium), he may well have had a hand in its conception, if not in the execution. Crespin's masterpiece has also been attributed to the hand of Augustine Courtauld; this suggestion is hard to understand in view of Courtauld's known conservatism.

During the last decade or so of his working life Crespin produced a quantity of small domestic items such as salvers, waiters, dishes and cakebaskets, all of superlative design and workmanship. On 22 January 1757 he entered his final mark, PC within an oval punch. In 1759, as we have

4. See chapter on De Lamerie, p. 54.

already seen, he retired, and went with his wife (who died there on 15 December 1775) and sixteen-year-old daughter Sarah to live in Southampton, where he died on 25 January 1770. In his will, drawn up on 17 December 1759, he is described as 'of the Parish of St. Ann's, Westminster, Silversmith'.

Thomas Heming
(*fl.* 1745–1782)

THE name of Thomas son of Richard Heming[1] is first recorded on 7 February 1737, when he became apprenticed to Edward Boddington, on the same day being made over to Peter Archambo Senr. He received his Freedom on 7 May 1746, and was elected to the Livery of the Goldsmiths' Company in June 1763. His earliest known workshop was in Piccadilly, from where he registered his first mark, TH in script, on

12 June 1744. In 1765 Heming moved from Piccadilly to Bond Street, from where he issued an elaborately engraved trade-card on which 'there is an ewer copied precisely from an engraving in Pierre Germain's *Eléments d'orfèvrerie* of 1748',[2] on which he states that:

Thomas Heming / Goldsmith to his Majesty / at the King's Arms in Bond Street / Facing Clifford Street / Makes and Sells all sorts of Gold & / Silver Plate in the highest Taste / Likewise all sorts of Jewellers work, Watches / Seals in Stone, Steel & Silver, Engrav'd / Mourning Rings &c, &c, &c, and at the most / reasonable Prices / NB. Gives most Money for the above Articles / or Lace, burnt or unburnt.

Also to be seen on Heming's trade-card is a soup-tureen which appears almost identical to one marked for 1763–4 in the Campbell Museum collection at Camden, New Jersey, which in 1973 was exhibited at the

1. Strangely, Thomas Heming has no known connection with Heming & Co. Ltd., Jewellers and Silversmiths of Conduit Street.
2. Honour, p. 204.

Victoria and Albert Museum. The bowl, which stands on four scrolling feet and has a gadrooned rim, is decorated with embossed drapery surrounding on one side the Royal arms and on the other those of Johnston impaling Collyet. The finial is in the form of a cast cauliflower head which lies on several large heavily-veined leaves. The weight of this piece is 153 oz., the length 16½ in., and the overall height 9½ in.

On the accession to the throne of George III in 1760 Heming was appointed to succeed John Boldero in the important position of Royal Goldsmith; in this capacity he was responsible for preparing the regalia and plate for the King's coronation, for providing him with new pieces of silver, and for caring for the Crown Jewels, Garter insignia and plate already in the Royal collection. Heming is the earliest Royal Goldsmith to have had a known registered maker's mark: a mark TH in script surmounted by a crown, although not recorded at Goldsmiths' Hall, is also presumed to be that of Heming, and dates from about 1770.

During the succeeding twenty years Heming supplied plate worth some £6,000 a year to the Jewel House, including a number of ecclesiastical items; in 1764, for example, he was commissioned to provide sets of Communion plate for Anglican churches in the American colonies; patens and chalices in the austere 'Queen Anne' style, popularized in the early years of the century, are still in Trinity Church, New York City, and Christ Church, Williamsburg, Virginia. A similar set was presented in 1765 to the Portland Chapel in Marylebone by the widow of the 2nd Duke of Portland; a rather less severe set was provided for use in the King's private chapel in Windsor Castle in 1779.

One of Heming's earliest pieces of work is a delicate two-handled cup and cover of 1753, in the collection of David H. H. Felix of Philadelphia: the body, stem and foot are wreathed all over with vine-leaves; the handles take the form of Bacchus rising out of C-shaped scrolls, holding aloft in his left hand a bunch of grapes, a motif which is repeated on the finial of the cover; an unusual feature is that each handle is left flying at its apex. An almost identical cup, dated 1760, is in the Victoria and Albert Museum. An attractive piece in the Royal collection is a small porringer; the finial of the cover is formed of four outward-scrolling Prince of Wales' feathers; it was made by Heming in 1763 for Queen Charlotte, as a present for her eldest son. Another item made by Heming for Queen Charlotte is a tea-kettle and stand dated 1761, which was included in the exhibition of Royal plate in London in 1954. The stand is decorated with an orderly pattern of chased scrolls, waves and shells; the kettle is ornamented with only a few swirls of engraving around the shoulders; it has a curving and delicately fluted spout with a bird's head terminal.

In 1766 Heming produced his most celebrated surviving pieces of work – twenty-three out of a total of thirty items in a silver-gilt toilet service made for Princess Caroline Matilda, posthumous daughter of Frederick, Prince of Wales, eldest son of George II, on her marriage at the age of fifteen to the dissolute and near-lunatic Christian VII of Denmark. The service, each piece of which bears the Queen's cypher, CR and the Royal Crown, consists of a large looking-glass, a pair of candlesticks, a ewer and basin, four brushes, a hand-bell, a tray, a pin-cushion-cum-box, and a number of other boxes and flasks; it is richly decorated in the floral style in vogue in English silver during the late rococo era; the chasing and modelling of the flower sprays is surprisingly realistic, and the fluidity of the scrollwork and the 'waves' on the lower portion of the ewer are of a remarkably high standard at a time when English chasing was, in general, at a low ebb. Curiously, the candlesticks, in sharp contrast to the remainder of the service, are pure Gothic; their stems, which are in the form of clustered columns, rise from quatrefoil bases ornamented with delicate tracery. The complete service packs into a brown leather nail-studded travelling-case, which contains a separate compartment for each item, and a drawer for the looking-glass.

After the death of Princess Caroline the service passed into the hands of her daughter Louisa Augusta (b. 7 July 1771; d. 1843) on her marriage in 1787 to Duke Frederik Christian of Schleswig-Holstein-Sonderborg-Augustenborg. Princess Louisa left it, on her death, to her second son, in whose family it remained until after the First World War. It was then acquired by the Meyer Fuld family, from whom it was bought in 1954 by the Kunstindustrimuseum (Museum of Decorative Arts) in Copenhagen, out of funds provided by the Ny Carlsberg Foundation.

Two years later, in 1768, Heming made an almost identical set in pale gilt for Henrietta, wife of Sir Watkin Williams-Wynn (1749–89), 4th Baronet; Heming clearly used the designs of the Royal set for the Williams-Wynn service, thereby endowing the latter with a certain cachet. In May 1967 Sotheby's sold a punch-bowl, decorated in typical 'Adam' style with rams' head masks and foliate and festoon swags, which Heming made for Williams-Wynn in 1771.

A two-handled cup-and-cover made by Heming, also in 1771 (now in Trinity Hall, Cambridge), is a strange combination of French rococo and English 'Adam' styles: the shape of the cup is that of a classic Greek urn, but the scrolling handles, which are entwined with snakes as favoured previously by Paul De Lamerie and subsequently by Paul Storr, are pure rococo. On the body of the cup is a round medallion depicting, in relief, three bewigged men in contemporary dress sitting around a table in a room, with an 'Adam' design looking-glass hanging on the wall behind them. The cup stands $11\frac{3}{4}$ in. high on a circular base which rests on a square sub-base decorated with a classic Greek key-pattern frieze. The finial of the lid, in startling contrast, is, like that of the Felix cup, in the form of an infant Bacchus holding aloft a bunch of grapes. The general impression is classical, with somewhat incongruous rococo elements.

A pair of candelabra, engraved with the Royal arms of George III and punched with the mark of Thomas Heming and the date-letter for 1774, were shown by H. R. Jessop Ltd., at the 'Fanfare for Europe' exhibition at Christie's in January 1973. Among the Jewel Office Accounts in the Public Record Office is the following note: 'The Rt. Hon. the Earl of Jersey as a gift from His Majesty at the christening of his child and were collected by John Walls on behalf of the Earl of Jersey 14th June 1774.'

In January 1967 Sotheby's illustrated in their sale catalogue a pair of superb parcel-gilt ewers, bearing the mark of Thomas Heming and the date-letter for 1777, the design for which was probably derived from the drawings of Sir William Hamilton, husband of Nelson's Emma and at one time British Ambassador in Naples.

On 2 March 1763 Thomas Heming's elder son, George, became apprenticed to his father; there is no record of whether George ever became Free of the Goldsmiths' Company, but this would not have been obligatory as his premises were outside the City. On 17 November 1774 George entered a joint mark (GH surmounted by W with C below within an urn-shaped shield) from No. 151 New Bond Street, with William Chawner, with whom he remained in partnership until about 1791. On 15 February 1781 the partners registered a second mark, GH over WC.

In 1775, on the advice of her Consul-General in London, Catherine the Great of Russia entrusted to George Heming and Chawner what must have been the largest commission ever given to an English goldsmith by a foreign patron: the two dinner and two dessert services which she ordered are said to have given employment to no fewer than four hundred craftsmen; they were made, incidentally, in the same year as another huge service was produced for Catherine as a present for her favourite, Count Orloff, by Jacques-Nicolas Roettiers.

The inventory of the Imperial Russian collection, drawn up in 1907, mentions thirty-eight candelabra made by Thomas Heming, but whether these were made before or after Catherine's table services is, unfortunately, unknown.

Thomas Heming's younger son, Thomas Junr., became his father's apprentice in 1767. In 1794 a Richard Heming, probably a grandson, was at 151 New Bond Street. Thomas Senr. died between 1795 (when his name is found in the Goldsmiths' Company Livery list for that year) and 1 January 1802, the date of the next list on which his name no longer appears.[4]

4. A warrant was drawn up in December 1782 appointing Thomas Heming 'Goldsmith in Ordinary to His Majesty', but the entry was deleted in the following year, when William Jones was appointed in his place. This may have been caused by the prices charged by Heming, which the Jewel Office Accounts Books show to have been undeniably high.

The Provincial Goldsmiths

OUTSIDE of London (where the town mark was introduced in 1300 and the maker's mark some sixty-three years later) a number of cities in England have, since early times, been centres of goldsmithery.

In 1423 a Statute of Henry VI gave seven English provincial cities the right to 'touch' or assay silver: Bristol, Coventry, Lincoln, Newcastle upon Tyne, Norwich, Salisbury and York. The Plate Assay Act of 1700, (12 and 13, William III, cap. 4), conferred statutory powers on five towns where mints had been 'lately erected for re-coining the money of the Kingdom'; Bristol, Chester, Exeter, Norwich and York. In 1773 Birmingham and Sheffield were added to the list of Assay Office cities. Elsewhere in England a number of flourishing centres of the goldsmiths' craft, although never officially authorized, marked their own silver. Today only London, Birmingham and Sheffield remain as English Assay Offices.

BRISTOL

Although named in both the Statute of 1423 and the Act of 1700, very little is known about silver made in Bristol. A spoon dredged from the River Avon bears the mark BR conjoined, which was used by the Bristol mint between 1643 and 1645. The earliest known piece bearing the town mark (a ship issuing from a castle) is a straining spoon (now in the collection of a Bristol church), dated 1730. In 1964 a plain pear-shaped beer-jug engraved with a crest, having a moulded lip and double scroll handle, appeared in a London sale-room; this piece also bears the ship and castle town mark, the maker's mark EM and the date-letter 'B' for 1740. A somewhat similar jug, probably made by Stephen Curtis, is in the collection of the Bristol City Art Gallery. During the eighteenth century no fewer than sixteen Bristol goldsmiths registered their marks at Goldsmiths' Hall in London.

EXETER

Although not give the right to its own Assay Office until 1701, one John de Wewlingworth is recorded as a goldsmith in Exeter in 1327. The earliest known piece of silver made in the city is a communion cup stamped with the first Exeter date-letter, a Roman 'A' within a shield, and the initials IONS (for John Jons or Jones), and bearing the pricked inscription 'The Parish of Trinitye in the yeare of our Lorde 1575'; another communion cup by Jons, standing $7\frac{1}{4}$ in. high and in the collection of Sidmouth Church, is marked with the letter 'B' and is dated 1576: Chanter describes its conical bowl as being engraved with 'a band of interlacing strapwork and arabesque foliation $\frac{3}{4}$ in. wide, with pendants around centre and tongue ornamentation at base; stem with knop and fillets, ornamented with hatching at top and bottom; foot domical, $3\frac{5}{8}$ in. diameter, with tongue ornamentation round base'. A number of other cups with a characteristically conical bowl and straight tapering sides, made by Jons and stamped with the early Exeter town mark, the letter X crowned and/or within a circle of pellets, are to be found in a number of churches in Devon, Cornwall and Somerset. Jons' most celebrated *oeuvre* which dates from about 1575 has the typical conical bowl, but a slightly everted lip; another of his cups, without the lip, is in the Glasgow City Art Gallery. Jons also made the mounts for a number of tigerware jugs which date from about 1580; a jug of that date with five silver mounts, stamped I YEDS, was made by John Eydes, and is now in the Victoria and Albert Museum; another similar jug by Eydes is in the Metropolitan Museum of Art in New York; yet another tigerware jug, with silver-gilt mounts and marked with the letter 'B' dating from about 1575 and possibly made by either Jons or Eydes, was sold at Sotheby's in June 1973 for £1,650.

Other fine sixteenth-century Exeter goldsmiths were Richard Osborn and Edward Anthony (both of whom appear to have specialized in making spoons), Jasper Radcliffe, and C. Easton who made a fine drum-shaped standing salt described by Mrs. Holland as being:

Eight and a quarter inches high, its body is heavily embossed with bunches of fruit, flowers and strapwork, with cartouches enclosing boldly stamped lions' heads, all set on three demi-horse feet. This fine body has a projecting cornice above, in which the salt was kept, with a domical cover, embossed with cartouches and garlands of fruit, ending in a vase-shaped finial with four scroll handles on which stands the figure of a man holding a spear and shield. It is a most ambitious piece, really well made.[1]

From 1701 the city arms of three castles was adopted as the Exeter

mark, and in the same year the city's most celebrated goldsmith, John Elston, registered his mark, EL, which is found on a quantity of domestic silver made in various styles: Elston could produce simple and even austere items in the 'Queen Anne' taste, or more elaborate pieces decorated with fluting and foliate chasing. An admirer of the simple baluster shape, in 1714 he made a fine plain jug for St. Mary's, Exeter, in this form, whose basic simplicity is relieved only by a narrow reeded rib, below which is a finely engraved coat-of-arms surrounded by the customary cartouche. A large monteith, on the other hand, beautifully fluted with flat-chased leaves, shells, foliage and scrolls, is basically baroque. A tankard by Elston dated 1704 has a moulded band encircling the cylindrical body, which is covered by a slightly domed lid with a serrated front edge; it has a scrolling handle and thumb-piece.

Six other fine Exeter goldsmiths of the period were John Avery, Edward Richards, Joseph Collier, John March, Peter Elliott and Sampson Bennett. Avery is known for a tankard of 1705 with a slightly domed cover and boldly scrolling handle. In 1718 Richards made a plain circular covered toilet-bowl, engraved 'St. David Exon. 1717', with two scrolling handles, standing on a circular moulded foot, $5\frac{1}{8}$ in. in diameter and weighing 14 oz. 7 dwt.: in June 1973 it sold at Christie's for £1,550. In 1723 Collier (who worked between about 1713 and 1730) made a coffee-pot weighing 24 oz. of which even the great Paul De Lamerie would not have been ashamed. March, in 1725, made a coffee-pot with the handle set at right-angles to the spout and with a high domed cover – both characteristics somewhat out of fashion by strict London standards. Elliott is responsible for a small brandy-warmer dated 1738, which has a shaped bowl with a moulded lip, and a straight ivory handle. Bennett, who lived in Falmouth

1. p. 42.

but had his work marked in Exeter, made a nice bullet tea-pot of conventional design dated 1759.

The end of the eighteenth century saw a decline in the number of manufacturing Exeter craftsmen, due no doubt in part at least to circumstances which led to a statement by the Exeter Assay Master for 1773, Matthew Skinner, that he 'had never received instructions from any man living how to assay', and that he 'bought all his plate from London'. One hundred and ten years later Exeter's Assay Office closed its doors.

BARNSTAPLE

Goldsmiths are known to have been active in the small Devon town of Barnstaple since 1370 when Hugh Holbrook and his wife Alice registered their makers' marks. The early town mark consists of a bird within a circular stamp, which was changed after 1625 to a castle surrounded by the Old English name, 'Barum'.

Thomas Mathew, whose son Robert was also a goldsmith, was one of the town's earliest craftsmen, stamping his products with his surname in full and a fruit or flower with decorative leaves. A fine cup by him, with a bell-shaped bowl supported on a knopped stem, bears the date 1576 in the centre of its lid which is decorated with flowing foliage. Mathew, who worked in Barnstaple for some fifty years, made a number of cups as well as apostle and seal-top spoons; two made in 1576 are in Truro Museum; in 1582 he made a fine ceremonial standing salt.

Another Barnstaple goldsmith was John Coton, who stamped his wares 'CoToN': a cup made by him for Stoke Rivers Church has a slender conical bowl rising from a domed foot; the cover is topped by a six-petalled flower finial.

Peter Quick (or Quyche) who was an apprentice of Coton, made a fine cup for Loxhore Church: its gracefully tapering conical bowl is decorated with panels of foliage within interlaced bands. Barnstaple was the home in the seventeenth century of no fewer than three goldsmiths named John Peard. After the Assay Act of 1700 Barnstaple silver was assayed in Exeter.

A small rat-tailed spoon with a flattened stem and a notched top, bearing the unknown maker's mark BP, possibly made in Truro in the late seventeenth century, was sold at Christie's in November 1973 for £100.

BRIDGWATER

The first mention of a goldsmith working in Bridgwater is in 1460 when one John Brooking had his premises searched by the town's wardens. The town mark was a castellated bridge over a river, surrounded by pellets.

BRUTON

A highly skilled goldsmith of Bruton, named Gabriel Felling, marked his wares with his initials contained within a rectangle. A tankard made by him in about 1710 with a slightly domed lid, a scrolling thumb-piece and skirted moulded base, was exhibited at the 1970 British Antique Dealers' Fair at Grosvenor House, London.

DORCHESTER

Lawrence Stratford is the only goldsmith known by name to have worked in Dorchester; he made at least thirty communion cups, which he punched with his initials.

LEWES

Two spoons are known bearing the maker's mark 'D' and the 'checky shield and lion rampant' of Lewes in Sussex.

PLYMOUTH

The silver-lead mines of the Tamar Valley to the north of Plymouth are known to have been worked since Roman times, but the first record of a goldsmith working in the city is not until 1281.

Plymouth's most celebrated goldsmith is Robert Rowe, who registered his mark RO at Exeter in 1701. His chief *oeuvre* is the famous Eddystone standing salt (in the City Museum, Plymouth), a 17 in. high model of the lighthouse which was completed in 1698 and destroyed in 1703. The salt, made in the 'Britannia' standard, bears the inscription 'Rowe, Plm° Britan' but not his registered mark, and was thus presumably made between 1698 and 1700. Rowe's mark is also found on a rose-water dish of 1704 in a private collection; a paten of the same year in Wembury Church near Plymouth; a flagon of 1706 at Whitchurch, and several other pieces dated 1711 near Yelverton.

A Plymouth goldsmith of the late seventeenth century who punched his wares with a cursive conjoined IM may have been one John Mortimer: he sometimes added the word 'Britannia' or 'Starling' or 'Sterling' to his mark. Another craftsman of the same period was Henry Muston; two spoons by him are pricked 1694, and are stamped with his mark, HM conjoined within a shield, the town mark of a saltire with four castles, and the word 'Sterling'. His best-known piece is a flat-topped posset pot made in about 1690, described by Mrs. Holland as being:

in the form of a tankard with plain straight sides and moulded base, and a tapering and curved spout set at right angles to the handle, like an American spout cup. It has a scroll handle and volute thumbpiece, and its cover also has a reeded edge, the overall impression being that of something squat, plain but really interesting. It is marked with a Plymouth saltire and maker's mark stamped twice on the body, the same reversed on the cover, 'HM' once, and the city arms twice.[2]

As can be imagined, there was a considerable interchange between the craftsmen of Plymouth and Exeter, and both Pentecost Symonds and Joseph Collier appear to have worked in each town. A pear-shaped teapot made by Symonds in 1713, 6½ in. high and weighing 21 oz. 5 dwt., has a simple rimmed foot, a polygonal curving spout, and a high domed cover with palm-leaves in cut-card work and pierced straps; it was sold in 1958 for more than £1,000. Three vase-shaped casters by the same maker, marked for 1720, have covers finely pierced in a symmetrical pattern of foliage and flowers.

Plymouth silver was sent for 'touching' to Exeter after the establishment there of an Assay Office on 29 September 1701.

POOLE

The arms of Poole (an escallop shell) are found on a number of seventeenth-century spoons of varying design.

SALISBURY

Although one of the original Assay centres established in 1423 there is, strangely, no record of any goldsmiths having actually worked in Salisbury.

2. p. 44.

SHERBORNE

Richard Orenge of Sherborne made a number of seal-top spoons (one is known dated about 1600) as well as several cups, including a fine example for the church of Gillingham: the boss inside the cover is inscribed '1574, GYLLYNGAM'.

TAUNTON

A group of apostle spoons stamped with a crowned rose in the bowl and on the stem made between about 1600 and 1640 were probably made in Taunton. The rebus of a T behind a Tun[3] appears on a number of pieces of silver made between about 1640 and 1690; the initials of three Taunton goldsmiths during this period are known: TD, SR and IS, but only the name of the first, Thomas Dare, has been established; among items bearing his mark and dating from about 1675 are a saucer-shaped sweetmeat-dish and a small and finely chased beaker.

NORWICH

The city of Norwich was established as an Assay Office centre by the Act of 1423, but as early as 1142 a lease of tenement in the parish of St. Peter Mancroft was granted by the Abbot of St. Benet to one Salamon, a goldsmith. Goldsmiths in some numbers are known to have been active in Norwich since 1285. The earliest known Norwich date-letter, for 1565,

was used in conjunction with the town mark, a lion surmounted by a

castle, which in 1624 was changed to a crowned rose. Some seven hundred marked pieces of Norwich silver are extant, and the names of a number of early, as well as later, craftsmen are known.[4] As can be imagined the

3. A large cask or barrel used for storing wine or beer.
4. The connections established between Norwich marks and the names of their users are largely due to the researches of Mr. G. J. Levine.

influence of Scandinavia and the Netherlands is very evident in Norwich silver, both as the result of trade and through the arrival of craftsmen who came as refugees from religious persecution in their own countries.

One of the earliest of Norwich goldsmiths was Valentine Ishbourne, whose mark was a heart surmounted by IV: this mark is found on a cup at St. Swithin's, Bintree, which stands 5 in. high and bears the following inscription on its bucket-shaped bowl: 'THIS. FOR. DE. THON. OF. BINTRI.'. Thomas Buttell adopted as his mark the rebus of a flat-fish within an oval;[5] this mark appears on a cup in St. Bartholomew's Church, Heigham, which is engraved on the bowl with a band of strap-work which forms four panels of stylized foliage; on the cover are the words 'SENT. BARTELMEVS. OF HAYHAM' surrounding the date 1567. Richard Shipden used a ship as his mark, and Christopher Tannor, who became Free in 1571, punched his initials in monogram form on a number of spoons and on a cup engraved with the date 1585.

The most famous goldsmith to have worked in the city of Norwich is undoubtedly William Cobbold, who was made Free in 1552, became Master of the city guild in 1564, and died in 1586; he used the orb and cross as his mark, as did his son Matthew (who became Free in 1593) after his death; in 1954 a delicate wine cup on a slender tapering stem decorated with acanthus leaves, 7 in. high and dating from 1595, by Matthew, appeared in a London sale-room. The same mark appears on the 'Attle-borough' cup, dated 1627, made by Richard Cobbold who was apprenticed to Timothy Skottowe (Warden of the Company of Norwich Goldsmiths in 1624, who died 1645) in 1622. The maker's mark of TS conjoined was at one time attributed to Skottowe; a simple beaker of about 1660 bearing this mark and standing on a spreading moulded foot, engraved below the everted rim with panels of interlacing foliage and scroll-work with three pendant floral sprays and a later crest, pricked beneath the base '1663', was however more likely made in Great Yarmouth; it stands $5\frac{1}{2}$ in. high, weighs 8 oz. 8 dwt., and is additionally punched with a *fleur-de-lis*, a leopard, and the letter G; in June 1973 it sold at Christie's for £1,350.

William Cobbold is responsible for the finest piece of English provincial plate extant, the famous silver-gilt 'Reade Salt' made in 1568 'to serve the Mayor and his successors for ever'. This superb example of the goldsmith's art, standing on a domed base, measures $15\frac{1}{4}$ in. in height. The

5. A butt is a species of flat-fish.

cylindrical body is covered with magnificent chased decoration of flowers, fruit, foliage and garlands. The tall domed cover has a large urn-shaped finial on which stands a soldier holding spear and shield. It bears the arms (originally enamelled) of Reade, Blenerhasset and Reade impaling Blenerhasset; this salt is lodged in Norwich City Hall, and is still used on ceremonial occasions. Cobbold also made the only two surviving pieces of plate bearing the city's earliest known date-letter, for 1565, two inverted bell-shaped communion cups made for St. Saviour's Church in Norwich, and St. Mary's, Diss. Two years later he made another cup, complete with paten, for St. Mary Colonsay, Norwich: it is ornamented around the bowl with a central band of stylized foliage set between raised ribs, and stands on a reel-shaped stem. On the paten are engraved the words 'SAYNCT MARYE OF COLSANYE Aº 1569', within a decorative cartouche. St. Peter Mancroft in Norwich possesses a silver-gilt cup and paten-cover by Cobbold of the same year; this also has a central encircling band of strapwork of stylized foliage, and the inscription 'SANCT. PETER. OF. MANCROFTE Aº 1569.' In 1575 Cobbold made a finely chased parcel-gilt covered jug, now in All Saints Church, Crostwight. Two, or possibly three, years later he produced four beakers, based on those brought to East Anglia from the Low Countries, described by Mrs. Holland as being:

7 in. tall, an unusual height, cylindrical with slightly everted lips, and . . . engraved with strapwork forming three panels filled with stylised flowers and foliage, a large spray, trefoil in design, being carried down from the intersections of the strapwork. Stamped ovolo and reeded moulding decorates the base, and the gift inscription surrounds the body, between rope-twist bands.[6]

One of these beakers is in the Castle Museum in Norwich; a second is in the Rijksmuseum, Amsterdam, and there are two in the Ashmolean Museum in Oxford.

Peter Petersen (also known as the 'Great' and the 'Dutchman') worked in Norwich between about 1560 and 1610, using "the Sun in his Splendour" as his maker's mark, which appears on forty-six extant pieces of plate, among which are thirty communion-cups. In 1574 Petersen was excused from all civic duties except that of 'Chamberlayne', i.e. treasurer, on payment of a fine of £40 and "a bol all gylte conteyning XVI ozs."

Towards the middle of the seventeenth century the Haselwood family

6. p. 119.

reigned supreme among the goldsmiths of Norwich.[7] The earliest member of the family was Arthur Haselwood (1593–1671) whose mark, AH, is first recorded in 1624, in which year he also became a warden of the city guild. He is known for a bucket-shaped cup and cover of 1633, with a cylindrical stem and everted lip, which he made for the church of St. Mary of Grace, Aspall; a wine-cup of 1638 with trumpet-shaped bowl rising from a thin baluster stem set on a domed foot; a communion cup and cover of 1647 made for St. Mary's, Blundeston, and a tankard of 1656.

His son Arthur II (1638–84) received his Freedom in 1661, and registered his maker's mark, AH conjoined, in the same year. Among the earliest pieces of silver made by Arthur II, dating from about 1662, is a set of communion plate, consisting of a cup and cover 9¼ in. high, a flagon 10½ in. high, and an alms dish, all engraved with the arms of Bishop Reynolds of Norwich. In 1670 Arthur II made three bucket-shaped cups with everted lips standing on a baluster stem which rises from a conical foot, known as the 'Spendlove Cups': they are engraved with the arms of the city of Norwich on the bowl, and with an inscription on the foot stating that they were 'the guyft of Mr. Tho Spendlove, sometyme one of ye Aldermen of this citty. Ye 3 bowles way 43 oz. 3 qz'. Not long ago there appeared in a London sale-room a tapering drum-shaped tankard by Arthur II of about 1673: it stands on a simple moulded base with a plain flat lid, and has a scrolling handle and thumb-piece. Arthur II continued to make considerable quantities of both ecclesiastical and secular plate – indeed he was the most prolific member of the Haslewood family of goldsmiths – until shortly before his death.

His widow, Elizabeth, continued the family tradition using as her mark her initials EH, crowned. A pair of simple tumbler-cups made by her in 1697 appeared a few years ago in a London auction-room. When Queen Elizabeth II opened the County Hall in Norwich in May 1968, Mr. Geoffrey N. Barrett of Hethersett presented to her, on behalf of the city, a plain beaker, 3½ in. high and standing on a moulded base, which was made by her namesake in about 1685.

Arthur III, son of Arthur II and Elizabeth, received his freedom in 1702 and died in 1740; he may have been responsible for one or more of the three pieces of Norwich silver of the 'Britannia' standard extant, all of which are punched with the letters HA. Other goldsmiths known to have used the same mark, however, are Robert Hartsonge (or Harsonage),

7. Information on the Haselwood family is largely the result of researches by Mr. Geoffrey Barrett.

who briefly held the office of Assay Master in 1701, and Thomas Havers who died in 1734. The only known piece of eighteenth-century Norwich silver extant is a communion paten in Kirkstead Church, Norfolk, which has been attributed to Hartsonge. Although Norwich was re-confirmed as one of the Assay Office centres by the Act of 1701, it did not in fact re-open for business due to lack of demand.

BURY ST. EDMUNDS

The first known goldsmith in Bury St. Edmunds was working there in 1270. The town's most celebrated craftsman, however, was Erasmus Cooke, who used as his maker's mark the sign of the *fleur-de-lis*: this punch appears on a number of communion cups and covers, mostly made in about 1570, which are either of the typical East Anglian inverted bell-shape with the usual engraved band of stylized foliage, or are straight-sided.

COLCHESTER

R. Hutchinson stamped his name in full on silver made in Colchester in the early 1720s. He also registered marks at Goldsmiths' Hall, and examples of his work bearing London marks are known.

IPSWICH

According to Casley the earliest craftsman known to have been working in Ipswich was one 'Agnes the Goldsmith' who was registered there in 1282. The town's most important craftsman, however, was Geoffrey Gilbert (c. 1530–79) who, after completing his apprenticeship to Matthew Garrarde, used as his mark a Roman 'G'. Gilbert produced a number of communion cups with inverted bell-shaped bowls, most of which are decorated with a central band of conventionalized foliage set between raised ribs. Martyn Denys (fl. c. 1575) and William Whiting (fl. c. 1600) are other goldsmiths known to have worked in Ipswich.

KING'S LYNN

The town mark of King's Lynn, consisting of three dragon's heads erased pierced by a dagger, is found on a cup in Middleton (near King's

Lynn) Church, with the maker's mark H over W, which may have belonged to William Howlett. Mrs. Holland describes this cup as follows:

The date of 1632 is known by the inscription running around the centre of the tall, bell-shaped bowl between two triple bands of laurel leaves, broken by an upright row of three rosettes, reading 'Elizabeth Willton gave 40s. and Mari Griffin gave 10s. touered this bowle for the Parish Church of Middletun in Norfolke Anno Dom 1632'.... This has a paten cover with additions to the type made in Elizabethan Norwich, such as acanthus leaves engraved on the spool knop used there, which is itself surmounted by a reel-shaped collar stamped with ovolo ornament above an edging of foliage in relief. It is a lovely and most unusual cover to a beautifully made bowl, plain except for its central band, allowing the eye to focus on the finely decorated foot, leading through a series of steps – engraved in turn with ovolo decoration, reeded moulding, engraved flowers, and a narrow band of foliage in relief – to a fine vase-shaped stem, with flutings radiating towards a knop, decorated with interlacing strapwork and surmounted by a spool decorated with small oval hollows ... this, 7½ in. high with another 2⅛ in. in the paten, is an exceptionally fine piece.[8]

Other pieces of silver bearing the mark of King's Lynn are a small communion cup in Lincoln Cathedral, also thought to have been made by Howlett, though London marked for 1642; a cup of 1635 inscribed 'The Quest of Thomas Clarke to the Church of Barmar' (near King's Lynn), also possibly by Howlett; a delicate cup dated 1640, standing on a baluster stem in St. Ethelreda's Church, Norwich, and a paten in the Chapel of St. Nicholas, King's Lynn, both stamped with a so far unidentified maker's mark.

COVENTRY

Granted its own Assay Office by the Statute of 1423 the city of Coventry was a centre of goldsmithing in England from the Middle Ages until the mid-seventeenth century; unfortunately, the names of none of its craftsmen are known today.

LINCOLN

The city of Lincoln, a centre of the goldsmiths' trade since 1125, was one of the Assay centres set up in 1423. A few surviving spoons and some

8. p. 108.

communion plate have been tentatively attributed to Lincoln goldsmiths, none of whose names, however, are recorded.

NEWCASTLE UPON TYNE

An ordinance of 1248 during the reign of Henry III required the bailiffs of Newcastle to choose officers for the 'Keeping of the King's mints', for the post of moneyers and for acting as assayers of the city's coinage; in 1423 the city was granted its right of 'touch'. In 1536 a group of tradesmen in Newcastle, glaziers, plumbers, painters, and pewterers, joined with five goldsmiths to form their own joint Company. Their founding-charter is still in existence, and shows that the Company was to be governed by four wardens, one of whom was a goldsmith, Thomas Cramer.

The earliest known piece of Newcastle silver is a chalice in St. Michael's Church, Ilderton, decorated with typically Elizabethan flat-chased inter-lacing strap-work enclosing stylized foliage; punched with the maker's mark VB for Valentine Baker, it is engraved on the cover 'Anno 1583'.

The city's first goldsmith of note was William Ramsey, who joined the Company in 1656. Two years later the early town mark of a single castle was adopted; two further castles were added in 1672. A peg-

tankard punched with this earlier mark and Ramsey's initials WR (both twice), dating from about 1670, stands on three ball feet from which rise stylized leaves. On the side opposite the plain 'S' handle is engraved a coat-of-arms within an elaborate cartouche. A certain amount of confusion has arisen over the initials WR, as in addition to Ramsey there were two William Robinsons, father and son, working in New-castle in the seventeenth century: Robinson Senr., who in 1635 'affirmeth that his marke wherewth hee stampeth his plate and ware is the Rose', was described on his son's apprenticeship indenture dated 1657 as a 'goulsmith, late of Newcastle, deceased'. Robinson Junr. became Free in 1666, and died in the same year as Ramsey, 1698. Pieces bearing the initials WR, and including in the punch a variety of devices, e.g. a bird or a crown, include a pear-shaped chocolate-pot of about 1695 and a number of communion-cups, flagons and tankards. Ramsey, as Robinson

Senr.'s son-in-law, may have taken over the rose mark after his father-in-law's death; alternatively, William Robinson II may have adopted his late father's mark. An 11 in. high flagon, dated 1670 and stamped WR, is a typical example of Newcastle work of the period; it has a slightly domed lid, a moulded foot, and a plain 'S'-shaped handle: on one side are engraved the arms of the city of Newcastle. In the year that it was made the flagon was presented to Thomas Davison, Mayor of Newcastle upon Tyne, who subsequently gave it to one of the city churches or guilds where it remained until 1745, the year of the Jacobite Rebellion, when it was removed to some unknown place for safe keeping. In the late 1740s or early '50s the flagon passed into the possession of one Edward Norton, a member of an old family from Sawley in the West Riding of Yorkshire, who was a Colonel in the Militia, and who had probably been posted to Newcastle to assist Marshal Wade. In 1756 Norton and three friends presented the flagon to Sawley parish church, where Norton was a church warden and his brother was rector. There it remained until 1952 when, in order to provide funds for restoration work, it was sold to the Laing Art Gallery and Museum in Newcastle. Another vertical-sided tankard, also made in the same year, probably by Ramsey, stands on ball-and-claw feet and exemplifies the Scandinavian taste commonly found in work from the east coast of England: it is now in the Victoria and Albert Museum.

An 8¼ in. high cup and paten (on which is pricked '1664') in Ryton Church, Co. Durham was made by John Wilkinson, who is also known for another and, conceivably, earlier cup, as well as for a tankard of 1668.

In 1917 a small cup, sold for scrap, was purchased in Carlisle and proved to be the work of John Dowthwaite, who made a number of other cups which are to be found in north-country churches. His best-known piece is a peg-tankard of about 1670, gilded inside, and engraved with the arms of Thorp; this piece is in the Laing Art Gallery. Two flagons 18 in. high, made by Thomas Hewitson in 1697 (the year he became Free) and 1698 are in the same collection. Each has a broad 'S' handle with finely modelled cherub thumb-piece. Hewitson is also known for a small two-handled porringer with fine fluting, dating from 1697.

Eli Bilton, who became Free in 1682, occupies a position of special importance in the history of Newcastle silver, for he was not only a gold-smith but, *rara avis*, a provincial engraver, who is responsible for a quantity of flat-chased engraving of fruit, flowers, birds and foliage in a kind of naïve *chinoiserie* style. His early mark EB, either plain, crowned, or surmounted by a star, appears on a chocolate-pot of 1694; a two-handled porringer of 1700 (in Carlisle Museum, on loan from the Taylors' Guild); a rat-tailed spoon, with trifid terminal of about 1694, and a number of communion cups in north-country churches. In 1964 a two-handled porringer with, unusually, a cover, appeared in Christie's sale-rooms: dating from about 1695 and bearing Bilton's mark, it stands on a low reeded foot from which rises the spreading bowl, the lower portion of which is finely chased with delicate fluting; the cover has a baluster finial rising from a fluted rosette.

To conform with legal requirements Bilton changed his mark after 1697 to the first two letters of his surname although on occasion (e.g. in the case of the Taylors' porringer mentioned above) he continued illegally to employ his old mark, EB. Pieces punched with his new mark, and of the 'Britannia' standard, include a spoon of 1699 and a mug of 1700. At the British Antique Dealers Fair of 1967 a tumbler-cup was exhibited decorated with twisted fluting, made by Bilton in 1703. In the same year he made a pair of communion cups for use in Stanhope Church, with vertical sides with a raised rib in place of an engraved band, rising from a dumpy stem set on a moulded foot. In 1704 Eli II, son of Eli's brother Josuah, became apprenticed to his uncle.

The goldsmiths of Newcastle suffered, along with their colleagues in other provincial centres, during the period between 1697 and 1701 when silver could only legally be assayed in the capital. Francis Batty, Free in 1674, led a deputation to Parliament which succeeded in obtaining the re-establishment of their city as an Assay Office (1 Anne, Cap. 9) in 1702, one year later than other provincial centres. Although the goldsmiths of Newcastle held regular meetings from 24 June 1702, it was not until 1716 that they broke finally from the 'Company' and formed their own 'Company of Goldsmiths of Newcastle upon Tyne'. A porringer made by Batty in 1722 and a punch-ladle possibly made by him in 1721 or '25, are in the Laing Art Gallery.

During the early 1700s Newcastle's craftsmen received commissions for ceremonial plate from a number of the various guilds of Carlisle. The Skinners' and Glovers' own a small Newcastle mug of 1701; the Taylors' possess a tumbler-cup made in 1707 by John Younghusband, who had obtained his Freedom in the previous year; these two pieces, together with a tankard by Isaac Cookson (1744), a two-handled cup and cover (1727) by Thomas Partis, and a covered tankard of 1722 by James Kirkup, are all still in Carlisle. In 1728 Kirkup made a rare two-handled gold cup for presentation as a racing prize in that town.

The work of Isaac Cookson appears throughout the north of England; the church of Bolton-by-Bolland in Yorkshire possesses a quart-sized covered flagon made by him in 1731. During the closure of York's Assay Office between 1716 and 1776, Cookson provided civic-plate for that city's Mansion House, including a set of casters engraved with the arms of the city, in 1735, and a tankard of 1738. He is, however, perhaps best known as a maker of coffee- and tea-pots: his early coffee-pots are mostly cylindrical in shape, with applied leafage around the sometimes swan-necked spout; his later coffee-pots are of baluster form. The Laing Art Gallery possesses a considerable collection of pieces made by Cookson; these include a small bullet tea-pot made by him in 1732, which has a curious spout which emerges almost horizontally, and then turns upwards at nearly a right angle; a two-handled orange-strainer pierced with a geometric design; a pair of waiters of 1742 with scalloped edges, each standing on three hoof feet; a salver made in 1739, with a scroll, leaf and moulded border, resting on three shell feet; another salver similarly decorated but with scrolling instead of shell feet, made in 1742; a pair of fluted sauce-boats of about 1745, with collet feet and scrolling handles; a spoon of 1732 with a ridged and channelled shaft engraved with a coat-of-arms and the inscription 'Frances [sic] Pemberton Esqr. Master 1734'; and a punch-ladle with a turned wooden handle and an acorn finial, of the same date and similarly engraved as the spoon. A large tea-kettle, with lamp and stand *en suite* made in 1732 is perhaps Cookson's *tour de force*: the kettle is decorated with finely executed flat-chasing around the cover, and a beautifully engraved coat-of-arms. Cookson, who is reputed to have sent for assay some 150,000 oz. of plate during his long and industrious life, died in 1754.

Thomas Partis (*fl.* 1720-34) is known for a nice coffee-pot made in 1726 and presented in that year as the prize for the 'Ladies' Plate' race at Carlisle. His son, William, who died in 1759, made a pretty little sugar-basket with swing-handle and a cup of 1755 with an encircling rib and scrolling handles, both of which are now in the Laing Art Gallery.

William Beilby (1706-65), who was born in Scarborough, worked first in Durham in partnership with Jonathan Bainbridge (presumably a relation of his wife Mary, *née* Bainbridge, whom he married in 1733), from 1739 until the partnership was dissolved in 1741. Beilby, who was never a member of any craft-guild, is chiefly remembered for two pieces

45   David Willaume: helmet-ewer, 1700. Victoria and Albert Museum. (*Crown Copyright.*)

46 David Willaume: teapot, 1706–7. The City Art Gallery, Manchester. (*Courtesy of the Trustees of the Assheton-Bennett Collection.*)

47 Extract from an account giving details of work carried out by David Willaume for Lady Irwyn in 1726. Leeds City Libraries.(*Photo: Warren Jepson & Co. Ltd.*)

48 Thomas Heming: tea-kettle and stand, 1761–62. The Royal Collection. (*Reproduced by gracious permission of Her Majesty the Queen.*)

49   Thomas Heming: silver-gilt toilet-service, 1766. Kunstindustriemuseum, Copenhagen.

50   William Cobbold: the Reade Salt, 1568. Norwich City Corporation.

51   Robert Rowe: the Eddystone Salt, 1698–1700. City Museum and Art Gallery, Plymouth.
(Photo: Tom Mollard Ltd.)

52 Nathaniel Bullen: tobacco-box, late seventeenth century. Victoria and Albert Museum.

53 Marmaduke Best: gold goblet, 1671. York City Corporation. (*Photo: courtesy of 'The Connoisseur'.*)

54 William Ramsey: tankard, *c.* 1670. Laing Art Gallery and Museum, Newcastle.

55   Portrait of George Lowe,
founder of the family firm of
Lowe and Sons, Chester.

56   Peter Edwardes: monteith,
1686–90. Grosvenor Museum,
Chester. (*Photo: courtesy of
Christie's.*)

57   Ralph Walley: punch-jug,
1690–92. Grosvenor Museum,
Chester. (*Photo courtesy of De
Havilland [Antiques] Ltd.*)

of plate – a cup of 1748 set with a gem ring which he made for the church of St. Mary-le-Bow, Durham, and a tankard with a domed cover of 1750. From about 1759 until his death Beilby worked as a goldsmith in Newcastle and Gateshead.

The Laing Art Gallery has on loan from the Incorporated Company of Tanners of Newcastle upon Tyne a tankard resting on a moulded base, with a domed cover, knurled thumb-piece and scrolling handle, made in 1721 by the fine Newcastle craftsman John Ramsay: the tankard is engraved with a coat-of-arms and the inscription 'Tristram Wilkinson, William Rowell, Thomas Bailif, William Woodhave, Stewards 1723'.

The brothers James and David Crawford were both apprenticed as goldsmiths in 1763, but appear never to have worked together. A tall pear-shaped tankard ornamented with twisting fluting, made in 1790 by James, is to be seen in the Laing Art Gallery. Robert Makepeace was another fine Newcastle goldsmith of the period, who received his Freedom in 1718 and worked in the city until about 1755, as did Peter Lambart who also made silver in Berwick and Montrose. A large plain tapering cylindrical coffee-pot standing $9\frac{7}{8}$ in. high on a moulded base, with a polygonal scrolling spout and a high domed cover with a corkscrew thumb-piece and an orb finial, made in 1728 by Makepeace, sold at Christie's in November 1973 for £1,650.

Newcastle's most famous eighteenth-century goldsmith was John Langlands: he was apprenticed in 1731 to Isaac Cookson, becoming Free in 1754, when he took over his late master's business and entered into partnership with John Goodriche (or Goodrick) who died three years later. Punched with Langlands' individual mark are a large quantity of fine pieces of plate, including a nice baluster tankard, dated 1757; a drum-shaped tea-pot (1773) and a tankard with double-scrolling handle made in 1774. Four years later Langlands went into partnership with John Robertson. The Laing Art Gallery has a number of pieces stamped with their joint mark, including a tankard with spiral fluting on the base and cover made in 1780; a pear-shaped coffee-pot of 1782 with a domed cover and a vase-shaped finial, with an ivory scrolling handle and thumb-piece, and a salver with a moulded rim made in 1791. In the same gallery, on loan from St. Andrew's Church, is an alms-bowl with a gadrooned rim, engraved with a figure of St. Andrew and the inscription 'St. Andrew's Parish Church, Newcastle, 1784'; and a pair of flagons, punched with the mark of Langlands only and the date-letter for 1774, with moulded rim feet, scrolling handles and pineapple finials, similarly

engraved and inscribed as the alms-bowl. After John Langlands' death in
1793 the business was continued by his son John until the latter's death
in 1804, and subsequently by Dorothy, John II's widow, until she retired
in 1814. John Robertson died two years after his partner, and was followed in the business by his son, also John, who entered his mark in the
same year (1795); John Robertson II's widow, Anne, registered her mark
after her husband's death in 1801, and remained in the firm until 1811.
John Robertson II was at one time in partnership with John Walton (fl.
1820–66) who was the most prolific nineteenth century Newcastle goldsmith, but was never a Freeman of the Company. Walton is responsible
for a flagon of 1794 (in the collection of St. Andrew's Church, on loan to
the Laing Art Gallery), with reeded decoration, a moulded rim foot, a
shell-topped scrolling handle with a palmette thumb-piece, and a pierced
cross finial; beneath the lip is applied a figure of St. Peter, and the inscription
'*In usum ecclesiae sancti Petri D.D. Dorothea Gothard A.S. MDCCCXLIII*'.

Thomas Watson (*fl.* 1793–1845) is the last of the great names of Newcastle goldsmithery – much of his later work providing a foretaste of the
Victorian era. From the end of Watson's career the fortunes of Newcastle's
goldsmiths declined, and in 1883 only 316 oz. of silver was assayed in the
city, much of it made by Reid & Sons, founded by Christian Ker Reid
in 1778. The following year (1884) saw the closure of Newcastle's Assay
Office.

CARLISLE

A guild of craftsmen, among whom were goldsmiths, was in existence
in Carlisle from the sixteenth century until 1728, though little if any
silver was wrought in the town after the siege of 1644–5. Ten communion
cups are still in existence, stamped with the initials ED conjoined for
Edward Dalton, and the town mark of a quatrefoil within a circle. Dating
from between about 1565 and 1570, these cups are somewhat crudely
made in the typically Elizabethan style. The Dalton family of goldsmiths
is mentioned in old records up until the time of the siege.

GATESHEAD

The rebus of a goat's head erased was used on silver made in the town of
Gateshead by Augustine Float, who punched his mark AF within an

oval. A tankard bearing these marks weighs 32 oz., stands 7 in. high and has a diameter of 5 in.; it has a flat lid with a moulded rim, a corkscrew thumb-piece, and scrolls of strapwork applied to the 'S'-shaped handle; down the side of the tankard, underneath the hinge and opposite the handle, runs a rat-tailed rib, characteristic of Newcastle and Gateshead work by Float, who is known to have worked in both towns. Float also made a half-pint mug with an everted rim, and with a *repoussé* band of leaf decoration below which is a band of chased leafage with alternating convex and concave spiral fluting; this mug, which has a reeded handle and is engraved with the inscription '*Ex dono XXX*', weighs 4 oz. and stands 3⅜ in. high; both of these items, which were made in about 1680, are in the Laing Art Gallery in Newcastle.

Exhibited at the British Antique Dealers Fair in 1967 was another fine tankard weighing 29 oz. and measuring 7 in. high, made by Float, this time in Newcastle in about 1690; it is similar to that described above, but has cut-card decoration on its broad handle with a feather type thumb-piece.

YORK

The goldsmiths of York are known to have formed themselves into a guild in about 1270, though the names of members are not recorded until 1313. As early as 1389 Richard II is recorded as having presented a York-made mace to the city. The 'Scrope Mazer' (now in the Chapter House of York Minister) may well have been the work of Henry Wyman, who received his Freedom in 1386 and was thrice Lord Mayor of the city; his widow Agnes presented it to the 'Guild of Corpus Christi', which was dissolved in 1546. This mazer subsequently passed into the hands of the Cordwainers' Company on whose authorization it was twice repaired, once by Peter Pearson and again, in 1669, by Philemon Marsh, who became Free in 1652.

York was granted the right to its own Assay Office by the statute of 1423: it was subsequently decreed that 'the pounce of this citie, called the halfe leopard head and half [*sic*] flowre-de-luyce', be instituted. In 1560

this ordinance was re-confirmed, together with the introduction of a date-letter; a seal-top spoon marked with the initials of Robert Beckwith, the letter 'C' for 1561–2 and the town mark, is the earliest known piece of accurately dated and fully marked provincial silver extant. Between 1632 and 1698 the town mark was changed to a 'half-rose, crowned', which

in turn gave way in 1701 to a 'cross charged with five lions passant', taken

from the arms of the city. In 1716 the York Assay Office closed, and until it re-opened in 1776 York silver was 'touched' at Newcastle.

The Plummer family provided some of York's most important early goldsmiths: the earliest member, James, became Free in 1619; thirty years later he made a typically austere Commonwealth tankard, with an exceptionally widely spreading foot and severely plain C-shaped handle. A lengthy inscription covers the entire foot as well as the top quarter of the body, on the side of which is an oval medallion containing the words 'Be faithful unto Death'.

James's brother John, younger by twenty-five years, obtained his Freedom in 1648; in 1675 he made what is perhaps the finest extant example of English provincial ecclesiastical plate, an altar set for use in Ripon Minster. Mrs. Holland describes it thus:

The pair of communion cups ... are taller, larger versions of the old Elizabethan style, set on stepped feet; on one side of each armorials surrounded by scrollwork are engraved, together with an inscription ... the chief features of the cups are the pictures engraved on the other side, showing Ripon Minster as it was before 1660. ...

The flagon ... a massive version (13 in. high) of the straight-sided tankard with widely splayed, torus-moulded base, also shows engravings of the Minster, while on its flat lid, as on the conventional Elizabethan covers of the cups, the Holy Lamb is shown with scroll-work and the Jennings crest.

There are also two patens ... simple plates in themselves, on round, truncated cone feet, on which the Minster is engraved centrally, with armorials and inscriptions below. What makes for rarity is that each has a cover, known as an 'aire', borrowed from Greek ritual, with a beautifully ornamented dome raised on three claw and ball feet, and surmounted by an orb and cross. The effect is magnificent, and the workmanship fine; sadly, one has evidently been lost and replaced by a rather inferior copy.[9]

John Plummer also made two important tankards, one in 1657 (in the Victoria and Albert Museum) and the other in 1673. The earlier tankard, a 'peg' version, is superbly engraved with flowers which include a large iris, and stands on three pomegranate feet with applied leafage above. The scrolling handle has a pair of pomegranates as a thumb-piece, with a shield terminal. The cover is also beautifully engraved with flowers surrounding the crest of Sayer. The later tankard stands on three lion feet, a motif which is repeated on the thumb-piece of the C-shaped handle which has an applied reeded rat-tail, typical of north-country craftsmen. The lid has a band of moulding which is repeated near the bottom of the tankard, on which are engraved the city arms.

Two other members of the Plummer family are known to have worked in York, Richard and Michael, and both obtained their Freedom in the same year, 1659.

The Huguenot family of Mangy were famous York goldsmiths, some of whom are known to have worked in Hull and Leeds. Christopher became Free in 1609, and is known for a small cup made for St. Cuthbert's in York; George obtained his Freedom in 1638; Henry in 1650; Edward in 1660; Thomas, the most productive of them all, in 1664; George Mangy II in 1675; Katherine in 1680; and Arthur, who made the Leeds town mace in 1694, in 1681; in 1696 this evidently 'black-sheep' of the family was hanged on the Knavesmire in York for counterfeiting and clipping coinage. Thomas is known for a fine tankard of 1679 in the Mansion House in York, and six so-called 'Death's Head' rat-tail spoons made for the Stricklands of Boynton and Howsham between about 1661 and 1682; these spoons bear the morbid mottoes 'Live to Die' and 'Die to Live'; were they, perhaps, given as mementoes at funerals?

The pair of altar candlesticks in the Lady Chapel at York Minster are the work of William Mascall, who made them in 1672. Six years previously this gifted craftsman made an impressive tankard ornamented with a heavily embossed design of flowers; it rests on three pomegranate feet from which rise applied leaves, and has the usual C-shaped handle with repeating pomegranate motif thumb-piece.

Marmaduke Best, Free in 1657, made in 1671 a beautiful gold goblet

9. pp. 55-6.

which he ornamented with fine cut-card decoration and cable moulding; on one side are engraved the arms of the city of York and on the other an inscription giving the name of the donor, Marmaduke Rawdon; from this cup the Lord Mayor of York drinks the Loyal toast at civic banquets.

In the previous year Rawdon had given Best a commission for a silver chamber-pot, which weighs 50 oz. and is today one of the most valued possessions in the collection in the Mansion House, York. On one side of this impressive piece, which cost Rawdon £10, are engraved the arms of the donor, and opposite them those of the city of York. Since these early chamber-pots, only a few of which are extant, were designed to be used *in situ* in the dining-room, it was naturally important that they should be of a suitably impressive nature.

In 1672 Best made a cylindrical tankard for presentation to the Fishmongers' Company, whose coat-of-arms are emblazoned on the front – one of the treasures in the Castle Museum, York. In 1673 Best made a tankard as a pair to that produced in the same year by John Plummer, which is described above.

Among other early York goldsmiths of note were Robert Williamson, who worked also in nearby Leeds; George Gibson; Christopher Harrington, who made a spoon in the Castle Museum dated 1599; and William Busfield, who appears to have specialized in making tumbler-cups which are usually of a more dumpy shape than those made in London: one dated 1685 is nicely engraved with initials, presumably of either the donor or recipient; a second, made in 1687, is in the collection of the Castle Museum. Busfield appears to have continued punching his wares with the old York mark during the years when provincial Assay Offices were officially closed.

Together with John Langwith, Joseph Buckle (Free 1715), and Charles Rhoades, Busfield was one of the few York craftsmen to re-register his mark and produce work in the 'Britannia' standard of a silver when the York Assay Office re-opened in 1701. Between 1716 and 1776 the York Office closed again, and the town's goldsmiths sent their work for 'touching' to Newcastle.

In 1776 the York Assay Office opened its doors once again, when it was used mainly by the firm of J. Hampston & J. Prince; two fine examples of the work of this partnership, both dated 1784, are in the Victoria and Albert Museum; one is a plain and nicely proportioned bullet-shaped tea-pot; the other is a tea-caddy, described by Mrs. Holland as:

oval, straight-sided ... with horizontal lines of decoration surrounding it at top and bottom, has a plain, smooth surface in between, relieved by bright-cut engraving (a typical feature of Adam silver in the neo-classic style), employing the garlands and bows and ribbons of symmetrical curves so frequently seen in Adam interior decoration. An exquisite piece, it is typical of an age when York was still producing more of quality than quantity.[10]

After Hampston's retirement in 1805 Prince, who had obtained his Freedom in 1771, took as his new partner George Cattle, who on Prince's retirement in 1808 in turn took into partnership James Barber (originally a partner of William Whitwell), who himself later formed an association with William North. The firm, now calling itself Prince & Co., continued to make wrought plate until the York Assay Office finally closed in 1857.

HULL

The names of goldsmiths of Hull are recorded from 1427. From about 1565 to 1700 the arms of the town, three ducal coronets, were used as the town mark in place of that previously employed, a Roman upper-case letter 'H'. One of the earliest pieces of Hull-marked plate is a cup of 1569 made by Peter Carlille, in Wooton Church, Lincolnshire. Another cup by him, with typically bell-shaped bowl and knopped-stem, and cover, of about 1580, can be seen in Beverley Minster; other chalices made by Carlille are in churches at Beeford, Cabourne, Catwick, and in his home town of Hull.

Edward Mangy, who also worked in York, made an exceptionally attractive communion cup for Hornsea parish church: its interlacing strapwork contains delicate quatrefoils, with a pendant of leafage and flowers at the intersections; between the pendants is an inscription in finely executed italics. Edward and Katherine Mangy are represented in the collection of Trinity House in Hull by a chalice and a paten respectively; they may have been the parents of Edward II who is known to have been working in Hull in 1724.

Thomas Hebden, who was working in Hull in the 1690s, made a delightful drum-shaped tankard with three pomegranate feet, each surmounted by a leaf in cut-card work, and flat lid, which is strongly reminiscent of work produced at the time in the Baltic States.

The finest goldsmith working in Hull during the 'Britannia' period was,

10. p. 68.

like the Mangys, of Huguenot extraction: Abraham Barachim received his Freedom in 1706 but, in common with a number of Huguenot craftsmen, produced a quantity of wrought plate before this, stamped with his maker's mark, A B crowned with a rose beneath. No goldsmiths were registered in Hull after 1774.

LEEDS

Leeds silver made between about 1650 and 1700 is marked with the sign of the 'golden fleece', taken from the arms of the city.

A chalice stamped with this mark, in the possession of Almondbury Church near Huddersfield, has a tapering bell-shaped bowl set on a conical stem: surrounding the bowl of the cup is a design of thistle-leaves. A tumbler-cup weighing a bare $1\frac{1}{2}$ oz. punched with the maker's mark T B and the 'golden fleece' was sold at Sotheby's in 1967 for £960. The date of these early pieces is uncertain.

Robert Williamson, who also worked in York, is responsible for a flat-topped tankard bearing the Leeds town mark: he also made, in 1685, a simple baluster chocolate-pot with a slender curving spout set at right-angles to the scrolling handle, from which a chain leads to the high domed cover surrounded by cut-card work; it was sold at Sotheby's in 1961 in the dispersal of the Makower collection.

Samuel Todd is another Leeds goldsmith known to have been working in the city in the late 1690s; he made a communion cup which is now in the church at Darrington. As we have already seen, Arthur Mangy, who also worked (and was hanged) in York, made the Leeds corporation mace in 1694.

CHESTER

The city of Chester was not mentioned in the statute of 1423, probably because both city and county – and doubtless her craftsmen also – were subject to the Earls of Chester rather than to the Crown from the creation of the earldom in 1071 to the reign of Henry VII. The city had been an important centre for coinage since A.D. 925, and the city's goldsmiths had, since the thirteenth century, been a powerful and self-governing body.

Controversy has raged over the years concerning what may or may not be the earliest piece of Chester-made silver in existence, the magnificent

'Dollgellau Chalice', which in 1890 was unearthed, complete with paten – the largest known in Britain – at Dollgellau in Merionethshire. Under the foot of this chalice is the inscription 'NICOL'US ME FECIT DE HERFORDIE'. In about 1270 a goldsmith known as 'Nicholas the Great' was working in Chester, and there has been much speculation as to whether or not he may have been the maker of this superb example of the goldsmiths' art. The reader who wishes to do so may see this beautiful piece of medieval craftsmanship (the property of the Queen) in the National Museum of Wales in Cardiff, and will find it fully described and discussed by Canon Maurice H. Ridgway,[11] who gives full details of every known Chester goldsmith and his work, and from whom much of the contents of this section have been drawn.

We have to wait for another three hundred years to find the earliest known definitely Chester-made piece – or rather pieces – of silver, four communion cups and patens made in the year 1570, and punched with the sheep's head rebus of William Mutton who became Free in 1555 and who lived and worked in Bridge Street, Chester. The finest of these, in the church of Holy Trinity, Chester, has a deep bowl set on a knopped stem which rises from a rounded base; the bowl itself is decorated with a pair of bands, one below the rim and one in the middle, containing an inscription taken from the Communion Service, each letter separated by a cross: this cup and paten cost the churchwardens £6. 18s. 10d. Another chalice by Mutton of the same year (1570) is in the parish church of Great Budworth, near Chester. Standing 8½ in. tall, the bell-shaped bowl, which has a broad flat rim with delicate engraving of flowers and foliage, rises from a rounded base. Two other cups by Mutton of 1570 are in the city churches of St. Michael and St. Mary. Mutton is known for several other similar cups made in or around 1574, most of which are on the Isle of Anglesey; he also made in about 1580 the only known Elizabethan Chester seal-top spoon. Mutton died in February 1583.

References are found in the early 1530s to a Guild of Goldsmiths in Chester; the first name recorded in the minute-book of the Chester Goldsmiths is that of Robert Smyth, who was sworn in on 23 October 1574; he had become a Freeman of the city on 23 May 1570. A minute of a meeting of the city's goldsmiths, dated about 1575, refers to a fine of 3s. 4d. imposed on any of their number offering for sale wrought-plate not bearing his mark.

Two other early Chester goldsmiths were Peter and Christopher

11. pp. 6–8, plates 4 and 5.

Conway, father and son. Peter became a Freeman on 13 February 1532: only one piece of plate is known made by him – a paten dated 1576 in Pott Shrigley Church. His son, Christopher, who was apprenticed to William Mutton, became a Freeman on 2 March 1583, and received the Freedom of the Company in the following year; he died in 1606.

Richard Gregorie, a member of the Company by 1584, probably helped to provide parts of the city mace which was re-made at the time of the Restoration and was then presented to the city by the Earl of Derby.

The goldsmith family of Lingley were active in Cheshire, Lancashire and North Wales between about 1574 and 1625; the forenames of two were John and of two others Joseph, and since all used the same maker's mark, IL, and since it is not certain exactly who worked where, they present a perplexing problem to the biographer. Of Joseph I little is known; John I was certainly working in 1573, when he was fined by the goldsmiths of London; he died in 1615. John II received his Freedom on 12 October 1592, and died in 1609; his brother, Joseph II, Free in 1615, carried on the family work alone. The most interesting and the only secular piece of Lingley silver extant, made, probably by John I or II in 1606, is a small mace at Kenyon Hall, Holt in Denbighshire; measuring 20 in. long, inscribed with the weight 'viii ounces' and known as the 'Queen's Mace', it surprisingly bears the Royal arms of James I on its head, which is surrounded by a scalloped rim; below this is a decoration described by Ridgway as 'consisting of coiled dolphin-like creatures placed back to back',[12] with underneath the inscription 'D SPEEDE MAIOR 1606' (it will be remembered that James' mother, Mary Queen of Scots, was at one time married to the French Dauphin, whose emblem was a dolphin); at the foot of this attractive little mace – more like a tipstaff in appearance – is a silver ball topped with acanthus foliage.

Another well-known family of Chester goldsmiths were the Edwardes: the two earliest members were both named Griffith, the father becoming Free on 19 May 1585 and his son (who after the death of his father completed his apprenticeship with Christopher Conway) in 1607; Griffith Senr., who died between 1603 and 1607, is known only for a small communion paten in Bunbury parish church; it bears his mark, GE above a rose within a trefoil shield. Griffith II made a cup 'waying 23 oz. 1 qr. and a dramme of Gilt plate' for £8. 6s. 8d. as a prize for Chester races in 1634. Between 1540 and 1609 archery and football contests and horse- and running-races were held annually on Shrove Tuesday on Chester's 'Roodee'. Silver

12. p. 48.

bells and cups and the 'broad arrows of Shrovetide', all of which were used as prizes, were made during this period, presumably by Chester craftsmen; since 1609 the horse-racing changed to St. George's Day, 23 April, and many more race-cups were produced by the goldsmiths of Chester.

Griffith Edwardes II married Katherine, daughter of Owen Jones of Gourton, Denbighshire, and died in 1637. Their son, Peter Edwardes, was apprenticed to his uncle, Gerrard Jones, and received his Freedom on 24 January 1654/5; he died in 1698; his only known surviving piece of plate is a communion cup and cover dated 1685 in Caerwys Church, Flintshire. His son, Peter II, became Free on 22 July 1680 and, from the four extant pieces of his work known today, was clearly a superlative craftsman. His most important *oeuvre* is a large monteith bearing the Chester date-letter 'A' for 1686–90; the rim has eight indentations (for holding the stems of wine-glasses) and is surrounded with applied acanthus foliage; below, on the body of the bowl, fluting runs down from the notches, and the arms of Holland are engraved within a floral cartouche. Ridgway describes it as 'one of the finest things ever made in Chester'.[13] In 1962 and 1965 it was sold at auction for £1,900 and £3,500 respectively.

In about 1664 so few goldsmiths were working in Chester (only Gerrard Jones, who died in 1665, Thomas Chapman and Edwardes, were members of their guild), that they decided to merge with the Watchmakers'; they were joined during the next twenty years by Nathaniel Bullen (whose early mark was a bull's head) in 1669; Peter Pemberton in 1676; Thomas Robinson in 1682; and Ralph Walley, also in 1682; three years later Walley was elected Warden of the company.

When the Chester goldsmiths re-organized themselves separately from the Watchmakers' they chose Peter Edwardes I as their Assay Master; he was Sheriff in 1673 and mayor in 1682. His son, Peter, and Walley were elected as wardens, who in 1682 were empowered to visit their members' premises 'once every week or as often as they see needful'. The town mark consisted of three garbs (wheat-sheaves) separated by a sword, an adaption of the crest of the city, a belted sword, which was used as a standard mark.

13. pp. 136–7.

Ralph Walley (1661–1703), who became Free of the Company on 15 November 1682, is known for eight pieces of plate: the most important is a jug of 1690/92 with a wooden handle attached at rather more than a right angle to the pear-shaped body, which rises from a moulded rim foot; there is a beaded rat-tail decoration under the lip; on the opposite side is an engraved coat-of-arms, possibly those of McCullough of Myreton. For some years this piece has been described as a 'mead-jug'; in view of the fact that it has a wooden handle, presumably for hot liquids, it is surely more likely that it was in fact made for punch. In 1973 it was acquired at Christie's for the sum of £4,500 by the Grosvenor Museum, Chester, with the help of a £750 grant from the National Art Collections Fund, and contributions from the Goldsmiths' Company, the Pilgrim Trust, the Mark Fitch Foundation, and the Victoria and Albert Museum; it had already been sold to a collector in Boston, Massachusetts, to whom an export licence was refused for four weeks in the expectation that the necessary funds would be forthcoming. In 1963 it had been sold at Sotheby's for £1,200. Walley's other pieces are a paten of about 1683, 9 in. in diameter, with fine engraving of berries and leaves around the rim and surrounding the central inscription 'John Thomason, Joseph Maddock, Churchwardens, 1683'; two spoons, and four tankards, all of a plain drum-shape set on a reeded base, with a flat-stepped cover having a saw-toothed front edge, below which is engraved a coat-of-arms within a decorative cartouche; the S-shaped handle has a feather type thumb-piece: one, made between 1686 and 1690, was recently sold for £4,000. Walley, who was the son of Peter Walley, a draper, lived and worked in Eastgate Street; he had six sons, three of whom became Freeman of the City of Chester, but none seems to have followed in his father's footsteps as a goldsmith.

Timothy Gardner became Free of the city in 1686 and of the Company in the following year; he is known only for a communion cup and paten at Llansadwrn, Anglesey. His son, Thomas, became Free in 1721. Alexander Pulford, an apprentice of Peter Edwards II, became Free in 1690, and served as Warden from 1692 to 1697; only four pieces bearing his mark, a monogram AP, are known, including a fine taperstick of 1705 engraved on the base with a lion rampant regardant. Thomas Robinson, who lived in Goss Street, became Free on 11 May 1682, and Warden with Peter Pemberton in 1697. From 1682 to 1701 his mark was TR conjoined; in 1702 he registered a new mark, Ro. Pieces bearing the earlier mark include Communion plate, a porringer, a jug, and a cup of 1690/92; the later mark is found on a number of spoons and ladles, tumbler cups, Communion plate, and a flagon-ring of 1711 which was exhibited at the 1973 Chester Festival.

Nathaniel Bullen, who became Free of the Chester Goldsmiths' Company on 19 October 1669 and was Assay Master in 1692, is known for some Communion cups, a number of spoons, a tankard, a tumbler cup of 1703, a small oval tobacco-box $3\frac{1}{2}$ in. long, in the Victoria and Albert Museum, and a large paten inscribed 'The gift of Thomas Barlow [a churchwarden, died 1683] to St. Mary's Church in Chester, 1683'. Bullen had his home and workshop, which he shared with Peter Edwardes I to whom he may have been apprenticed, on the east side of Bridge Street. His marks were NB conjoined, the rebus of a bull's head, and after 1701 Bu.

One of Bullen's apprentices was Bartholomew Duke, who received his Freedom on 16 March 1716, and was admitted to the Company in the following year; he died in 1729 and was buried in St. Mary's Church, Chester; his mark was Du within an indented punch; his son, Thomas, was admitted to the Company in March 1772, when Bartholomew's nephew, Joseph, was Warden, a position which he occupied until 1809. Joseph had been admitted to the Company in 1764 and had become Free in 1769: his mark was ID separated by a mullet, and that of Thomas TD within a deckled shield. The last Chester Assay Master, Mr. A. Vincent Ward, is a descendant of the Duke family.

Another apprentice of Bullen was Peter Pemberton, a Freeman in 1676/7, admitted to the Goldsmiths' Company on 31 July 1677 and elected Warden in 1699. He was the founder of a family of fine Chester goldsmiths; his best-known piece is a 'Queen Anne' style chocolate-pot of 1703; the simple swan's neck spout, which emerges from a plain baluster body, relieved only by bands of reeding around the foot and neck, is set at right angles to the wooden handle which has a silver strap with crested edges; the acorn finial and the cover are attached to the handle by chains. This pot crossed the Atlantic to the United States in 1958 for £1,200. In the same year Pemberton made a fine tankard with a boldly scrolling handle and a corkscrew thumb-piece, which in 1973 was exhibited at the Chester Festival. Peter Pemberton, who worked in Eastgate Street, had two brothers, Thomas and Benjamin, three sons, Peter II, Samuel and Benjamin II, and two grandsons. Benjamin II made in 1725 a small tumbler cup, gilded inside, and engraved with its owner's initials; another piece, made in the same year, is a christening-mug inscribed 'IANE

IONES, MARCHE YE 1st. 1726.7'. Also made by Benjamin in 1725 is a cream-jug – an unusual item for a provincial goldsmith – described in Sotheby's catalogue (19 October 1961) as having an 'inverted pear-shaped body chased at the shoulders and foot with diaper scale ornament, scrolls and leafage, the narrow neck chased under the lip with a shell motif and at the upper handle terminal, capped with a satyr mask and a leaf at the lower end of the serpent, on spreading circular base, 5 in. high: 6 oz. 4 dwts.'; it sold for £150. Peter Pemberton II died in 1727 leaving a son, Peter III, who became Free in 1756/7. Samuel's son, William, received his Freedom in 1770. Benjamin II appears to have died in 1754.

John Bingley, who was apprenticed to Timothy Gardner in 1692 and was admitted to the Company on 9 September 1702, was the first Chester goldsmith to join the Company after the Act of 1701; he is known for only one piece of silver, the Communion cup at Church Minshull, which bears his mark, Bi in script beneath an arrow. Charles Bird, who also used the letters Bi but without the arrow, was apprenticed to Thomas Robinson and became Free in 1697; his family came from the village of Broxton, some twelve miles south-west of Chester.

Another prominent family of eighteenth-century Chester goldsmiths were the Richardsons, who also appear to have taken an active part in civic affairs. Richard Richardson I, the son of John Richardson of Knightwick, Worcestershire, became Free in 1703 and Sheriff of the city in 1714. Richard Richardson, who was born in 1674, was himself apprenticed to Ralph Walley; he was evidently sufficiently well thought of to receive a grant of £25 from the City Council after completion of his articles of apprenticeship, to enable him to set up in business on his own account. After his death in 1730 the business passed into the hands of his eighteen-year-old son, Richard II (1712–69), Mayor of Chester in 1751, and subsequently to his grandson, Richard III, who remained in the business until 1823; the name of the firm was at some later date changed to Butt & Co.

Richard Richardson I, who worked in Eastgate Street, was the most prolific member of the family, and is thought to have made more ecclesiastical plate than any other provincial goldsmith since the sixteenth century. In addition he made an enormous quantity of ceremonial civic plate, among which the pair of maces made for the use of Caernarvon Corporation are usually regarded as his most important oeuvre. Each mace measures 29 in. in length, and is capped by a bowl resting on a ribbed knop, surmounted by an engraved border set between a pair of ribs, and an ornamental frieze in which is incorporated the Prince of Wales' feathers. A crown of arches rises over all, with an orb-and-cross finial. The bowls are finely engraved with two coats-of-arms and an inscription stating that the maces were the gift of 'Captain George Twistleton of Ilyar Esqr. to the Ancient and Loyal Corporation of Carnarvan, 1718'. One mace was fashioned from silver taken from an old London-made mace of about 1650, and both are marked with Richardson's mark, RI within an oval.

Among civic items made by Richardson and now owned by the city of Chester is an oval tobacco-box of 1704, made from silver obtained by melting down a (presumably) smaller box of 1673. Richardson's box, $5\frac{3}{4}$ in. long, stands on four ball feet and is engraved on the cover with the city's coat-of-arms, and the inscription 'Edward Partington Mayor 1704'; inside is a pipe-stopper engraved with the date 1673 which must have come from the original box: in 1742 this box was repaired by Thomas Maddock. Also in the civic collection is the 'Chester City Oar' made by Richardson in 1719. It is 14 in. in length with a plain blade and a square shaft. On one side are engraved the city arms and 'Rd. STUBS' 1752'; the second bears a coat-of-arms and the motto 'EITHER FOR EVER', and the third the inscription 'James Meakin 17 MARCH 1812'; the fourth side is unmarked. In 1721 Richardson was commissioned to provide a silver head for the 6 ft. 3 in. long Mayor's Porter's Staff: this head is $5\frac{1}{4}$ in. deep and is beautifully embossed with the arms of the city – both old and new versions – and representations of the city's sword and mace contained within cartouches, and the inscription 'Thos. Edwards, Esq. Mayor. 1721'. Chester Corporation also possess two rat-tailed spoons made by Richardson in 1712, with the crest of a bull's head on their necks.

Richardson did not, however, disdain to make ordinary everyday domestic items, among which are a taperstick of 1704, now owned by Magdalen College; a $2\frac{1}{4}$ in. high tumbler-cup (of which he made a number), dated 1721, belonging to the Shoemakers' Guild of Carlisle, and now in the Tuillie House Museum in that city; and a 2 in. high mug of 1721 in the same collection.

Richard Richardson II was apprenticed to his father, Richard I, and became Free in 1732; he made a fine pair of tumbler-cups, dated 1748, which were exhibited at the 1970 British Antique Dealers Fair: each weighs 2 oz. and is engraved in italics, the one with 'The Sheriff's Office', the other with 'The Foreman's Oath'. Richardson is also known for a number of small mugs, mostly made between about 1748 and 1765. His son, Richard IV, became Free in 1779 and was elected Assay Master in 1785, but resigned in 1791.

William Richardson, Richard I's youngest brother, became Free in 1720 and was a warden of the Goldsmiths' Company of Chester in 1724; in 1722 he made the silver bowl of a wooden-handled spoon, now in the collection of Chester Corporation. This spoon is some 18 in. in length overall, with a bowl measuring approximately 3 in. by 4 in. and is punched on the back with William's mark, RI distinguished by a half-moon over the 'I'. A silver-mounted coconut-cup bound with three vertical silver straps and with engraved scalloped borders to the mounts, rising from a circular domed foot, punched six times with William's mark but with no standard mark or date-letter, but of about 1730, sold at Christie's in November 1973 for £180. William died in about 1750: his elder son, William II, became apprenticed to his father in 1734; his younger son, Richard III, did not join the Goldsmiths' Company until 1773, from which it has been deduced that he entered the business during the inter-regnum between the death of Richard II in 1769 and 1779 when Richard IV became Free.

Thomas Maddock (1700–61) became Free in 1720 and in the following year joined the Company; he was elected Warden in 1723 and Assay Master six years later; he became Mayor of Chester in 1744. Maddock's marks were Ma and TM within an oval punch; in 1730 he made a fine seal for St. John's Hospital, Chester.

George Walker was apprenticed to Richard Richardson II and became Free in 1767: he was elected to the Company on 19 July 1770, became Warden in 1773, and Assay Master in 1791. Four pieces by him were exhibited during the 1973 Chester Festival: a porringer and a beaker (1769); a sauce-boat (1784); and a papboat (1789) – all bearing his mark GW within a rectangle. His son, George II, joined the Company in 1794 and became Free in 1779.

George Lowe (1738–1814), father of the founder of the firm of Lowe & Sons which still flourishes today in Bridge Street Row, Chester, was the son of William Lowe of Guilden Sutton and the grandson of Ralph Lowe. George and his wife, Mary (née Bennett), had eight children: the eldest, George II (1768–1841), was apprenticed as a goldsmith and received his Freedom in 1791. George's younger brother Edward (1773–1856) became a watchcase maker in 1792/3. George II was appointed to the post of Assay Master in the year before his death, and was followed by his son

RICHARDSON PEDIGREE

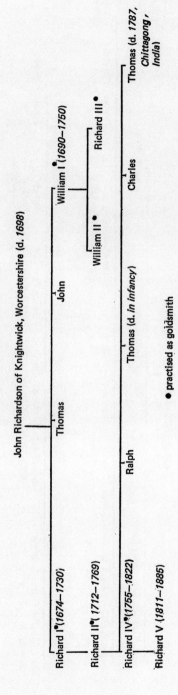

John Richardson of Knightwick, Worcestershire (d. *1698*)

Thomas

John

William I *(1690–1750)*

William II ●

Richard III ●

Charles

Thomas (d. *1787, Chittagong, India*)

Richard I ● *(1674–1730)*

Richard II ● *(1712–1769)*

Richard IV ● *(1755–1822)*

Richard V *(1811–1885)*

Ralph

Thomas (d. *in infancy*)

● practised as goldsmith

LOWE PEDIGREE

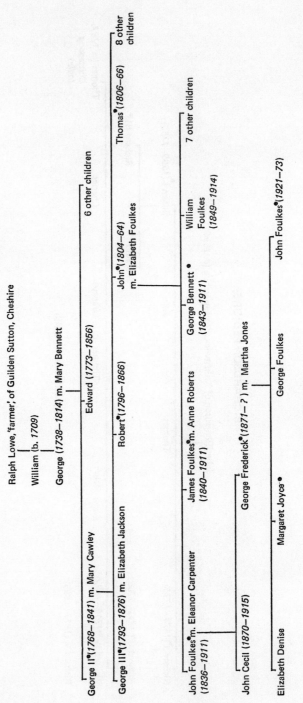

Ralph Lowe, 'farmer', of Guilden Sutton, Cheshire

William (b. *1709*)

George (*1738–1814*) m. Mary Bennett

Edward (*1773–1856*)   6 other children

George II• (*1768–1841*) m. Mary Cawley

Thomas• (*1806–66*)   8 other children

Robert• (*1796–1866*)

John• (*1804–64*) m. Elizabeth Foulkes

George III• (*1793–1876*) m. Elizabeth Jackson

George Bennett• (*1843–1911*)

William Foulkes (*1849–1914*)   7 other children

James Foulkes• m. Anne Roberts (*1840–1911*)

John Foulkes• m. Eleanor Carpenter (*1836–1911*)

George Frederick• (*1871–?*) m. Martha Jones

John Cecil (*1870–1915*)

George Foulkes

John Foulkes• (*1921–73*)

Margaret Joyce•

Elizabeth Denise

• practised as goldsmith

Thomas (1806–66), who held office until 1864. George II's eldest son, George III (1793–1876), became a goldsmith in Gloucester, and his second son, Robert (1796–1866), a goldsmith in Birmingham. George II's third and fourth sons, John (1804–64) and Thomas, took over their father's business after his death, the former becoming both Prime Warden of the Goldsmiths' Company and Sheriff in 1841. John's eldest son, John Foulkes (1836–1911), followed his father in both these posts in 1897; John's second son, James Foulkes (1840–1911), was Assay Master from 1865–1910. The family business was continued by John Foulke's younger son, George Frederick, who married Martha Jones of Towyn; their fourth child, John Foulkes (1921–73) continued the business with his younger sister, Margaret Joyce. The Lowes' marks were variations of GL, JL, and TL, sometimes separated by a pellet; GF Lo below a mullet within a Maltese cross, and JL over JL for John and Joyce Lowe.

Prior to the opening of Assay Offices at Birmingham and Sheffield in 1773, Chester was responsible for 'touching' the products of those and other Midland and northern towns. In 1773 a Parliamentary Committee inspecting provincial Assay Offices reported that 'it appears to this Committee that the Assay Office at Chester has been conducted with fidelity and skill'. After that date, however, and with the mass production methods introduced during the Industrial Revolution of the late eighteenth and early nineteenth centuries, and the invention of 'Sheffield' plate, Chester regrettably declined as a centre of the goldsmith's trade. In 1959 the Hallmarking Committee recommended the closure of the Chester Assay Office, which took place three years later.

LIVERPOOL

A number of excellent goldsmiths are known to have worked in Liverpool, and to have marked their own silver during the period when the Chester Assay Office was closed between 1716 and 1776. Benjamin Brancker, who was admitted to the Freedom of Chester in 1715, used as his early mark his initials within an oval, to which he later added a 'liver' (an heraldic cormorant) taken from the city arms. The Corporation of Liverpool own a nice little collection of his silver which includes a coffee-pot, a jug and a tankard; Brancker also made a communion cup for the church of St. Nicholas, Liverpool. A tiny brandy-warming saucepan made by him in about 1700 appeared in a London sale-room in 1967. His son, John, also worked in Liverpool; a saucepan of 1741 bearing the maker's mark JB in upper-case Gothic letters may have been made by him; he died in 1752. His business in Water Street, Liverpool, was taken over by a former employee, Robert Jones, who died in 1756. The business then passed to his widow, Maria, who in 1760 married Joseph Walley (fl. *c.* 1760–1801), who used as his mark I W separated by a pellet. After Maria's death in 1789 Walley was joined by his stepson, Robert Jones II, who started his own business in 1772. In 1970 a magnificent cylindrical coffee-pot, its swan's-neck spout set at right-angles to a wooden handle, also made around 1700, by Robert Shields of Liverpool, sold in New York for over £7,000. The domed and chained cover has a nicely gadrooned border, and the body, near the spout and handle, is decorated with cut-card work. Robert Boulger, Free in 1782, made a delightfully simple pair of beakers with mouldings encircling the rim and base, in 1802.

Among other notable Liverpool goldsmiths were John Gilbert (fl. *c.* 1755); Nicholas Cunliffe (fl. *c.* 1800); John Sutters, whose mark J S within an indented punch appears on a number of spoons, ladles and forks between about 1835 and 1846; and William Smith, who was working in Liverpool in about 1880 using as his mark an incised W S.

MANCHESTER

During the nineteenth century a number of manufacturing goldsmiths worked in Manchester but had their wares assayed in Chester. Among them were Thomas Appleby (fl. *c.* 1810), John Crossley (fl. *c.* 1807) and perhaps John Ollivant who in about 1795 used as his mark the letters I O within a rectangular punch.

BIRMINGHAM AND SHEFFIELD

The cities of Birmingham and Sheffield (which adopted as their mark an anchor and a crown respectively) were granted the right to their own

Assay Offices on 18 May 1773, when they formed companies known as 'The Guardians of the Standard of Wrought Plate within the Town of Birmingham [or Sheffield]', as the case might be. This was due, directly in the case of Birmingham and indirectly in that of Sheffield, to the efforts

of Matthew Boulton whose life and work have been discussed in another chapter.

As previously mentioned James Jackson became Birmingham's first Assay Master, and to him Boulton and his partner John Fothergill sent for assaying on the first day that his office was open, 31 August 1773, 841 oz. of plate. Heading the list is a neo-classical design tea-urn on a square stand, now in the Birmingham City Museum and Art Gallery. The first entry in the books of the Sheffield Assay Office, dated 20 September 1773, is for a 'Britannia' standard two-handled cup and cover with a pineapple finial, weighing 20 oz. 7 dwt. 18 gr. made by Henry Tudor and Thomas Leader; it was followed by a chased cup of 'Sterling' standard silver weighing 29 oz. 14 dwt. by Fenton, Creswick & Co. (Matthew Fenton and Richard Creswick). A Gothic letter 'E' was selected for the 1773 date-letter, reputedly as a tribute to the Earl of Effingham, first Chairman of the Assay Office. Henry Tudor was one of the early guardians of the Sheffield Assay Office, registering his mark in London prior to 1773, and he and his partner were among the finest craftsmen in the early days of Sheffield goldsmithery; they are said to have been induced to come to Sheffield from London by a Dr. Sherburn.

Well executed bright-cut engraving and delicate pierced work are characteristics associated with early Sheffield silver: a cylindrical gravy-argyle with a swan-neck spout made by J. Hoyland & Co. in 1777 bears a good example of the former type of decoration, while a neo-classic cake-basket, made in 1779 by John Younge & Co. and presented five years later to the Royal Academy by J. F. Rigaud as his 'election gift', exemplifies the skill of Sheffield hand-cut saw-piercing.

Between 1773 and about 1832 Sheffield was perhaps best known for its production of candlesticks and candelabra. One of the earliest known Sheffield-made candlesticks is one dated 1774, by George Ashforth & Co.; the square base with gadrooned edging is hung with laurel swags between rams' head masks: the spool-shaped fluted shaft is divided in the middle by a band of moulding, and around the base of the sconce is a complementary band of classical Greek key-pattern design. A fine and typically Sheffield set of six 11 in. high candlesticks was made by John Winter & Co. in 1780; in these examples the stepped bases are circular and are bead-edged; the classically tapering and fluted columns are divided from the inverted bell-shaped sconces, which have beaded rims, by a broad plain band on which are S-shaped swags. Around the turn of the century telescopic candlesticks, which could be shortened or lengthened at will with piston-like precision, were introduced. Other well-known early Sheffield goldsmithing firms were Luke Proctor & Co., and John Roberts & Co. In the 1780s and '90s the partnership of Samuel Roberts and George Cadman, who invented the 'silver thread' edging to Sheffield plate, produced silver second only to that of the great Matthew Boulton.

The cities of both Birmingham and Sheffield produced large quantities of small silver 'toys';[14] the best-known exponent of the art of producing these delicate pieces was Matthew Linwood of Birmingham, who specialized in the production of wine labels; in 1794 Linwood produced the earliest die-stamped wine labels made from beautifully cut casts which produced labels of exceptional quality. A fine snuff-box made by Linwood in 1810 has a view of Battle Abbey embossed on the lid.

Joseph Willmore was another Birmingham craftsman who produced work of an invariably high standard. He is perhaps best known for a number of beautifully chased die struck caddy spoons. In 1838 he made a lovely little snuff-box decorated overall with rococo motifs, among which are a fox, birds, leaves and foliage. His father, Thomas, made in 1791 a most unusual caddy spoon in the shape of a harebell: the wide bell-shaped bowl is nicely chased with a most lifelike swirl of petals.

Joseph Taylor of Birmingham specialized in jockey-cap design caddy spoons which he made in a variety of patterns – halved, plain, quartered or geometric – frequently with a star on the top and bright-cut engraving on the peak. Taylor also produced at least one filigree jockey-cap caddy spoon which he stamped with his initials, although filigree work is normally unmarked; perhaps he was especially proud of this particular piece.

Samuel Pemberton appears to have made a speciality of small boxes for snuff, patches, or toothpicks, with which he sometimes combined a vinaigrette. Nathaniel Mills was another noted box-maker; a box made by him in 1840 has a cast scene of a mounted huntsman, a fox and four hounds on the cover.

Although Birmingham may be said to have produced the bulk of these small pieces, Sheffield too possessed craftsmen skilled in this delicate work, such as Thomas Law in the middle and late 1770s; Matthew Fenton & Co. a few years later, and Roger Gainsford after the turn of the century. Law, who was the most prolific candlestick-maker in Sheffield, was also

14. 'Gold and Silver Toy Makers, who make Trinkets, Seals, Tweezers and Tooth Pick cases, Smelling Bottles, Snuff Boxes and Fillegree Work, such as Toilets, Tea Chests, Inkstands &c. &c.' (*Sketchley's Birmingham Directory*, 1767, p. 56).

a Master Cutler in 1753, and numbered among his apprentices Matthew Fenton and John Winter. Towards the end of his career he was in partnership with John Parsons who from 1783 continued the business as John Parsons & Co.

Among early Victorian firms working in Sheffield were Thomas Bradbury & Sons (who purchased some of the dies of the Boulton Plate Company in 1848), and James Dixon and Sons, both of which survived until the present century. The Sheffield collection of civic plate includes an elaborate centrepiece of 1881, and a tea- and coffee-service of 1883 decorated with flamboyant spread-eagles and masks, both by Dixon & Sons; these pieces were on view at the Sheffield City Museum during the exhibition held in 1973 to celebrate the bi-centenary of the opening of the Assay Office. Also in the exhibition were a magnificent centrepiece presented to James Dixon by his workmen on his retirement in 1845; a fine pair of rococo candlesticks by Matthew Fenton & Co. (1773); another pair, in the neo-classical style, by John Rowbotham & Co. (1775); and an interesting pair of telescopic candlesticks made in 1806 by John Roberts & Co. Other firms working in Sheffield during the first half of the nineteenth century included T. & J. Creswick; I. & I. Waterhouse & Co.; Padley, Parkin & Co.; Henry Wilkinson & Co.; Roberts, Smith & Co., who in 1848 became Smith, Sissons and Co.; Gainsford & Nicholson; and Hawkesworth, Eyre & Co.[15]

15. Marks struck on Old Sheffield Plate by craftsmen mentioned above include:

Joseph Hancock	1755	IOS[H] HANCOCK SHEFFIELD
Thomas Law	1758	TH[O] LAW (or) LAW (or) T.L (in script)
Tudor & Leader	1760	HT & Co. (in script)
John Hoyland	1764	JH & Co. (in script)
Boulton & Fothergill	1764	B & F (between two crowns)
John Winter	1765	IW (followed by a crown)
John Parsons	1784	IOHN PARSONS & CO. (followed by crossed keys)
George Ashforth	1784	ASHFORTH & Co. (followed by a pair of scales)
Matthew Boulton	1784	Twin Suns
Roberts, Cadman & Co.	1785	ROBERTS & CADMAN (followed by a bell)
M. Linwood & Sons	1808	LIN WOOD (between two castles)
T. & J. Creswick	1811	CRESWICK (followed by crossed arrows)
I. & I. Waterhouse & Co.	1833	I & IW & Co. (surmounted by a *fleur-de-lis*)
James Dixon	1835	DS (separated by a flower) (or) DIXON J (or) GR (with a crown between) (or) DIXONS IMPERIAL
Henry Wilkinson	1836	Crossed keys
Smith, Sissons & Co.	1848	A bell
Padley, Parkin & Co.	1849	A hand

George Richards Elkington, born in Birmingham on 17 October 1801, was destined to revolutionize the goldsmiths' craft. From his father, James, he inherited a small 'toy' manufactory in St. Paul's Square, Birmingham, where, after his father's death, he worked in partnership with his cousin Henry Elkington.

In 1836 G. R. Elkington applied for the first of a number of patents for 'an improved method of gilding copper, brass, and other metals or alloys of metals' by means of electrolysis. Two years later he took out a patent jointly with O. W. Barratt for coating metals with zinc.

In 1839 Elkington exhibited in Paris jewellery and bronze *objets d'art* 'gilt without mercury'; on 3 December of the same year he wrote to Benjamin Smith, the London goldsmith, on whose behalf he had been conducting a number of experiments, that 'the four candlesticks you ordered are now ready for silvering and shall be done as richly as possible upon the method we have in use if you wish it. It is uncertain how soon we can complete the improvement we contemplate, but ultimately I have no doubt of effecting it.' More headway was made in the development of this new process than he had anticipated, for three days later he was able to write to Smith that 'We have made sufficient progress to speak positively as to the success, but it will probably take us some weeks before we can commence in earnest as the system is quite different to what we before have had in use.'

On 24 March 1840 Elkington took out a patent on this new process of depositing silver by electrolysis, a discovery which he had made in collaboration with John Wright, a Birmingham surgeon whom he later took into partnership, and a scientist named Alexander Parkes. In the following year they licensed Charles Christofle (1805–63) to manufacture electro-plate in France.

In 1840–41 the cousins entered into agreements with Smith (whose son married G. R. Elkington's daughter), whereby Elkingtons undertook to supply plated goods from their new factory in Newhall Street to Smith alone among London's goldsmiths; Smith agreed to make and sell plated wares in London, while the Elkingtons were to do the same in Birmingham; the profits were to be divided equally.

A few years later Elkington wrote:

The recent discovery of the Electrotype process has already worked important changes in many branches of the arts and results hitherto unobtainable have in most astonishing perfection been accomplished. . . . There is scarcely an article of domestic use but is required by a rapidly increasing portion of the community to assume an historic form. . . . Every encouragement should be given to this growing desire.

Accordingly, in 1845, Elkington commissioned Sir Benjamin Schlick, who had recently arrived in this country after working on the Continent, to satisfy 'this growing desire' by providing the firm with drawings based on designs of ancient Greece and Rome.

By the middle of the 1840s most English Midland manufacturing goldsmiths were employing Elkingtons' process under licence. In their catalogue of 1847 Elkingtons proudly claimed that electro-plate possessed 'all the advantages of silver, in utility and beauty of effect, and at very much less cost to the consumer', and that it had already withstood 'the most severe test of wear in the vessels of the Royal Mail Steam Packet Company, the Peninsular and Orient Company and numerous Club Houses, Hotels and Private houses in every part of the Kingdom'. Their initial prices ranged from £2. 4s. od. for a dozen table forks through £16. 5s. od. for a plain tea-kettle (£17. 10s. od. for an engraved one) to £30 for a candelabrum and £32 for an engraved tea-tray. The firm's early profits arose from the manufacture of these and other domestic items, but they soon sought to rival such firms as Hunt & Roskell and Garrards in the production of massive sculptural centrepieces.

In 1848 Elkingtons bought Benjamin Smith out of his interest in their London branches in Regent Street and Moorgate. They closed down the Moorgate branch and re-opened the Regent Street address as 'Elkington & Co.'. In Birmingham the firm had been known as 'Elkington, Mason & Co.' since 1842, when Josiah Mason joined the cousins as a third partner.

In 1853 Elkingtons were given special authorization to make electrotypes of works of art contained in the museum at Marlborough House.

Among designers employed by Elkingtons were Aimé Chesneau, at one time the master of Albert-Ernest Carrier-Belleuse, and Pierre Emile Jeannest who worked for them from 1853 to 1858 at a salary of £450 per annum, and who specialized in Renaissance and Classical designs, sometimes containing a hint of lobate decoration as developed by the van Vianens; he also designed a small statue of Lady Godiva for the Prince Consort; a group of Queen Elizabeth I and the Earl of Leicester; and a figure of Charles I at Edgehill. Albert Willms, who had at one time worked in Paris for Christofle and François-Désiré Froment-Meurice (1802–55), joined Elkingtons in 1855 and produced designs in the Byzantine and Gothic taste. The firm's most noted artist, however, was Léonard

16

Morel-Ladeuil who worked for Elkingtons from 1859, when he was earning £400 per annum, until his death in 1888: his finest work is the magnificent oval 'Milton Shield' (now in the Victoria and Albert Museum), made by Elkingtons in silver and damascened iron, which won a gold medal at the 1867 Paris Exhibition.

When he died in 1865 at the age of sixty-four George Elkington left the sum of £350,000, most of which had been made out of the profits of the firm bearing his name, and a prosperous business which supplied work for well over a thousand employees. Ten years later the *Art Journal* was of the opinion that 'Elkington & Co. are still the leading producers of this kind of ware ... electroplating has encouraged it [artistic development] by permitting the manufacture of works of Art at a relatively low-price ... electroplated goods of white alloys are practically little inferior to those made of solid silver.' In 1889 the same publication reported that 'Messers. Elkington & Co. have not only been content to make a reputation, they have been careful to sustain it.'

Today, two hundred years after they were granted their right of 'touch', Birmingham and Sheffield are the only remaining provincial English Assay Offices.

Bibliography

Paul De Lamerie

BANISTER, J. *Old English Silver*; London (1965).

CARRINGTON, J. B. AND HUGHES, G. R. *The Plate of the Worshipful Company of Goldsmiths*; London (1926).

EVANS, J. 'Huguenot Goldsmiths in England and Ireland' in *Proceedings of the Huguenot Society* XIV (1933). 'Huguenot Goldsmiths of London' in *Proceedings of the Huguenot Society* XV (1936).

GRIMWADE, A. G. *Rococo Silver 1727–1765*; London (1974).

HAYWARD, J. F. *Huguenot Silver in England 1688–1727*; London (1959).

HONOUR, H. *Goldsmiths and Silversmiths*; London (1971).

MCNAB, D. J. *Metropolitan Museum Bulletin* XXVI, pp. 174–9 (1967–8).

PHILLIPS, P. H. S. *Paul De Lamerie*; London (1935).

SELVIG, F. *The Minneapolis Institute of Arts Bulletin*, LI, pp. 72–7 (1962).

Hester Bateman and her Family

BANISTER, J. *Old English Silver*; London (1965).

OMAN, C. *English Domestic Silver*; London (1962).

ROWE, R. *Adam Silver, 1765–95*; London (1965).

SHURE, D. S. *Hester Bateman, Queen of English Silversmiths*; London (1959).

TAYLOR, G. *Silver*; London (1956).

Matthew Boulton

DELIEB, E. *The Great Silver Manufactory: Matthew Boulton and the Birmingham Silversmiths*; London (1971).

DICKINSON, H. W. *Matthew Boulton*; Cambridge (1937).

GALE, W. K. V. *Boulton, Watt, and the Soho undertakings*; City of Birmingham Museum and Art Gallery, Department of Science and Industry (1952).

GOODISON, N. 'Matthew Boulton and the King's Clock Case' in *The Connoisseur*, pp. 77–84 (June 1970).

HOLLAND, M. *Old Country Silver* (1971).

HONOUR, H. *Goldsmiths and Silversmiths*; London (1971).

HUGHES, G. B. *Antique Sheffield Plate*; London (1970).

ROBINSON, E. 'Matthew Boulton's Marketing Techniques' in *The Economic History Review*, 2nd series, XVI, pp. 39–60 (1963). 'Matthew Boulton, Patron of the Arts' in *Annals of Science* IX (1953).

ROWE, R. *Adam Silver, 1765–1795*; London (1965).

SEABY, W. A. AND HETHERINGTON, R. S. 'The Matthew Boulton Pattern Books' in *Apollo* (February and March 1950).

SMILES, DR. S. *Lives of Boulton and Watt* (1865).

Boulton's will in the Public Record Office.

Boulton papers in the Birmingham Assay Office

Boulton and Watt Collection in the Birmingham Public Reference Library.

Paul Storr

ANON. *Memoirs of the late Philip Rundell Esq., Goldsmith and Jeweller to His Majesty and the Royal Family, late of the Golden Salmon, Ludgate Hill, who by industry and perseverance accumulated the immense fortune of One Million and a Half, Interspersed with Anecdotes. To which is added his Will.* By a Gentleman many years connected with the firm; London (1827).

BANISTER, J. *Old English Silver*; London (1965).

CARRINGTON, J. B. AND HUGHES, G. R. *The Plate of the Worshipful Company of Goldsmiths*; London (1926).

DORAN, W. An undated and pirated edition of the *Memoirs . . .*, reproduced by E. A. Jones in 'A Royal Goldsmith – Memoirs of Philip Rundell, Esq.' in *Apollo* (September 1942).

FOX, G. MS memoirs in the library of the Victoria and Albert Museum (1843–6).

HONOUR, H. *Goldsmiths and Silversmiths*; London (1971).

PENZER, N. M. *Paul Storr*; London (1954).

SITWELL, H. D. W. 'The Jewel House and the Royal Goldsmiths' in the *Archaeological Journal* CXVII, pp. 131–55 (1960).

Augustine Courtauld and his Family

CHESTER, J. L. *Some Earlier History of the Family of Courtauld* (1911).

COURTAULD, S. L. *The Huguenot Family of Courtauld* I; London (1957).

HAYWARD, J. F. *The Courtauld Silver* (1966): *Huguenot Silver in England 1688–1727*; London (1959).

JONES, E. A. *Some Silver Wrought by the Courtauld Family of London Goldsmiths in the Eighteenth Century*; Oxford (1940).

ROWE, R. *Adam Silver, 1765–95*; London (1965).

EVANS, J. 'The Huguenot Goldsmiths in England and Ireland' in *Proceedings of the Huguenot Society* XIV, pp. 496–554.

Garrard and Co.

A.M.B. *The Story of Garrards, Goldsmiths and Jewellers to Six Sovereigns in three centuries, 1721–1911*; London (1912).

GRIMWADE, A. G. 'The Garrard Ledgers' in the *Proceedings of Society of Silver Collectors* (10 April 1961).

HONOUR, H. *Goldsmiths and Silversmiths*; London (1971).

SITWELL, H. D. W. 'The Jewel House and the Royal Goldsmiths' in the *Archaeological Journal* CXVII, pp. 131–55 (1960).

WARDLE, P. *Victorian Silver and Silver Plate*; London (1963).

The ledgers of the company in the possession of Messrs. Garrard & Co. and the library of the Victoria and Albert Museum.

Family papers etc. in the possession of Mrs. Jean Meade-Fetherstonhaugh.

The Hennell Family

BANISTER, J. 'Silversmiths for five generations: Hennell family' in *Country Life*, p. 976 (April 1973).

HENNELL, P. G. 'The Hennells identified' in *The Connoisseur* (December 1955). 'Masterpieces in Metal: Silver ... and the Hennells' in the *Anvil* – house journal of the Davy-Ashmore Group (Winter 1968 issue). 'The Hennells, a continuity of craftsmanship' in *The Connoisseur* (February 1973).

Family papers etc. in the possession of Mr. P. G. Hennell.

Anthony Nelme

HAYWARD, J. F. *Huguenot Silver in England, 1688–1727*; London (1959).

HONOUR, H. *Goldsmiths and Silversmiths*; London (1971).

HUSSEY, C. *Country Life* (14 May 1964 and 21 December 1972).

JONES, E. A. *The Plate of St. George's Chapel, Windsor Castle* (1939).

David Willaume

HAYWARD, J. F. *Huguenot Silver in England, 1688–1727*; London (1959).

HONOUR, H. *Goldsmiths and Silversmiths*; London (1971).
EVANS, J. *Proceedings of the Huguenot Society of London* XIV, pp. 496–554 (1929–33) and XLV, pp. 4–14 (1965).
Lady Irwin's account in Leeds Public Library.
Willaume's will in the Public Record Office.

Paul Crespin

BANISTER, J. 'Silver with a special flourish: the work of Paul Crespin' in *Country Life Annual*, pp. 11–13 (1971).
BARRAUD, E. M. *Barraud – the story of a family*; London (1967).
JONES, E. A. 'Paul Crespin, Huguenot Goldsmith' in *Proceedings of the Huguenot Society of London* XVI, No. 3 (1940).
ROWE, R. *Adam Silver, 1765–95*; London (1965).
SYMONDS, R. W. *The Connoisseur* (June 1940).
WENHAM, E. *The Antique Collector* (November–December 1945).

Thomas Heming

GRIMWADE, A. G. *The Connoisseur* CXXXVII, pp. 175–8 (1956).
HONOUR, H. *Goldsmiths and Silversmiths*; London (1971).
OMAN, C. *English Church Plate, 597–1830*; London (1957). *Country Life*, pp. 1850–51 (5 November 1954).
ROWE, R. *Adam Silver, 1765–95*; London (1965).
SITWELL, H. D. W. 'The Jewel House and the Royal Goldsmiths' in *The Archaeological Journal* CXVII, pp. 131–55 (1960).
THIEME, U. AND BECKER, F. *Allgemeines Lexikon der bildenden Künstler*; Leipzig XVI, p. 361, (1907–50).
ZAHLE, E. *Det Danske Kunstindustri-museum Virkomted*, pp. 14–34 (1954–9).

Provincial Goldsmiths

BALL, S. 'Ancient Chester Goldsmiths and their Work' in *The Connoisseur* (May 1932).
BANISTER, J. *Old English Silver*; London (1965). 'Silver at the Chester Festival' in *Country Life* (28 June 1973).
BOARD OF TRADE. *Report of the Departmental Committee on Hallmarking*; H.M.S.O. (1959).
BOYLE, J. R. 'Goldsmiths of Newcastle' in *Archaeologia Aeliana* (1894).
BRADBURY, F. *History of Old Sheffield Plate* (1912).
CASLEY, H. C. 'An Ipswich Worker of Elizabethan Church Plate' in *Proceedings of Suffolk Institute of Archaeology* XII.

CHANTER, J. 'Devon Church Plate' XXXVII, 'Barnstaple' XLIX, and 'Plymouth' (1936–7) in *Report and Transactions of Devonshire Association*.

DICKINSON, H. W. *Matthew Boulton*; Cambridge (1936).

FALLOW, T. W. *Yorkshire Church Plate* I and II.

HOLLAND, M. *Old Country Silver* (1971).

HUGHES, G. B. 'Hallmarks on British Provincial Silver' in *Country Life* (9 April 1959). *Antique Sheffield Plate*; London (1970).

HUGHES, G. B. AND T. '200 Years of the Sheffield Hallmark' in *Country Life* (26 July 1973).

LEE, W. 'Rare Yorkshire Church Plate' and 'Civic and Other Silver Plate in York' in *The Antique Collector* (April, May, June, October and November 1967).

OMAN, C. 'Civic Plate and Insignia of the City of Norwich' in *The Connoisseur* CLVI (1964). 'Civic Plate and Insignia of York' in *The Connoisseur* (October and November 1967).

PRATTENT, O. J. 'Marks of the Plymouth Goldsmiths' in *Country Life* (20 October 1960).

REID, C. L. 'Old Newcastle Goldsmiths' in the *Newcastle and Gateshead Chamber of Commerce Journal* (March 1928).

RIDGWAY, M. H. *Some Chester Goldsmiths and their Marks* (1973). *Chester Goldsmiths from early times to 1726* (1968).

SMITH, M. A. *The Bi-centenary of the Family Firm of Lowe and Sons* (1970).

WARDLE, P. *Victorian Silver and Silver Plate*; London (1963).

Elkington Records in the Department of Metalwork, Victoria and Albert Museum, London.

Catalogues

CHESTER FESTIVAL, 1973. *Silver on view at the Grosvenor Museum*.

DEVON FESTIVAL, 1957. *Exeter Silversmiths' Domestic Silver of the Sixteenth–Eighteenth Centuries*; Royal Albert Museum, Exeter.

LOAN EXHIBITION, CASTLE MUSEUM, NORWICH. *Norwich Silver, 1563–1706*. Introduction by G. N. Barrett.

SOCIETY OF ANTIQUARIES OF NEWCASTLE UPON TYNE. *Exhibition of Silver Plate of Newcastle manufacture at the Black Gate Museum* (1897).

General

BANISTER, J. *Old English Silver*; London (1965).

CHAFFERS, W. *Gilda Aurifabrorum: a History of London Goldsmiths and Plateworkers and their Marks stamped on Plate*; London (1883).

FALLON, J. P. *Marks of London Goldsmiths and Silversmiths* (1972).

HEAL, A. *London Goldsmiths, 1200–1800*; Cambridge (1935).

JACKSON, SIR C. *English Goldsmiths and their Marks*; London (1921).

JONES, E. A. *The Gold and Silver of Windsor Castle*; London (1911).

OMAN, C. *English Domestic Silver*; London (1962).

TAYLOR, G. *Silver*; London (1965).

Index

Acts of the Apostles, the, 16
Adam, Robert, 85–86, 88, 89
Aelfric, 'The Grammarian', 16
Albert, Prince, 153, 155, 176
Albemarle, Earl of, 193
Alexandra, Queen, 150–151
Anecdotes of William Hogarth written by himself, 30
Anglesey, Marquess of, 152, 154
Anthony, Edward, 202
Appleby, Thomas, 236
Apprenticeship Books of the Royal Society of Genealogists, 190
Archambo, Peter, 53
Archives départmentalles de La Rochelle, 126
Art Journal, the, 242
Ascalon, Battle of, 154
Ashburnham, John, Earl of, 44
Ashforth, George & Co., 237
Ashmolean Museum, Oxford, 35, 44
Assay Bill, 82
Avery, John, 203

Bailey, Henry, 61
Baker, Valentine, 213
Barachim, Abraham, 224
Bardin, Anne, 129
Barnstaple, 204
Barratt, 240
Barraud, E. M., *The Story of a Family*, 190
Bateman, Ann, 64–65
Bateman, Hester, 57–64
   birth of, 57
   marries John Bateman, 57
   children of, 58, 59
   widowhood of, 59
   maker's marks of, 61, 62
   retirement of, 63
   death of, 64
Bateman, John, 57, 58, 59
Bateman, John Jnr., 58, 59, 60, 63
Bateman, Jonathan, 59, 62, 63
Bateman, Jonathan Jnr, 63, 65
Bateman, Peter, 58–60

   apprenticeship of, 60
   Freeman of the City of London, 60
   maker's mark of, 63, 64
   marries Elizabeth Beaver, 61
   family business left to, (with Jonathan), 63
Bateman, Peter and Ann, 64, 71–72
Bateman, Peter and William, 65
Bateman, William, 58, 62
Bateman, William Jnr, 65, 66, 67
Battle of the Nile Cup, the (*see* Paul Storr)
Batty, Francis, 215
Beaver, Elizabeth, 61
Beckwith, Robert, 220
Beilby, William, 216, 217
Bennett, Sampson, 203
Bérain, Jean, 50
Berrow's Worcester Journal, 84
Best, Marmaduke, 221, 222
Best, William, 64
Beyer, Elizabeth Susanna, 102, 113
Bilfrith, Saint, 16
Bilton, Eli, 214, 215
Bingley, John, 230
Bird, Charles, 230
Birmingham, 75, 201
   right of touch granted to, 75
   town mark, 236
   City Museum and Art Gallery, 86
   Reference Library, 88, 91
Board of Ordnance, 183
Boldero, John, 197
Borough of Holborn, 173, 178
Boulger, Robert, 236
Boulton, Matthew, 74–96
   family of, 75
   birth of, 75
   marries (1) Mary Robinson, 75
   marries (2) Anne Robinson, 76
   children of, 76
   founds new business in Soho, 77
   maker's marks of, 78, 82–83
   work in Sheffield plate, 78–79
   work in silver, 79–80
   partnership with John Fothergill, 77

Boulton, Matthew,—cont.
  Chester marked silver by, 83
  agitation for Assay Office at Birmingham,
    79–82
  cassolette at Temple Newsam, Leeds, 86–87
  death of, 92
  funeral of, 92
  will of, 92
  portraits, busts of, 94–95
  honours awarded to, 94
Boulton & Fothergill, 77, 78, 79, 82, 86
  silver designed by Robert Adam for, 86, 87,
    88
  silver designed by James Wyatt for, 89–90
Boyle, Henry, 33
Bradbury, Thomas & Sons, 239
Bradley, Samuel, 84
Brancker, Benjamin, 235
Brancker, John, 235–236
Bridge, John, 121–123
Bridge, John Gawler, 43
Bridgwater, 205
Bristol, 201–202
Bristol City Art Gallery, 176, 201
Bristol, 1st Earl of, 187
Britten, F. J., Old Clocks and Watches and their
    Makers, 125
Bronowski, Dr. Jacob, The Ascent of Man, 17–18
Bruno, C. L., 174, 176, 178
Bruton, 205
Buccleuch, Duke of, 152
Buckle, Joseph, 222
Bull, History of Newport Pagnell, 163
Bullen, Nathaniel, 227, 229
Burlington, Earl of, 193
Bury St. Edmunds, 211
Busfield, William, 222
Buttell, Thomas, 208

Cadman, George, 78, 238
Campbell Museum, the, 42, 124, 152, 187, 196
Canterbury, Archbishop of, 146
Carlille, Peter, 223
Carlisle, 218
Caroline, Princess, 198
Carrington, J. B. and Hughes, G. R., The Plate of
    the Worshipful Company of Goldsmiths,
    43–44, 45, 110
Carter, John, 81
Catherine, Empress of Russia, 191
Chamberlain's Court at the Guildhall, the, 26
Chapman, Thomas, 227
Charles II, King,
Chawner, William, 199
Cheltenham Spa, 92
Chernock, Sir Pysent, Bt., 188
Chesneau, Aimé, 241
Chester, 201, 224–235
Chester, guild of, 225, 227
Chesterman, Charles, 166
Child, Sir Francis, 15
Child, Sir Josiah, Discourse on Trade, 15

Christie's, 29, 47, 48, 146, 149, 186, 188, 193,
    199, 217
Christofle, Charles, 240
Civil List of the Crown, 23
Claes, Thomas, 60
Clare College, Cambridge, 44
Clark, Kenneth, Civilization, 17
Clarke, Richard, 60, 62
Clifford, Charlotte, Baroness, 193
Clinton, Lord George, 36
Clotaire II, King of the Franks, 16
Cobbold, Matthew, 208
Cobbold, Richard, 208
Cobbold, William, 208, 209
Coeur de Lion, Richard, 154
Colchester, 211
Collier, Joseph, 203, 206
Composite Order, 93
Conway, Christopher, 225–226
Conway, Peter, 225–226
Cook, James, 91
Cooke, Erasmus, 211
Cookson, Isaac, 215, 216, 217
Coton, John, 204
Cotterill, 153, 154, 155, 156
Council of the Stock Exchange, 177
Courtauld, Augustin, 126–128
Courtauld, Augustine, 129–134
  apprenticeship of, 127–128
  maker's marks of, 129–130
  Free, by service, of the Worshipful Company
    of Goldsmiths, 129
  apprentices of, 130
  marries Anne Bardin, 129
  children of, 129, 130, 134
  State Salt of the Corporation of the City of
    London, by, 133
  death of, 130
  will of, 130
  portraits of, 130–131
  assessment of work of, 131–133
Courtauld, Augustine Jnr, 127, 128
Courtauld, Louisa, 136–138
  widowhood of, 136
  maker's marks of, 135–137, 138
  partnership with George Cowles, 137
  partnership with her son, Samuel, 138
  portrait of, by Zoffany, 137
  Fitzgibbon Cup, by Samuel and, 138
  death of, 138
Courtauld, Peter, 128–129
Courtauld, Samuel, 134–136
  apprenticeship of, 134
  maker's marks of, 134
  marriage to Louisa Perina Ogier, 134
  apprentice of, 135
  assessment of work of, 135–136
  death of, 136
  toilet service probably for member of Russian
    court, by, 136
Courtauld, Samuel Jnr, 138
Coventry, 212
Cowles, George, 81, 137

Cramer, Thomas, 213
Cranbourne, Lord, 79
Crawford, David and James, 217
Crespell, Sebastian and James, 148
Crespin, Paul, 190–195
  family of, 190
  marriage to Mary Branboeuf, 192
  children of, 192, 195
  maker's marks of, 190, 191, 194, 195
  portrait of, 192
Creswick, T. & J., 239
Cripps, William, 188
Crossley, John, 236
Cumberland, Duke of, 146
Cunliffe, Nicholas, 236
Curtis, Stephen, 201
Cutlers' Company, the, 80
Czars of Russia, the, 29

Daily Advertiser, the, 49
Daily Journal, the, 38
Daily Post, the, 38
Dalton, Edward, 218
Dare, Thomas, 207
Dartmouth, Lord, 79
Davison, Thomas, 214
De Lamerie, Paul, 21–55
  family of, 21–22
  baptism of, 22
  apprenticeship of, 25
  apprentices of, 34–35
  maker's marks of, 26, 39, 43
  marries Louisa Juliott, 27
  Elected to the Livery of his guild, 28
  children of, 28
  commissioned to make silver-plate for the
    Czars of Russia, 29
  Great Seal Salver, by, 31
  Armory v. Delamirie case and, 33–35
  Treby dressing-table service by, 35
  Assistant of the Goldsmiths' Company, 38
  appointed to committee of the Goldsmiths'
    Company, 42
  Ashburnham Cup by, 44
  Newdigate Centrepiece, by, 46
  Wardenships of the Goldsmiths' Company
    held by, 47
  work in the Chinoiserie fashion, 47
  work in the Hogarthian style, 31
  work in the Rococo style
  death of, 48
  evaluation of the work of, 51–55
  will of, 49, 50
Denys, Martyn, 211
Design Registry, the, 168
Devlin, Stuart, 177
Devonshire, Duke of, 151, 193
Dictionary of National Biography, the, 20
Dixon, Gilbert, 80
Dixon, James & Sons, 239
Dolgellau Chalice, the, 225
Dorchester, 205
Dowling, Ann, 62

Dowthwaite, John, 214
Duke, Bartholomew, 229
Duke, Joseph, 229
Duke, Thomas, 229
Duleep Singh, Maharajah, 156
Dunstan, Saint, 16
'Duty-Dodgers', the, 40

Easton, C., 202
Edgar, King, 16
Edict of Nantes, 21
  revocation of the, 27
Edward VII, King, 159
  and Queen Alexandra, 158
Edwardes family, 226, 227, 228, 229
Elizabeth II, Queen, 170
Elkington, George, 240, 241, 242
Elkington, Henry, 240
Elliott, Peter, 203
Eloi, Saint, 16
Elson, Anthony, 174, 177
Elston, John, 203
Exeter, 202–203
Eydes, John, 202

Farrer collection,
Felix, David H. H., 197
Felling, Gabriel, 205
Fenton, Matthew, 238, 239
Fitzgibbon Cup (see Courtauld, Samuel)
Float, Augustus, 218, 219
Fogelberg, Andrew, 99–100
Fothergill, John, 77
Fox, George, An Account of the History of Rundell,
    Bridge & Rundell, 120, 122–123
Franklin, Benjamin, 93
Frazer & Haws Ltd., 174
Frederick, Duke of York, 109
Frederick, Prince of Wales, 141, 143
Frisbee, William, and Storr, Paul, 100

Gainsford & Nicholson, 234
Gainsford, Roger, 238
Gardner, Thomas, 228
Gardner, Timothy, 228
Garrard & Co., 140–161
  foundation of, 149
  commemorative medals by, 151
  Crown Jewellers, 152, 153
  pieces exhibited at the Great Exhibition by, 153
  Royal commissions executed by, 153, 155,
    156, 157, 160
  Great Railway Salver by, 155
  sporting Trophies by, 151, 153, 154, 155, 156,
    158, 160
  work on coronation regalia by, 158, 159
Garrard, Henry, 157
Garrard, James Mortimer, 157
Garrard, Robert, 149–150
Garrard, Robert II,
  apprenticed to father, 150
  becomes Liveryman, 150
  maker's marks of, 150–151
  marries Esther Whippy, 151

Garrard, Robert II,—*cont.*
  children of, 150, 157
  elected to the Court of the Worshipful Company of Goldsmiths, 151
  elected Master of the Worshipful Company of Goldsmiths, 151
  elected Warden of the Worshipful Company of Goldsmiths, 151
  death of, 157
Garrard, Sebastian, Henry, 157, 159
Gateshead, 218, 219
Gay, John, *Trivia, or the Art of Walking the Streets of London*, 39
George II, King, 31, 186
George III, King, 72, 79, 114, 197, 199
  as Frederick, Prince of Wales, 141–142
George IV, King, 151
Germaine, Pierre, *Eléments d'orfevrerie*, 196
Gibson, George, 222
Gilbert, Geoffrey, 211
Gilbert, John, 236
Gilbert, Stephen, 145
Goldsmiths' Company, the, 25, 26, 28, 34, 40, 63, 81, 145, 165, 232
Goldsmiths' Hall, 25, 26, 47, 65, 113, 127, 128, 140, 145, 147, 163, 165, 171, 174, 194, 197
Goodriche, John, 217
Grafton, Duke of, 80
Granville, George, 1st Duke of Sutherland, 28
Great Exhibition, the 153
Great Railway Salver, the (*see* Garrard & Co.)
Gregorie, Richard, 226
Gribelin Simon, 33
Grimwade, A. G., 'Silver at Althorp III, The Huguenot Period', 132–133
Grimwade, A. G., 'Silver at Althorp IV, The Rococo and Regency Periods', 108–109
Grimwade, A. G., *The Garrard Ledgers*, 145, 148–149, 169–170
Guild of Goldsmiths, the, 24, 25

Hampston & Prince, 222
Hanck, Berenk of Hampstead, 99
Hanwell, Robert (*see* Hennell, Robert)
Harache, Pierre, 53
Harbord, Sir Harbord, 85
Harrington, Christopher, 222
Harsonage (*see* Hartsonge)
Hartsonge, Robert, 210, 211
Haselwood, Arthur, 210
Haselwood, Arthur II, 210
Haselwood, Arthur III, 210
Haselwood, Elizabeth, 210
Haver, Thomas, 211
Hawksworth, Eyre & Co., 239
Hebden, Thomas, 223
Heming, George, 199
Heming, Thomas, 196–200
  apprenticeship of, 196
  receives Freedom of the Goldsmiths' Company, 196
  elected to the Livery of the Goldsmiths' Company, 196

appointed Royal Goldsmith, 197
maker's marks of, 196, 197
partnership with William Chawner, 199
children of, 199–200
dinner and dessert services for Catherine the Great by, 199
death of, 200
Heming, Thomas, Jnr., 200
Hennell & Co., 172
Hennell, Charles, 173
Hennell, David, 163–165
  birth of, 163
  apprenticeship of, 163
  maker's marks of, 163, 165
  receives Freedom of the Worshipful Company of Goldsmiths, 163
  elected to Livery of the Goldsmiths' Company, 165
  retires, 165
Hennell, David II, 166–167, 171
Hennell family, the, 163–178
  of Foster Lane, 169–173
  of Newport Pagnell, 167–169
  exhibition of silver and jewellery by, 174–178
Hennell, James Barclay, 169, 176
Hennell, John, 165, 166
Hennell Ltd., maker's marks of, 173–175
Hennell, Percy Garnett, 173
Hennell, Robert, 163, 173
Hennell, Robert II, 164, 165, 166, 169, 170, 171, 172
  children of, 166–167, 170
  maker's marks of, 169, 170, 171, 172
Hennell, Robert III, 166–170
  apprenticeship of, 167
  maker's marks of, 167, 168, 170
  ambassadorial services made by, 168
Hennell, Robert IV, 167, 170, 171
Hennell, Robert V, 168, 169, 176
Hennell, Robert VI, 168, 169, 176
Hennell, R. G. & Sons, 173
Hennell, Robert George, 172, 173
Hennell, Samuel, 167, 170. 171, 172
Hennell, Samuel, II, 172
Hennell's Stock Books, 174
Hennell, William, 164 (half-brother of David Hennell)
Hennell, William, 166 (younger brother of Robert III Hennell)
Henry VI, statute of granting assay, 201
Henry, Prince, 146
Hermitage Museum, 191
Hewitson, Thomas, 214
Higden, Ranulf, *Polychronicon*, 16
Hogarth, William, 30–31, 33
Holbrook, Hugh and Alice, 204
Holland, M., *Old Country Silver*, 202, 206, 209, 212, 220–221, 222–223
Holmes, Geoffrey, *The Trial of Doctor Sacheverell*, 150
Honour, Hugh, *Goldsmiths and Silversmiths*, 185, 196
Honourable Artillery Company, the, 41

Hope, H. T., 154
Horse's Head Ewer (*see* Storr, Paul)
Household Cavalry, 72
Howell, James, 58
Howlett, William, 212
Hoyland, J. & Co., 237
Huguenots, the, 18, 19, 21
    complaints against emigré, 182
    as refugees, 22, 23
Hull, 223, 224
    town mark, 223
Hunt, Samuel, 110, 113
Hutchinson, R., 211

Illustrated London News, the, 153, 154
Imperial Russian collection, 199
Inwood, William and Henry, 109
Ipswich, 211
Isaac, J. W., 160
Ishbourne, Valentine, 208

Jackson, Sir Charles, *English Goldsmiths and their
    Marks*, 61, 131, 190
Jeannest, Pierre Emile, 241
Jones, E. A., *Proceedings of the Huguenot Society
    XVI (1940)*, 193
Jones, Gerrard, 227
Jones, Robert II, 236
Jons, 202
Jons Cup, the, 202
Journal of Design, the, 154
Juliott, André, 27
Juliott, Louisa, 27

Kandler, Charles and Frederick, 53
Kent, Duke of, 151
Kent, William, 142
King, Commander W. D., 177
King's Lynn, 211–212
Kirkup, James, 215, 216
Koh-i-Noor diamond, cutting of the, 155
Kremlin, the, 30
Kunstindustrimuseum, the, 199

Laing Art Gallery and Museum, the, 214, 215,
    216, 217
Lambert, Peter, 217
Lansdowne, Battle of, 154
Langworth, John, 222
Law, Thomas, 238, 239
Leader, Thomas, 237
Leeds, 224
Lempster, Sophia, Baroness, 47
Lennox, Duke of, 79
Le Roux, Jean, 22
Leveson-Gower, John, 1st Earl Gower, 28
Lewes, 205
Lewes, Sir Walter, 84
Lincoln, 212–213
Lincoln, Lord, 33, 36
Lingley, family, 226
Linwood, Matthew, 238
Liverpool, 235–236

Liverpool, Earl of, 48
Lloyd Lawrence E., firm of, 174
London Evening Post, the, 49
Londonderry, Marquess of, 171
Londonderry Trust, the, 171
London Gazette, the, 168
Louis XI, King, 22
Louis, XIV, King of France, 21
Lowe family, of Chester, 232, 235
Lukin, William, 33
Lunar Society, members of the, 94

Maddock, Thomas, 232
Majou, Margueritte, 27
Makepeace, Robert, 217
Manchester, 236
Manchester City Art Gallery, the, 181
Mangy, Arthur, 224
Mangy, Christopher, 221
Mangy, Edward, 221, 223
Mangy, George, 221
Mangy, George II, 221
Mangy, Henry, 221
Mangy, Katherine, 223
Mangy, Thomas, 221
March, John, 203
Marsh, Philemon, 219
Mary, Queen, 158, 159
Mascall, William, 221
Mason, Josiah, 241
Matthew, Thomas, 204
Meath, 5th Earl of, 186
Mecklenburg, Prince of, 146
Memoirs of Phillip Rundell, 121, 123
Metropolitan Museum of Art, New York, the,
    202
Mettayer, Louis, 53
Mettayer, Marie, 53
Mills, Nathaniel, 238
Milton, Shield, 242
Minors, Thomas, 36
Morel-Ladeuil, Leonard, 242
Mortime , John, 109, 110, 113
Mortimer, John (of Storr & Mortimer), 206
Museum of Fine Arts, Boston, 63
Muston, Henry, 206
Mutton, William, 225

National Maritime Museum, Greenwich, 101,
    170
Needham, Thomas and Anne, 57
Nelme, Anthony, 181–184
    family of, 181
    maker's marks of, 181
    becomes Free of the Goldsmiths' Company,
        181
    becomes Second Warden of the Goldsmiths'
        Company, 181
    sons of, 181, 184
    commissioned to make candlesticks for St.
        George's Chapel, Windsor Castle, 182
    commissioned to make domestic items for
        Board of Ordnance, 183

Nelme Francis, 181, 184
Nelson, Admiral Lord, 104
Netherton, Samuel, 144
Newcastle, Duke of (*see* Lord Lincoln)
Newcastle upon Tyne, 213–218
    town mark, 213
Newdigate, Sir Roger and Lady, 47
New Sterling Act, 26
John Nichols, *Biographical Anecdotes of William
    Hogarth*, 31, 32–33
Nightingale, Florence, 151
Northumberland, Duke of, 79
Norwich, 207–211
    town mark, 207
Ny Carlsberg Foundation, the, 198

Ogier, Louisa Perina (*see* Courtauld, Louisa)
Ogier, Pierre and Catherine, 134
Ollivant, John, 236
Oman, Charles, 194
Orange, William of, 18
Orenge, Richard, 207
Orloff, Count, 198
Osborn, Richard, 202
Oxford English Dictionary, the, 15, 20

Padley, Parkin & Co., 239
Pantin, Simon, 127–128
Parker, John, 144–145, 146
Parkes, Alexander, 240
Partis, Thomas, 215, 216
Partis, William, 216
Peard, John, 204
Pemberton, Benjamin, 229
Pemberton, Benjamin II, 229, 230
Pemberton, Peter, 227
Pemberton, Peter II, 229, 230
Pemberton, Peter III, 230
Pemberton, Samuel, 229, 238
Pemberton, Thomas, 229
Pennant, Thomas, 15
Pennant, Thomas, *Account of London*, 47
Penzer, N. M., *Paul Storr*, 97, 98, 100–101, 104–
    105, 106, 107, 109, 110, 112, 119, 125
Peter I, the Great, 29
Petersen, Peter, 209
Philadelphia Museum of Art, 72
Phillips, P. H. S., *Paul de Lamerie*, 29, 31, 37, 46
Pickett, William, 119–120
Plate Assay Act, 1700, 202
Platel, Peter, 25
Plohn Collection, the, 188
Plummer, James, 220
Plummer, John, 220, 221
Plummer, Michael, 221
Plummer, Richard, 221
Plymouth, 205–206
Pontaine, Simon (*see* Pantin, Simon)
Poole, 206
Portland, Duke of, 100, 191, 193, 197
Portland Font (*see* Storr, Paul)
Prince & Co., 223
Prince Consort (*see* Prince Albert)

Proctor, Luke & Co., 238
Provincial Goldsmiths, 200–242
Pulford, Alexander, 228

Quennell, Peter, *Hogarth's Progress*, 30
Quick, Peter, 204
Quyche (*see* Quick)

Radcliffe, Jasper, 202
Ramsay, John, 217
Ramsey, William, 213, 214
Reade Salt, 208, 209
Reid, Christian Ker, 218
Relief List of the Royal Bounty, the, 24
Reminiscences of Francis Storr, 109
Rhoades, Charles, 222
Richards, Edward, 203
Richardson, Richard I, 230, 231
Richardson, Richard II, 230, 231, 232
Richardson, Richard III, 231, 232
Richardson, Richard IV, 232
Richardson, William, 232
Richmond, Duke of, 79, 80
Ridgway, Canon Maurice H., *Some Chester
    Goldsmiths and their Marks*, 225, 226, 227
Roberts, John & Co., 238, 239
Roberts, Samuel, 78, 238
Roberts, Smith & Co., 239
Robertson, Anne, 218
Robertson, John, 217
Robertson, John II, 218
Robinson, Matthew, 93
Robinson, Thomas, 228
Robinson, William, 213
Rockingham, Earl of, 193
Roebuck, John, 93
Roettiers, Jacques-Nicholas, 199
Roll of Denizations, the, 24
Romer, John Christian, 98
Rowbotham, John & Co., 239
Rowe, Robert, 205
Royal collection, the, 106, 107, 153, 170
Royal Mint, the, 74
Royal Society, the, 94
Rundell, Bridge & Rundell, 103, 105, 107–108,
    120–125, 152, 153, 167
Rundell, Phillip, 103, 108, 117, 119–125
Ruskin, John, 20

Salisbury, 206
Saunders Vase, the, 176
Schlick, Sir Benjamin, 241
Scott, Sir Walter, *The Fortunes of Nigel*, 15
Scott, Sir Walter, *Talisman*, 153–154
Scrope Mazer, the, 219
Shaw, William, 60
Sheffield, 201, 236–242
Sheffield Old Plate, marks of, 234
Sherborne, 207
Shipden, Richard, 208
Shure, D. S., *Hester Bateman, Queen of English
    Goldsmiths*, 61

Silver, old and new standards of, 39–40
Simpson, Joseph, 33
Skottowe, Timothy, 208
Small, Dr. William, 93
Smith, Benjamin, 240, 241
Smith, *Leading Cases*, 33
Smith, William, 236
Smithin, Samuel, 36
Smyth, Robert, 225
Society of Arts, the, 154
Society of Dilettanti, the, 67
Soho, 91, 92
Somerset, Duke of, 193
Somerset House, 27
Sophia, Queen, 79
Sotheby's, 29, 146, 188, 198, 199, 202, 207
Souchay de la Merie, Paul, 22
Spencer, Earl, 37
Spencer, W. F., 156
Spendlove Cups, the, 210
Spendlove, Thomas, 210
Sprimont, Nicholas, 53, 194
Stapleton, Edward, 102
Steele, Sir Richard, *Guardian*, 15
Storr, Paul, 95–125
  ancestry of, 97–98
  birth of, 99
  apprenticeship of, 99
  marries Elizabeth Susanna Beyer, 102
  children of, 102–103, 109
  partner in firm of Rundell, Bridge & Rundell, 103
  partnership with William Frisbee, 100
  maker's marks of, 100, 101, 103, 107, 108, 110
  resigns partnership with Rundell, Bridge & Rundell, 108
  firm of 'Storr & Mortimer, Gold and Silver Smiths' formed by, 109, 110
  partnership with Mortimer and Hunt, 110, 113
  Portland Font by, 100
  Battle of the Nile Cup by, 101
  work on the table-service for the Duke of Wellington, 104
  Theocritus Cup by, 106
  Horse's Head Ewer by, 110–111
  retirement of, 113
  death of, 113
  will of, 113
  assessment of work of, 114–118
  portraits of, 102
Styles, Alex, 159
Stratford, Lawrence, 205
Sussex, Duke of, 151
Sutherland Wine Cistern, the, 29
Sutton, John, 236
Symonds, Pentecost, 206

Tannor, Christopher, 208
Tatham, Charles Heathcote, *Designs for Ornamental Plate*, 114–115
Taunton, 207
Taylor, John, 147–148, 149

Taylor, Joseph, 238
Temple Newsam, Leeds, 86
Terry, John, 172
Theocritus Cup, the (*see* Storr, Paul)
Titchfield, William Henry, Marquess of, 100
Todd, Samuel, 224
Townsend, the Right Honourable, the Lord Viscount, 193
Treby, Right Honourable George, 35, 36
Treby Punch Bowl, the, 36–37
Trial of the Pyx, 41
Tudor, Henry, 237
Tutt, A. W., 174

Vianen, Christian van, 18
Vedeau, Aymé, 188
Victoria, Queen, 153, 155, 156
Victoria and Albert Museum, the, 42, 47, 124, 143, 143, 174, 175, 187, 197, 202
Vyner, Sir Robert, 45

Wakelin, Edward, 144–149
  maker's marks of, 144, 145, 147
  partnership with George Wickes, 144–145
  partnership with John Parker, 145–146
  partnership with Robert Garrard, 149
  death of, 148
Wakelin, E., and Taylor, J., work of, under joint mark, 147–148
Wales, Prince of, Investiture of at Carnarvon, 159
Wakelin, John, 147
Walker, George I, 232
Walker, George II, 232
Walley, Joseph, 236
Walley, Ralph, 227, 228
Walpole, Horace, 79
Walton, John, 218
Warwick Vase, the, 107
Waterhouse & Co., I. and I., 239
Watson, Thomas, 212
Watt, James, 74, 95
Wedgwood, Josiah, 79, 93
Weekly Journal or British Gazetteer, the, 191
Wellington, Duke of, 104
  ambassadorial service presented to, 167–168
  and the cutting of the Koh-i-Noor diamond, 155
  museum at Apsley House, 105
Wewlingworth, John de, 202
Whiting, William, 211
Wickes, George, 140–148
  family of, 140
  marks of, 140, 142, 145
  receives freedom of the Worshipful Company of Goldsmiths
  partnership with John Craig, 140
  appointed 'Goldsmith Jeweller & Silversmith' to Frederick, Prince of Wales, 140–141
  Royal commissions of, 141–142
  apprentices of, 144–145
  partnership with Samuel Netherton, 144
  partnership with Edward Wakelin, 144
  death of, 148

Wilkinson, Henry, & Co., 239
Wilkinson, John, 214
Willaume, David, 185–189
  family of, 185
  becomes free of the Goldsmiths' Company,
    185
  elected to livery of the Goldsmiths' Company,
    185
  marries Marie Mettayer, 185
  children of, 185
  apprentices of, 185
  maker's marks of, 186, 188
  pieces by, 186–187
  death of, 188
  will of, 188
Willaume, David Jnr., 185, 188
Williams-Wynn, Sir Watkin, Bt., 198
William III, of Orange, Stadholder of the
  Netherlands, 22
William IV, King, 152
Williamson, Robert, 222, 224
Willmore, Joseph, 238

Willmore, Thomas, 238
Willms, Albert, 241
Windsor Castle, pair of candlesticks for St.
  George's Chapel, 182
Winter, John, & Co., 237
Wood, Edward, 164, 165
Wood, William, 15
Worshipful Company of Goldsmiths, the, 16,
  24, 43, 45, 48, 60, 99, 111, 135, 153, 165,
  188
  Court of Assistants at, 66
  books of Apprenticeship and Fredom of, 163
Wright, Charles, 81
Wright, John, 240
Wrought Plate Act, 39
Wyatt, James, 85–86, 89–90, 93
Wyman, Henry, 219

Younge, John, & Co., 237
Younghusband, John, 215
York, 219–223
  town mark, 219, 220